1984

THE STATE AND REVOLUTION IN IRAN

The State and Revolution in Iran
1962-1982

Hossein Bashiriyeh

CROOM HELM
London & Canberra

ST. MARTIN'S PRESS
New York

© 1984 Hossein Bashiriyeh
Croom Helm Ltd, Provident House, Burrell Row,
Beckenham, Kent BR3 1AT

Croom Helm Australia Pty Ltd,
28 Kembla Street, Fyshwick,
ACT 2609, Australia

British Library Cataloguing in Publication Data

Bashiriyeh, Hossein
    The state and revolution in Iran, 1962–1982
    1. Iran, Politics and government
    I. Title
    955'.05   DS318
    ISBN 0-7099-3214-6

All rights reserved. For information, write:
St. Martin's Press, Inc., 175 Fifth Avenue, New York, NY 10010
Printed in Great Britain
First published in the United States of America in 1984

Library of Congress Cataloging in Publication Data

Bashiriyeh, Hossein.
    The state and revolution in Iran, 1962-1982.

    Bibliography: p.
    Includes index.
    1. Iran—Politics and government—1941-1979.
2. Iran—Politics and government—1979-
I. Title.
DS318.B337 1984 955'.053 83-19218

    ISBN 0-312-75612-7

Printed and bound in Great Britain

CONTENTS

TO MY PARENTS

PREFACE

The present book is in the main an outgrowth of research originally carried out for my doctoral thesis in Iran in 1980. Apart from personal observations, contacts and travels, especially in the western provinces in connection with the question of the minorities, I conducted interviews with the Plan Organisation and the Ministries of Commerce and Economy on government-business relations. The Statistical Centre and the Central Bank were helpful in providing government data and information and the Ministry of National Guidance allowed me to use its archives. For the newspapers and sources prior to the revolution, I used the Library of the Majles and the Central Library of Tehran University, as well as the Library of the School of Oriental and African Studies in London.

I would like to express my thanks to Dr Barry Munslow of the University of Liverpool, Dr David Pool of the University of Manchester, Mr Hans Schadee, and Professor Nikki Keddie of the University of California for their intellectual support and incisive comments. Professor Keddie read the manuscript for the publishers and made helpful comments on the structure of the study, which were gratefully taken into consideration in the rewrite.

Finally, I owe a special debt to my sister, Moulood, for her assistance with the laborious job of going through piles of numerous newspapers published after the revolution.

Currency and Calendar

One pound sterling = 140 rials, approximately.
The Iranian year starts on 21 March (1 Farvardin) and ends on 20 March (30 Esfand).
To find the equivalent year on the Christian calendar, add 621 years to the Persian calendar.

INTRODUCTION: ANALYTICAL FRAMEWORK

The revolution which broke out in Iran in 1978 and led to the fall of the monarchy and the establishment of an Islamic republic forms one of the major episodes of conflict in the political history of twentieth-century Iran. The focus of the present study is to explain the causes of that revolution and the phases which it has gone through, by putting emphasis on the social aspects of the conflict. In this endeavour the introductory Chapter 1 analyses the evolution of the state structure in Iran from the beginning of this century to the consolidation of the Shah's regime in 1963. It thus puts the Islamic Revolution of 1978-9 in a longer historical context of political conflict arising from the Constitutional Revolution of 1905-11. In Chapter 2 the nature of the royal regime obtaining before the revolution will be studied in terms of its foundations of power and stability in the 1963-78 period. Oil wealth, economic stabilisation, cooperation between the state and the upper class, repression and US political support formed the bases of the Shah's power. In turn, the crumbling of these foundations of power eventually led to the disintegration of his regime. In Chapters 3, 4 and 5 we will seek to explain the major causes of the revolution. To do this, we will use a concept that will bring together several factors which by themselves are insufficient to explain the revolution. They include the development of a revolutionary ideology portraying a better possible society in a decade or so before the revolution; the economic crisis of 1973-8 leading to the generation of economic discontent and grievances on a mass scale; the emergence of some fundamental conflicts of interest between the state and the upper bourgeoisie; the disintegration of the regime's foreign support; the revolutionary mobilisation of the masses by a network of mobilising organisations; and the occurrence of a political alliance between diverse forces of opposition to the monarchy. Thus we will treat the revolution as a conjuncture taking into account the internal contradictions of the state such as its conflict with the upper class and the disintegration of the army, and the external revolutionary pressures brought to bear on the regime such as political mobilisation and political alliances.

The significance of this concept of revolution as a primarily political event becomes evident when it is contrasted with modern anti-political theories of revolution which divert attention from the political conjunctural nature of revolutionary situations. The modern theories of revolution fall into two main categories: psychological and functionalist sociological. J. Davies, Ted Gurr, D. Schwartz and S. Huntington, among others, employ primarily psychological concepts such as 'relative deprivation' and 'rising expectations' to explain revolutions.[1] On the other hand, N. Smelser, C. Johnson and M. Hagopian rely on functionalist sociology.[2] The psychological theories confine themselves mainly to the question of how grievances are generated, assuming that once discontent and grievances are created they are automatically transformed into concerted action, violence and revolution. These theories suffer from two basic flaws. First, they assume an automatic relationship between a hypothetical state of anger and the eruption of violence. Secondly, they take it for granted that violence is the same as revolution. They thus ignore the fundamental fact that the mere existence of individual discontent does not account for the occurrence and the success of a revolution. The psychological theories seek the cause of revolution in men's 'psychic disorder'. In the same vein, the functionalist approach explains revolutions as pathologies of the body politic and seeks their cause in the state of 'disequilibrium' and 'dissynchronisation'. The functionalist theories assume that society is like some hypothetical system and then they analyse the system which is made up. They deal neither with the constituent interests of the state and society nor with the world of the immediate consciousness of men. On the whole, these theories do not offer any explanation as far as revolution is concerned.[3]

Chapters 6 and 7 will explain the course of the revolution after the fall of the Shah and the consolidation of the clerical state under Ayatollah Ruhollah Khomeini. One of the major characteristics of all revolutions, which distinguishes them from other forms of abrupt political change such as military *coups d'état* and 'palace revolutions', is the gap in time which occurs between the fall of the old regime and the consolidation of the new one. As Peter Amann has explained, 'revolution may be said to be a breakdown, momentary or prolonged, of the state's monopoly of power. Revolution prevails when the state's monopoly of power is effectively challenged and persists until a new monopoly of power is re-established.'[4] In the meantime, revolutions are marked by political conflicts and class struggles for power. Classical studies of revolution, notably those by Edwards, Pettee and Brinton,[5] have sought to develop a paradigm for the *course* of all revolutions by generalising that of the French Revolution. They have discerned four phases in revolutions: 'the rule of the moderates', 'the ascendancy of the extremists', 'the reign of terror and virtue' and '*Thermidor*'. Whereas the 'moderates' are generally from the upper class and reflect the views of the propertied class, the 'extremists' are egalitarian and are from a lower class position.[6] The 'moderates' who first come to power are more than satisfied with the political revolution and seek to preserve the power apparatuses of the old regime. They finally lose out because they are unable to cope with the participation of new groups. The 'extremists' win out because they mobilise the popular forces. With their rise, dual power comes to an end as the new revolutionary clubs and committees are merged with the organisations of the old regime. They thus monopolise state power and create the machinery of 'terror and virtue'. Finally, the revolution ends in a 'Thermidor', which signifies the institutionalisation of the work of the revolution and the transfer of power to a new group or class.

The Islamic revolution in Iran has followed this classical model of revolution and hence we will explain its course accordingly. Like all classical revolutions, it has been a 'self-fulfilling' as opposed to a 'plan-fulfilling' revolution. In the 'plan-fulfilling' type, the revolution starts in the countryside and ends in the capital. It is part of a clearly thought-out plan for the reconstruction of the state, and thus the post-revolutionary period does not witness the succession of moderates and extremists (like the Chinese Revolution). By contrast in the 'self-fulfilling' type, there is little prior planning; hence the unpredictability of the aftermath of the revolution and the succession of the moderates and the extremists (as in the French Revolution).[7] The Iranian revolution was of the 'self-fulfilling' type in that there was no specific plan as to the actual political arrangements and social goals to be achieved after the revolution.

Having described the aim and major contents of the study, we now come to a brief discussion of the concepts underlying the analysis. Our focus will be essentially on social classes and class conflict. After the Constitutional Revolution of 1905-11, a plurality of classes and class-fragments emerged and occupied the power bloc.[8] From then on several political regimes were established on the basis of the shifting alliances of the social classes and political forces. The conception of social class used in this study should be clarified here.

Karl Marx's notion of class as it appears in his political works[9] has it-self been subject to diverse interpretations, among which two schools of thought in particular stand out: the economist conception and the politicist conception. According to the economist interpretation social classes are economic categories defined by their relations to the means of production. They are exclusively determined by economic considerations, and through their economic organisations they appear as the agents of conflict over economic interests. Hence the class conflicts at the political level are the direct reflections of these conflicts in the economic process. In short, classes exist before their conflicts are reflected at the political level. By contrast, the politicist interpretation maintains that classes acquire effective existence only at the political level. Accordingly, conflict between economic organisations of classes is not class conflict. Instead social classes emerge at the political level only by constituting for themselves a political ideology and a political party and engaging in political conflict.[10]

The concept of class used in this study is neither of these two extremes. Rather it is based on a third interpretation, that of Nicos Poulantzas, according to which classes are *'the result of an ensemble of structures and of their relations*, firstly at the economic level, secondly at the political level and thirdly at the ideological level. A social class can be identified either at the economic level, at the political level, or at the ideological level.'[11] The significance of this definition for this study is, first, that a class in power can be located in economic, political as well as ideological terms, and, secondly, that social class does not effectively emerge only when it represents its interests through a political organisation and ideology; classes at the economic level are not absent from the political class struggle so far as they are represented and articulated at the political level. In the latter sense, social classes are usually subject to mobilisation, as happens under corporatism, populism and fascism.[12]

On the basis of these concepts, within the Iranian social formation it is the upper classes (the landed nobility, the upper bourgeoisie, the high-ranking clergy) and the middle classes (the traditional bazaar petty bourgeoisie and the new petty bourgeoisie) which have developed political ideologies and organisations of their own and along with the royal court and the army have composed the power bloc. On the other hand, the lower classes – the working class and the peasantry – have been mainly subject to intermittent efforts at mass mobilisation. After the Constitutional Revolution, the upper classes advocated a liberal-constitutional order based on a parliamentary system with a weak executive. Hence, when the nobility was the hegemonic segment in the power bloc, the parliament, itself dominated by the oligarchy, became the central political institution and political administration was decentralised. The high-ranking clergy, as a fraction of the upper class which was given special constitutional prerogatives after the Constitutional Revolution, also advocated liberal-constitutionalism and was opposed to anti-liberal hegemony in the power bloc. The new petty bourgeoisie advocated democracy, administrative reform, electoral reform (the vote to be confined to the educated people) and industrialisation. By contrast, the traditional bazaar petty bourgeoisie in association with the lower clergy supported non-liberal fundamentalism. And finally, the radical intelligentsia associated with the working class advocated popular socialism which led to the emergence of a strong labour movement in the 1940s. Thus, although these diverse classes were at times united against the Shah's regime (as during the early phase of the Islamic Revolution in 1978-9) these different class ideologies advocated different types of socio-political order. Also, even when the regime was bureaucratic-military under the Shah, its nature is still explained in terms of the cooperation of the dominant classes in the power bloc and the model of class mobilisation utilised by the regime. The Shah articulated his own corporatist ideology of class harmony (in line with nineteenth-century corporatist social thought), and in terms of the model of mobilisation of class support at times oscillated between corporatism and populist-fascism — depending on the stability or instability of the political conditions.

On the whole, the class analysis underlying this study covers the following aspects: class identification of political parties; class background of social thought; class conflict for power; economic conflict of classes; class-state relations; and classes in power.

Finally, it should be noted here that because Iranian politics in general and the revolution of 1978-9 in particular have been mainly centred in the capital city, Tehran, the view taken in this study is mainly one from this centre of politics.

Notes

1. The major studies in this category are: James Davies (ed.), *When Men Revolt and Why* (New York, 1971); Ted Robert Gurr, *Why Men Rebel* (Princeton, 1970); *idem*, 'A Causal Model of Civil Strife', *American Political Science Review*, vol. 62 (December 1968), pp. 1104-24; I. Feirerabend *et al.* (eds.), *Anger, Violence and Politics: Theories and Research* (Englewood Cliffs, NJ, 1972); D. Schwartz, 'Political Alienation, the Psychology of Revolution's First Stage', in ibid.; D. Morrison, 'Some Notes Towards a Theory of Relative Deprivation, Social Movement and Social Change', *American Behavioral Scientist*, vol. 14 (1971), pp. 675-90; S.P. Huntington, *Political Order in Changing Societies* (New Haven, 1968) (especially pp. 54-7); and J. Davies, 'Towards a Theory of Revolution', *American Sociological Review*, vol. 27 (1962), pp. 5-19.

2. See Chalmers Johnson, *Revolutionary Change* (Boston, 1966); Neil Smelser, *Theory of Collective Behavior* (New York, 1963); and Mak Hagopian, *The Phenomenon of Revolution* (New York, 1974).

3. For critiques of these theories see: Rod Aya, 'Theories of Revolution Reconsidered', *Theory and Society*, vol. 8 (1979), pp. 39-99; J. Goldstone, 'Theories of Revolution: The Third Generation', *World Politics*, vol. 32 (1979-80), pp. 425-53; M. Freeman, 'Theories of Revolution', *British Journal of Political Science*, vol. 2 (1972), pp. 339-58; and F.G. Hutchins, 'On Winning and Losing by Revolution', *Public Policy*, vol. 18 (1969), pp. 1-40.

4. Peter Amann, 'Revolution: A Redefinition', *Political Science Quarterly*, vol. 77 (1962), pp. 36-56; pp. 38-9.

5. L. Edwards, *The Natural History of Revolution* (Chicago, 1970); G. Pettee, *The Process of Revolution* (New York, 1938); and C. Brinton, *The Anatomy of Revolution* (New York, 1960).

6. See, for example, D. Underdown, *Pride's Purge* (Oxford, 1971), and Brinton, *Anatomy of Revolution*, pp. 122, 129, for a discussion of the higher class position of the moderates and the lower social status of the radicals in the English and French revolutions.

7. This basic distinction has been made by F.G. Hutchins, 'On Winning and Losing', pp. 8-16. This typology partly corresponds to S.P. Huntington's distinction between 'Eastern' and 'Western' revolutions. In the Western type the revolution begins in the capital and is largely spontaneous, whereas in the Eastern type, the revolution begins in the countryside and ends with the capture of power in the capital by organised groups and quasi-armies: Huntington, *Political Order*, pp. 266ff.

8. The concept of power bloc which is used in this study has been formulated by Antonio Gramsci and developed by Nicos Poulantzas. It refers to the situation in which power is held by an alliance of dominant classes, of which the hegemonic segment organises consent to the state through its political and ideological practices. See N. Poulantzas, *Political Power and Social Classes* (London, 1973), pp. 229-45; E. Laclau, *Politics and Ideology in Marxist Theory: Capitalism, Fascism, Populism* (London, 1979); and G. Williams, 'The Concept of "Egemonia" in the Thought of Antonio Gramsci', *Journal of Historical Ideas*, vol. 21, no. 4 (1960).

9. 'The Class Struggles in France, 1848-1850' and 'The Eighteenth Brumaire of Louis Bonaparte' in K. Marx and F. Engels, *Selected Works* (Moscow, 1958).

10. The politicist interpretation is best presented by G. Lukács, *History and Class Consciousness* (London, 1971). The opposite economist interpretation is the orthodox Marxist interpretation associated especially with the Second and Third Internationals.

11. Poulantzas, *Political Power*, p. 63.

12. The concepts of populism and fascism are specified by N. Poulantzas, *Fascism and Dictatorship* (London, 1970), and Laclau, *Politics and Ideology*; and those of corporatism and clientelism have been recently discussed in J. Malloy (ed.), *Authoritarianism and Corporatism in Latin America* (Pittsburgh, 1977); P. Schmitter, 'Still the Century of Corporatism?' *Review of Politics*, vol. 30 (1974), pp. 85-131; and L. Panitch, 'Recent Theorizations of Corporatism', *British Journal of Sociology*, vol. 31 (1980), pp. 159-87.

1 THE EVOLUTION OF THE STATE STRUCTURE

In order to arrive at an analysis of the state which was overthrown in the 1979 revolution, this chapter investigates the major historical changes in the structure of Iranian polity and society since the turn of the century, as well as the more recent origins of the pre-revolutionary state.

The Break-up of Absolutism

During the second half of the nineteenth century or the so-called 'Age of Imperialism', Iranian society passed through a process of fundamental change which amounted to a significant break with its past. The reverberations of those changes have since formed the political history of Iran.

The traditional Iranian state had been based on an absolutist power structure in which the Shahs wielded supreme political authority. In times of strength, the royal court (*darbār*) subdued all society to its power, and in times of relative weakness, it manipulated and neutralised all contending sources of power. The structure of authority was patrimonial and the kings made grants and commissions as acts of grace.[1] This political absolutism was founded on the absence of legal private property and the existence of state-communal property.[2] The Persian despot was in possession of the means of production, i.e. land, and as a result, in Persian absolutism in contrast to Western feudalism, no established hereditary landed nobility developed.[3] Land-holding was bureaucratic and the ruler granted land assignments (*tuyūl*). But this was temporary in nature and there was no contract between the ruler and the assignee (*tuyūldār*).[4] The political upheavals characteristic of Persian history, i.e. internal tribal fighting and foreign invasions, also contributed to this social instability. Besides bureaucratic land-holding, absolutism also meant the interference of the state in trade and commerce. The bazaar guilds, originally imposed from above, were channels for the administration of the bazaars, which were subordinated to the absolutist state.[5]

This picture of absolutism is only the ideal type of the pre-modern history of Iran. At times, Iranian polity fluctuated between despotism and feudalism, especially during the rule of foreign invaders when feudal land-holdings were established.[6] After a long period of invasions and weakness, a strong despotic state was established under the first Shiite dynasty, the Safavids (1501-1722) who subdued the *tuyūldārān* and extended state control of the bazaar.[7] The absolutist state structure began to disintegrate, however, under the Qajar dynasty (1796-1925) due to compounded external and internal causes. During the nineteenth century, classes with independent sources of power and wealth began to emerge. In this period, the state was in need of money in order to buy Western arms to defend itself. This led to the systematisation of the sale of state lands and offices and consequently to the growing power of the landed classes, the mercantile bourgeoisie and the clergy.[8] Furthermore, the expansion of the world economy and Western imperialism accelerated the process of the disintegration of absolutism. Although the state was saved from outright foreign control due mainly to a conflict of interests between the two great powers, Britain and Russia, its hold over society declined. The system of *tuyūldārī* began to disintegrate and the state became increasingly dependent on foreign powers.[9] Also, due to a growth in foreign trade resulting from the increasing incorporation of Iran into the capitalist exchange system, the merchant class prospered and a number of big business families rose to prominence.[10] Another consequence of the disintegration of the Qajar state was an increase in the power of the *'Ulamā* and the *Mujtaheds* (the learned men of Islam and doctors of divinity). Under the Safavids who established the first Shiite state in Iran and who imported clerics from Arab lands to legitimise their claim to religious authority, the Ulama were closely associated with the rulers and were also in charge of religious endowments (*ouqāf*). No conflict occurred between the kings and the Ulama in the Safavid era, in spite of the fact that Shiism had originally been an opposition movement in Islam, and the main point of its opposition concerned the qualities of the political leader. Theoretically, all temporal power was illegitimate and legitimate authority belonged to Imams from the line of 'Ali (the first Shiite Imam), and since the Occultation of the last Imam, Mahdī in AD 874, the Ulama were considered to be the 'general agency' of the Absent Imam.[11] However, despite the persisting ambiguity of the theoretical relationship between temporal and religious powers, under the Safavids the Mujtaheds emerged as a major power elite and cooperated with the kings.

During the Qajar era, a rift began to arise between the rulers and the Ulama. Paradoxically, the increasing foreign influence contributed more to a rise in the power of the Ulama than to their weakness. They were opposed to Western penetration and the ensuing secularisation of traditional institutions. The reaction of the Ulama to Western influence gave them a new position of power, and they emerged as the proponents of the rising indigenous nationalism which was expressed in terms of Islam. Thus, the increasing power and opposition of the Ulama were more functions of rising nationalism in the face of Western imperialism than the imperatives of Shiite political theory.[12] The Ulama also had strong connections with the bazaar through the religious taxes they received for the financing of mosques and seminaries. In addition, law and education were the prerogatives of the Ulama.[13] Another important consequence of increasing contact with the West was the emergence of the modern intelligentsia which as a constitutionalist and secularist class-fragment posed a new challenge to the traditional order.

On the whole, under the Qajars the structures of the traditional state began to dissolve.[14] The fragmentation of the Qajar polity into contending classes and interests finally led to the Constitutional Revolution of 1905. It began with the protests of merchants and the Ulama about the influence of foreign officials in the government and led to the introduction of a constitution (adapted from the 1830 Belgian Constitution) and the establishment of a parliament. The revolution was the result of an alliance among the bazaar bourgeoisie, the Ulama, the modern intelligentsia and some landed nobles and tribal chiefs.[15] The Constitution granted all participants prerogatives and rights while limiting the power of the court. The 1906 Electoral Law gave the vote to the Qajar tribe, the Ulama, nobles, merchants, landowners and the guilds and distributed Majles seats among the same classes.[16] Of the deputies of the First Majles, 21 per cent were landlords, 37 per cent were from the bazaar guilds, 17 per cent were from the Ulama and 25 per cent were state employees and professionals.[17] The Ulama obtained a significant prerogative. A parliamentary committee of five Mujtaheds was to be formed in order to ensure the conformity of legislation with Islamic law. As to the landlords, one of the early Acts of the Majles abolished the *tuyūldārī* system and established private property on land. Thus the majority of villages fell under landlord ownership and most peasants became landless share-croppers.[18] On the whole, several classes came to occupy the power bloc which was born out of the revolution. The landed nobility, the Ulama and the bazaar emerged as forces to be reckoned with. As the royal court under the young son of the exiled Mohammad Ali Shah continued to weaken in the 1910s, the landed class emerged as the dominant force. In the 1907-21 period, the number of landed Majles deputies increased from 21 to 50 per cent; that of the guilds declined from 37 to 5 per cent; that of the Ulama also declined from 17 to 13 per cent; and the number of professional deputies rose from 25 to 31 per cent.[19]

The constitutional system gave rise to factionalism and party politics. After 1909, two main parties, representing the main classes in the power bloc, dominated the Majles. The intelligentsia formed the Social Democrats Party, a secularist minority faction advocating land reform and the creation of an army. And the landed and Ulama deputies formed the Social Moderates Party, the conservative majority faction in the Majles.[20]

Although the aim of the Constitution was to establish a liberal regime, due to a number of factors, a military authoritarian regime emerged in the 1920s. The outbreak of the First World War; the weakening of the central administration; the suspension of the Majles; the outbreak of local rebellions in Gilān, Āzarbāyjān and Khorāsān; the growing influence of Great Britain in Iran after the October Revolution in Russia; and the declining influence of the Qajar court — all these contributed to a transfer of power in 1921, in a British-backed *coup d'état*, to Reza Khan, a colonel in the Cossack Brigade. With the Qajar court in ruins, the Majles proposed, in 1924, to declare a republic. But in the face of opposition to this from the Ulama and the bazaar, Reza Khan was declared king as the founder of the Pahlavi dynasty.

Under Reza Shah's authoritarian regime (1925-41) an attempt was made to centralise the state and to secularise society. Although the landed class became firmly established in its estates, it was politically subordinated to the military. The bazaar guilds were also suppressed and the public sector in the modern sense began to emerge in the context of the world economic crisis of the 1930s. In particular, the influence of the Ulama was severely undermined. Religious practices were discouraged and the anti-clerical integral nationalism of the state put emphasis on pre-Islamic Iranian culture. The Ulama were denied their constitutional right of appointing a parliamentary commission to supervise legislation, and in 1934 the state extended its hold over pious endowment lands. Reza Shah's authoritarian regime was, of course, not the restoration of traditional absolutism. It was rather the first such regime to develop in the context of the new social formation ushered in by the Constitutional Revolution. Unlike the regimes which followed it, however, Reza Shah's regime was a traditional authoritarian regime which ruled over a rather politically inert population, resulting in the political exclusion of social classes rather than in their incorporation in a political party. The rule of Reza Shah came to an abrupt end after the occupation of Iran by the Allies during the Second World War, due to Iran's pro-German sympathies. He was succeeded to the throne by his twenty-year-old son, Mohammad Reza Pahlavi (1941-79).

Despite the emergence of authoritarianism, the work of the Constitutional Revolution was accomplished, in that Iranian society was delivered from oriental despotism to a new social formation, in which the concepts of freedom and rights of the civil society became predominant, i.e. the capitalist social formation. Once the absolutist state crumbled, several classes and class-fractions came to the fore to shape the emerging state. Thus we enter into a class conception of Iranian politics.

The Emerging Social Classes and Political Forces

After the Constitutional Revolution, the specific interests of the social classes which thus came to the fore, and the political ideologies maintained by those classes, led to the emergence of a number of political parties. With regard to the social organisation of production, the social structure was composed of the following classes: the landed and tribal nobility (including the royal family), the high Ulama and the emerging upper bourgeoisie who were in possession of the main means of production, i.e. land and mercantile capital; the bazaar national and petty bourgeoisie; the rising salaried new petty bourgeoisie; the working class and the peasantry. The political ideological system which emerged after the revolution comprised four ideologies: liberal conservatism, democracy, non-liberal clerical fundamentalism (political Islam) and popular socialism. It was mainly the upper and middle classes which developed ideologies of their own; there were no peasant and few working-class traditions. Liberalism was the ideology of the landed and merchant class, advocating a strong parliamentary system but no major social changes. The majority of the Ulama also advocated liberal-constitutionalism as provided for by the Constitution. As we shall see in some detail, the major constitutionalist Ulama during and after the revolution, such as Ayatollahs Behbehani, Tabatabai, Khorasani and Naini, accepted the legitimacy of a secular-constitutional state based on a combination of divine and man-made laws. After the revolution, a minority of the Ulama, however, called for the adoption of Islamic law (*Shariat*) rather than a Western constitution as the law of the state; this was the ideological origin of fundamentalist Islam. The bazaar petty bourgeoisie was close to the Ulama and supported their liberalism and traditionalism, but in association with the lower clergy and religious students, it also gave rise to the non-liberal extremist political Islam advocating the establishment of an Islamic social order. This ideology was extremely nationalistic and anti-imperialist and had originally developed in reaction to Western encroachments and the secularism of the new petty bourgeoisie. The latter advocated democracy and social reform on the Western model. And finally, the radical intelligentsia allied to the urban masses advocated popular socialism.

The above four ideologies represented specific class interests and gave rise to several factions and parties. On the other hand, the royal court developed its own corporatist ideology seeking to create an equilibrium of classes. Thus the court parties were to represent this corporatist ideology.

The social structure itself was in a process of transformation from a mainly agrarian-based economy to a semi-industrial society as a result of the changing mode of production and state economic policies of land reform and industrialisation. Prior to the land reforms of the 1960s, there were four categories of land-holding: Crown lands comprising 2,000 villages, or 4 per cent of all villages; state lands (*khālesejāt*) comprising 3,000 villages or 6 per cent of all villages; endowment lands (*ouqāf*) comprising 6,000 villages or 12 per cent of all villages; and private lands comprising 40,000 villages or 80 per cent of all villages. Of the latter, 19,000 villages were owned by large landowners (*'omdeh-mālekīn*) which comprised 37 large families. Medium landowners owned 7,000 villages, and the remaining 15,000 villages were owned by small landowners (*khoedeh-mālekīn*) and peasant proprietors. The latter owned 10 per cent of all the villages.[21]

The nobility were from the ranks of the *'omdeh-mālekīn*. Between 1943 and 1960, a period in which the landed class retained a good deal of power, an average of 56 per cent of the Majles deputies were from that class. Within the same period, of 17 prime ministers who formed cabinets 15 were prominent members of landed families and two were from the military elite.[22] Thus the nobility was less in need of parties than were those classes outside the power bloc. However, after the fall of Reza Shah, when parliament was at the centre of power, a number of groups and factions were formed by the nobility to counter the newly emerging parties of the intelligentsia and the new petty bourgeoisie.[23] The most important party formed by the nobility was the Iran Democrat Party which was created in 1946 by Premier Ahmad Qavām of the old Qajar nobility.[24] The party was not a long-lasting experiment, however, and later when the landed nobility lost much of its power to the army and the court, it was much less capable of organisation and ideological articulation. With the rise of industry, members of landed families became engaged in industrial and mercantile ventures or turned to free professions. For instance, members of the Firuz-Farmanfarma landed family were to be found in several modern business enterprises.[25]

The high financial and industrial (comprador) bourgeoisie which became dominant in the 1970s was drawn partly from the landed class and partly from the bazaar. Under Reza Shah, this modern bourgeoisie had identified itself with the integral nationalism of the state whereas the bazaar mercantile (national) bourgeoisie had remained ideologically close to the Ulama.[26] Similarly from 1963, the state was to encourage the expansion of the modern bourgeoisie which established local monopoly industries and owned almost 70 per cent of all financial and industrial institutions, all at the expense of the bazaar bourgeoisie.

In contrast to the modern bourgeoisie, the traditional bazaar petty bourgeoisie had been in a process of decline since the late nineteenth century due to the penetration of Western interests in Iran and the growing dependency of the local economy. The class consisted of traders, craftsmen, artisans, shopkeepers, brokers and manufacturers residing in the bazaar which was an integrated socio-economic organisation encompassing trading houses, mosques and religious schools. The bazaaris were close to the religious community through the payment of religious taxes and the financing of mosques. Mullahs and religious students taught and resided in nearby schools and sometimes also owned shops in the bazaar.[27] In the 1940s and 1950s, the bazaars reorganised their guilds and in alliance with the lower clergy, formed a number of non-liberal fundamentalist parties. The Islamic petty bourgeois parties emerged mainly in the Tehran bazaar, which has been the stronghold of Islam as a political ideology. The first major such party was the Fedāiyān-e Islām, which was formed in 1946 by a number of theology students led by Navvāb Safavī. It was opposed to Western democracy and the secular intelligentsia, and planned and carried out several political assassinations. In particular, the party was opposed to any political or military alliance between Iran and the West, at a time when Iran was increasingly integrated into the Western political, economic and military network. A similarly fundamentalist and nationalist party was the Mojāhedīn-e Islām, which was led by Ayatollah Abul Qāssem Kāshānī and had widespread influence in the bazaar guilds in the 1950s. Kashani was extremely anti-imperialist and called on the Ulama to participate actively in politics. In this he followed Hasan Modarres, a nationalist religious leader of the Reza Shah period who had opposed the 1919 Anglo-Persian Agreement and had called for a policy of 'negative balancing' in foreign policy.[28] In 1960, another fundamentalist party called the

Party of Islamic Nations was formed by a number of theology students. It advocated the establishment of an Islamic state and taught its members the tactics of guerrilla warfare. Its objectives were 'the capture of political power, the creation of a communal economy and the establishment of a dictatorship based on a single party'.[29] Later, after its suppression, the remnants of the party formed the Party of God (Hezbollāh) in 1971. On the whole political Islam was the movement of the lower clergy associated with the bazaar and had little appeal among the high-ranking Ulama who, as constitutionalists, advocated an institutional separation between politics and religion.

In contrast to the bazaaris, the new petty bourgeoisie, consisting of civil servants, professionals, lawyers, judges, teachers, engineers, doctors and clerks, advocated Western-style democracy and secular politics. Numerically, it was a small class. In 1966, out of a population of 25 million, it numbered around 416,000. By 1976, it had expanded to around 1,560,000 out of a population of 33 million.[30] Politically, however, the new petty bourgeoisie was the most active among the political forces. The major democratic party formed by the new petty bourgeoisie was the Iran Party (originally the Association of Engineers) which was organised by a group of foreign-educated engineers in 1942. Among party leaders were engineers Golamhossein Farivar and Mehdi Bazargan, Karim Sanjabi (a lawyer) and Allahyar Saleh (a judge). The Iran Party was the party of 'doctors, lawyers, engineers, journalists, professors and teachers'.[31] Two major splinter groups broke away from the party to form the more Islamically oriented Freedom Movement (led by engineers Bazargan, Samii, Atai and Sahabi) and the more socialistically oriented Mardom-e Iran Party, composed of mostly younger professionals. The new petty bourgeoisie also formed a number of Pan-Iranist fascist parties such as the Sumka and Arya parties which had appeal amongst army officers and students. Another important party formed by the modern intelligentsia was the Toilers' Party, led by Dr Baqai Kermani and a leading group of socialist intellectuals.

The new petty bourgeois parties were small elite-dominated parties with few links to the working class and peasantry which formed the bulk of the population. In the 1950s, the working class numbered around 2 million. It was employed in the oil industry (37,000), textile factories, manufacture and crafts, the construction sector and manual services. Modern industries employed 19 per cent of the working class. By the mid-1970s, the class had expanded to 4 million.[32] Prior to the land reforms of 1962-7, more than half of the economically active population were peasant share-croppers, living in 50,000 villages scattered throughout the country. Relations between peasants and landlords were regulated on the basis of the 'five-element formula' according to which labour, land, water, seed and animals were taken as the basis of the division of the produce and usually the peasant retained one-third of the crop. Some landlords leased the land to the peasants for a fixed rent and some 7 per cent of peasant families were themselves proprietors.[33] The rural population was divided into two main sections: the sitting peasants or *nasaqdār* families comprising 1.9 million families; and the *khoshneshinhā* (rural artisans, craftsmen and shopkeepers) and agricultural labourers comprising 1.3 million families.[34] As we will see in more detail, in 1963 the state undertook a major mass mobilisation effort and, at a time of important transformations in the power bloc, instituted land reforms. Under the reform scheme, some 1 million *nasaqdār* families obtained some land, and as a direct result of the scheme, a rural middle class began to emerge in the 1960s.

On the whole, the countryside remained the stronghold of tradition and political indifference.[35] By contrast, the urban working class was more active and exerted some pressure on those in power. The popular working-class ideology was for the first time represented on an organised basis by the Tudeh (masses) Party of Iran which originated in a group of Western-educated intellectuals led by Dr Taqi Arani, who circulated Marxist ideas in Reza Shah's Iran. The party was established in 1941 and during and after the Second World War it succeeded in mobilising the masses on a large scale. In 1944, it organised the Central United Council of Trade Unions, encompassing 47 trade unions with 50,000 members.[36] Party members numbered around 25,000, of whom 23 per cent were intellectuals and professionals, 75 per cent workers and 2 per cent peasants.[37] In 1952, the party declared itself the party of the working class alone and called for the overthrow of the monarchy. In the 1960s, however, the Tudeh became more of a constitutionalist and reformist party. This led to a number of divisions within the party and the emergence of radical splinter groups such as the Maoist Revolutionary Organisation, the Tufan Organisation and the Red Star.[38] The more important of the radical groups was the Fedaiyan-e Khalq Guerrilla Organisation, which was formed in 1970 by a group of Marxist intellectuals defecting from the Tudeh and other parties.[39] Early in the period, however, the Tudeh Party established the popular working-class ideology which was to be of relevance in the subsequent articulation of state ideology.

The political parties were thus built on the basis of the class ideologies and represented diverse class interests which had come to the fore after the break-up of the traditional state. They made and broke alliances in the course of the ensuing political conflicts on the basis of such issues as nationalism, constitutionalism, secularism and traditionalism.

The Rise and Demise of Liberalism

The fall of Reza Shah in 1941 led to the disintegration of his authoritarian regime and ushered in a period of limited political participation and economic and political liberalism. As one fragment among the political forces, the new Shah tried to hold his place against challenges for power from all classes in the period 1941-62. Only in the 1963-79 period did he emerge as unquestioned ruler. In the former period, power was decentralised. The composition of the 14th Majles, the first parliament which was convened after Reza Shah, pointed to the dominant forces in the power bloc: of the deputies, 59 per cent were landed magnates, 11 per cent were from the bazaar, 27 per cent from the upper bureaucracy (partly landlords), 2 per cent from the Ulama and 1 per cent from the lower classes.[40] The period was characterised by the rapid political activation of the popular sector as a result of mobilisation by the Tudeh Party, as well as by the expansion of the national mercantile bourgeoisie as a major fraction of the power bloc. After the war, the decline of the role of the state in the economy, the abolition of government monopolies, the release of previously suppressed demand and the advent of financial resources through foreign grants led to heavy imports which greatly benefited the merchant class. In the government, liberal economic policy was predominant and later attempts at reorganising the public sector through economic planning met with the opposition of mercantile interests. Private investment increased by 20 per cent annually and the number of business enterprises increased from 45,000 in 1956 to 70,000 in 1960.[41] The merchant class also acquired great influence in the government and parliament.[42]

Confronted with powerful groups and strong parliaments, the Shah sought to consolidate his power position by reorganising the army. In general, under Allied occupation and from a position of weakness, the Iranian state had to reconsider its foreign relations against the background of the new international situation. Taking advantage of this new situation, the Shah pressed for Western, especially US, economic and military assistance, and became increasingly dependent upon this support. A number of US military missions, associated with various branches of the Iranian army, assisted in the task of expanding and training the armed forces. In 1946, the army under the Shah and with US help defeated the two autonomous communist regimes which had been set up in Azarbayjan and Kurdestan under the aegis of the Red Army. The event enhanced the influence of the Shah. Furthermore, in 1949 the Shah succeeded in setting up a constituent assembly to revise Article 48 of the Constitution and grant him the right of dissolving the Majles, on the pretext that it was interfering in areas outside its jurisdiction.

The power of the Shah continued to increase until the emergence of the National Front of Dr Mohammad Mosaddeq in 1949. As a grouping of constitutionalist and nationalist politicians, the National Front was opposed to the increasing power of the court and demanded electoral reform (including female enfranchisement) in order to widen and democratise the political system; new liberal press laws; the reinterpretation of the revised Article 48 of the Constitution to curb the power of the Shah; and a change of martial law requirements to prevent the interference of the army in politics.[43] Later, the Front launched the movement for the nationalisation of the Anglo-Iranian Oil Company which since 1907 had exploited Iranian oil resources on the basis of a concessionary agreement. Earlier in 1944, Dr Mosaddeq, as a member of the Majles, had proposed a parliamentary bill forbidding the granting of any oil concessions to foreign powers. In the 16th Majles, he headed the committee which recommended the nationalisation of the oil industry and was finally carried to power on a wave of popular support and was made Premier in May 1951.[44] Mosaddeq's National Front thus attracted widespread support and became a coalition of parties. The coalition was made up of the Iran Party, the Pan-Iranist Party, the Toilers' Party, the People of Iran Party and the Mojahedin-e Islam Party. It thus brought together a broad set of interests and in the main represented the national bazaar bourgeoisie allied to the Ulama and the parties of the new petty bourgeoisie. The alliance was based on the issues of constitutionalism and nationalism and was opposed to authoritarianism and imperialism.

So long as the nationalist cause was alive, the National Front remained united and the government subdued the power of the court and the army. However, as the oil dispute with Great Britain remained unresolved despite US attempts at mediation between the two countries, and as the financial situation deteriorated and imports declined, the National Front was faced with more opposition from landed and mercantile interests, especially with regard to its economic policy. And despite Mosaddeq's success in obtaining extraordinary decree powers from parliament to deal with the economic problems and in wresting the control of the army from the Shah, the National Front splintered into squabbling factions. The major split was between the secular parties of the modern intelligentsia and the bazaar clerical parties led by the Ulama. Quarrels ended in defections from the coalition in reaction to Mosaddeq's assumption of plenary powers, his toleration of the Tudeh Party and his appeals to the United States for support and financial assistance in Iran's dispute with Great Britain. In particular, the defection of Ayatollah Kashani, the Speaker of the 17th Majles, and his bazaar-based Mojahedin Party made the government's base of support much slimmer. He accused Mosaddeq of collaborating with the US in the latter's attempt to take over the control of Iran's oil resources from the British.[45] On the other hand, the Shah, heartened by the National Front's disintegration, emerged from his seclusion, but his first attempt to oust Mosaddeq failed, leading to the Shah's flight abroad. But the royalist army officers who had been purged by Mosaddeq continued their anti-government activities while receiving financial support and advice from the US embassy and CIA agents in Iran.[46] The US government helped topple Mosaddeq because he had posed a challenge to Western interests in Iran at the height of the Cold War, and he also seemed to be drifting to the left. As the National Front disintegrated, some clerics sided with the Shah, and in the day of confrontation between the army and Mosaddeq, they managed to register some popular support for the royalists while the army distributed cash among the crowds. Finally, on 19 August 1953, the National Front was removed from power in a US-backed *coup d'état* which brought the army and the Shah to power.

As a liberal nationalist government, the National Front had set out to introduce land, press and constitutional reforms and to ensure Iran's economic independence from the West, and had it not been overthrown, Iran could have developed on a pattern similar to that of post-independence India. But the external threat did not apparently seem strong enough to hold the diverse domestic forces together. The coalition of the forces which brought Mosaddeq down (the court, the army and some clerical, mercantile and landed interests) was to form the subsequent regime.

The Emergence of Authoritarianism in the Context of a Closer Integration of Iran into the Western Economic and Political Structure

From the beginning of his reign, the Shah had actively encouraged Western and especially US interest in the rebuilding of a strong Iranian state. In the wake of the war, US military aid proved essential for the reorganisation of the Iranian army. With the defeat of the nationalisation movement in the US-backed *coup d'état* of 1953, the American interest in Iran and in the institution of monarchy acquired new dimensions. The spoils of Iranian oil were distributed among the major Western countries, including the US. An international consortium of Western oil companies took over the control of the production, pricing and marketing of oil from the Anglo-Iranian Oil Company. Furthermore, in the 1950s, American economic and financial aid to Iran was expanded.[47] US financial advisers and investors became increasingly involved in directing economic development plans and American investment in Iran began to increase substantially from the early 1960s.[48] In 1957, the US assisted the army in establishing the security police (SAVAK), and in 1959 the Shah succeeded in concluding a bilateral military treaty with the US which made the latter directly committed to the defence of Iran. Thus, by the late 1950s, Iran became closely integrated into the Western political and military system and this greatly bolstered the power position of the Shah.

However, following the fall of Mosaddeq, the power bloc was occupied by the upper-class groups, and the power of the Shah depended on support from the military elite, the landed class and the high Ulama.[49] In particular, the Shah frequently paid lip-service to Islam and visited Ayatollah Borujerdi, the highest-ranking religious leader, at his home in Qum. There was no open conflict between the state and the Ulama in this period.[50] The landed class was also well entrenched in the state,[51] and the court was not able to bypass the local influence of landed deputies in the Majles. The 19th Majles elections, held in 1959 under Premier Ala, a landed aristocrat, bore witness to the cooperation of the court and the government with the landed class: the deputies were all nominated by the government and 61 per cent of them were landed magnates. The court had so far asserted its monopoly over the means of coercion and had been assured of foreign support, but in order to mobilise mass support and shake itself free of the power of entrenched interests, it needed a transformation in the power bloc. The situation which prompted the court was provided by both external pressures and internal causes. Externally, this was a time when many other similar praetorian states in peripheral capitalist countries confronting economic crises and political instability were attempting some social reforms and economic change which required the establishment of strong corporatist-authoritarian regimes. These attempts at a closer incorporation of the local economies into the central capitalist economy were instigated by the IMF and the central capitalist states, especially the US.

More generally, in all such peripheral countries, this process led to the emergence of a new type of developmentalist state which embarked upon a process of 'deepening' the capitalist economy.[52] In the case of Iran, the Kennedy administration, concerned with the way in which US financial aid to Iran was spent, demanded a greater emphasis on economic development than simply on the regime's political strength.[53] The internal political situation, however, provided the main cause for a restructuring of the state through a fascist-type mass mobilisation or a 'revolution from above' in order to consolidate the power basis of the Shah. The situation which prompted the Shah was the resurgence of large-scale political opposition and activism by the middle-class groups and parties in the early 1960s, and the expressed discontent of the popular sector as a result of an economic crisis (1957-61). This was caused by the liberal economic policy which had been in operation since the fall of Reza Shah. From 1955, with the reactivation of the oil industry and the advent of foreign grants, imports increased heavily (fivefold between 1955 and 1960) and the credit market expanded sevenfold. The result was trade deficit and inflation. In 1957, the government devalued to restore the balance of trade, but that caused more inflation. Between 1957 and 1961, at least twenty major strikes occurred. In the same period peasant unrest took place in several areas, especially in Gilan and Azarbayjan.[54]

Prompted by external and internal pressures, the Shah embarked upon a power struggle with various political forces which, after a period of two and a half years, ended in his hegemony. He first tried to impose his control over the parliament, which was dominated by the nobility. This was to take place through electoral manoeuvres, by introducing two court parties, in order to create a situation of controlled competition in the 1960 elections. The majority of candidates nominated by these parties were from the middle classes – professionals and civil servants – indicating the Shah's attempt at recruiting a dependent clientele.[55] Landed, military and clerical deputies, however, stood for re-election to the Majles as 'independents'. This led to the interference of the government in the elections to ensure the victory of court candidates, causing widespread protest among the political parties. The Shah had to cancel the election results. In the repeat elections, compromises had to be made with the old deputies.[56] Failing to dominate the Majles through fraudulent means, the Shah sought to curb its power through a strong reform cabinet. In May 1961, he called on Dr Ali Amini, a veteran landed politician, to form a reform cabinet. Amini widened the social basis of the cabinet by recruiting men like Dr Arsanjani, a socialist and an advocate of land reforms, Dr Darakhshesh, leader of the Teachers' Association, and Nuroddin Alamuti, one of the original founders of the Tudeh Party. The reform cabinet launched a campaign against 'feudalism' and the Shah stepped up his mass mobilisation by dissolving the Majles and mandating the government 'to guarantee welfare for state employees; to implement the land reform law; to guarantee workers' welfare through their participation in the factory's profit; and to assist factory owners by protecting domestic industry'.[57]

The centrepieces of the Shah's mobilisation effort were, first, land redistribution, which aimed at building a rural base of support among the small-holding peasants for the regime; and, secondly, to effect a shift in the power bloc through the adoption of a new economic policy. This was to lead to an alliance between the state and the high modern bourgeoisie on the basis of the 'deepening' of the economy. According to the Land Reform Law of 1962, landlords could retain only one village, and the rest of their holdings were subject to redistribution. The Law thus affected large land-holdings, covering 14,000 out of the 50,000 villages, and was first implemented in the large estates of Azarbayjan. Travelling around the country, the Shah himself handed over title deeds to the peasants. The land reforms were to continue in three phases until 1971 under further Acts covering lands exempted by the 1962 Law.[58]

The new economic policy which the government adopted in response to the economic crisis discussed above and the rise of the new authoritarian regime were closely intertwined.[59] In the previous two decades, the policy of economic liberalism had led to a substantial increase in foreign trade and resulted in a growth of the mercantile bourgeoisie, causing a decline in economic growth rates and a balance-of-payment crisis. With the 1962 prescription of the IMF, the government was forced to attempt major economic stabilisation efforts. Credit was tightened, foreign trade came under government control and the regime put emphasis on 'internal production'. This indicated a shift in the power bloc from an alliance between the national commercial bourgeoisie and the state to one emerging between the new regime and the modern dependent industrial bourgeoisie. The Shah directed the government to assist industrialists in order to raise domestic production. In 1963, the government held an 'Economic Conference' with industrialists, in which state development priorities were clarified. The emerging authoritarian regime began to intervene in the economy on a large scale, and to regulate private enterprise by protecting the industrial upper bourgeoisie at the expense of landed and commercial interests. The economic growth of the 1950s had been erratic; the new drive was towards the closer incorporation of the Iranian economy into the central capitalist economies. Despite the short-term opposition which it caused among mercantile interests, the new economic policy of stabilisation and growth was to be one of the cornerstones of the emerging authoritarian regime under the Shah.

In his attempt to transform the political system, the Shah sought to mobilise every segment of the population. Thus along with peasants and workers, he also undertook a mobilisation of women by amending the Electoral Law and giving them the right to vote.

To complete his consolidation of power, the Shah then disposed of Amini and his intellectual colleagues and replaced them with a loyal courtier, Assadollah Alam, and others of a similar disposition. Further, in January 1963, he ordered the government to convene a National Congress of Peasants in order to keep up the mobilisation and demonstrate his new-found support. The congress was followed by the holding of a national referendum, as a new source of populist legitimacy, to approve the Shah's measures. Then the Shah began to recruit a new dependent clientele to carry out his reforms, from among a group of 300 (mostly US-educated) civil servants and technocrats. They formed a grouping called the 'Progressive Centre'. This was soon converted into the official ruling party, the New Iran Party. The new party then nominated candidates from among its members for the elections of the 21st Majles, which had been postponed for more than two years. Not unexpectedly, the Shah's party emerged as the majority faction of the Majles and obtained all the cabinet posts. Thus the Shah succeeded in replacing the post-war practice of competitive elections and came to dominate all the major institutions of the state: the army, the Prime Minister's office, the cabinet, parliament, government and the ruling party.

The Shah's consolidation of an authoritarian regime and the suppression of the Constitution created a great deal of opposition which was expressed mainly in terms of support for the Constitution. The opposition of the landed class to the land reforms was not very formidable because there had already been warnings of land redistribution as well as some attempts at its implementation, such as the sale of the Crown lands, the Mosaddeq reforms and the ratification of a Land Reform Law by the Majles in 1959. In particular the opposition of absentee landlords was much less formidable than that of those who resided in their estates. For instance, in Azarbayjan there were 290 large absentee landlords affected by the 1962 Law: they were merchants, government employees and professional men, and of them only 238 retained a village as permitted by the Law; the rest sold off all their holdings.[60] By contrast, the landlords of Fars, who were more dependent on the land revenues, engaged in open conflict with the regime. Furthermore, from 1963, when more opposition was expressed by smaller land-holders in reaction to Arsanjani's warning of thorough land reforms, the Shah slowed down the reforms. Hence, the Law of the second phase of the reforms concerning lands exempted by the 1962 Law gave a number of options to the landlords: they could either rent or sell their lands to the peasants, or divide them between themselves and their peasants. On the whole, the reform aimed at dispersing the grand landowners and when it came to smaller landowners, they were slowed down. Landed aristocrats such as Sardar Hekmat, the Speaker of the 19th Majles, Mohsen Sadr, the President of the Senate, Ahmad Bahmanyar, the Finance Minister, and Hossein Ala, the former Premier and others expressed their opposition to the suspension of the Constitution and the land reforms, but this generation of landed nobility increasingly dropped into the background.

The bazaar and the commercial bourgeoisie expressed strong opposition to the rise of the Shah and his new policies. The increasing intervention of the state in the economy to regulate private enterprise and redirect mercantile capital into productive ventures hit powerful interests who had been benefiting from the post-war policy of tariff concessions and open trade.[61] In October 1961, hundreds of traders in the Tehran bazaar organised a meeting and set up a Union for the Safeguarding of the Constitution and Individual Rights. It expressed its vehement opposition to the reform cabinet and the suspension of parliament, and called for the scrapping of the new economic policies.[62]

The most vehement opposition to the ascendancy of the Shah, the suppression of the Constitution and the increasing integration of Iran into the Western political and economic system was expressed by the Ulama. The main body of the Ulama supported the Constitution which had defined the realm of secular power and recognised the prerogatives of the Ulama, especially in legislation affecting Islamic law. However, some of the Ulama, for example Ayatollahs Borujerdi and Behbehani, were conservative and anti-reformist; a few, for example Ayatollahs Taleqani and Zanjani, joined democratic parties; and others, for example Ayatollahs Kashani and Khomeini, were intensely nationalist and anti-imperialist and spoke of the revival of the Islamic social order. In times of conflict with the state, however, they all supported the Constitution. Thus in their opposition to the rise of authoritarianism, they supported the constitutional *status quo*. But there were also other issues involved. The conservative Ulama objected to female enfranchisement and opposed the land reforms as being contrary to Islamic juridical theory. The first Land Reform Law of 1959 had brought about the opposition of Ayatollah Borujerdi, although it had excluded the *ouqāf* lands. The 1962 Law also excluded the latter, but the 1963 Amendments to the Law extended the reforms to these lands. This further intensified the opposition of the Ulama as it was expressed by Ayatollah Behbehani of Tehran, who sent a letter of protest to the government.[63] Other Ulama, Ayatollahs Khomeini and Milani for example, did not express opposition to the land reforms[64] and put emphasis on the constitutional issue. In the light of this issue, they also objected to a government bill which abrogated the constitutional provision for candidates in local elections to be Moslem and gave the vote to women. Much more importantly, the opposition of the Ulama was an expression of the awakening of Iran's indigenous religious nationalism in reaction to the increasing incorporation of Iran into the Western political and economic system under the authoritarian rule of the Shah. Thus when in 1964 the Majles, dominated by the Shah, approved the Status of Forces Agreement between Iran and the USA, thereby extending diplomatic immunity to US military personnel in Iran in exchange for a $200 million US military credit, the Ulama opposition was further aggravated.[65] Of this religious nationalism Ayatollah Khomeini became the most outspoken representative.

The emergence of the authoritarian regime under the Shah thus antagonised landed, mercantile and clerical interests and led to open conflict between the army and the opposition. Preaching against the rule of the Shah and the domination of Iran by the West, Ayatollah Khomeini accused the regime of violating Islam and the Constitution and collaborating with imperialism. In the mourning month of Muharram (June 1963), the Ulama turned religious rituals into political protests which led to the arrest of the senior Ulama and a bloody suppression of bazaar crowds by the army. Some four hundred bazaaris were arrested and a few were executed. Thus the opposition to the rise of royal power was defeated; this was to mark the eclipse of political opposition until the revolution of 1978-9.

Thus, from a position of relative weakness and insecurity dating back to 1941, the Shah emerged into the limelight of politics as autocratic ruler by 1963. With the army under his firm control, the reform and referendum as his contrived source of legitimacy and a party of subservient lieutenants to carry out his policies, the Shah had now at his disposal all the ingredients of absolute rulership. In the following chapter, we shall discuss the major characteristics of the Shah's dependent authoritarian regime.

Notes

1. For a discussion of the traditional Persian power structure see A.K.S. Lambton, *Landlord and Peasant in Persia* (London, 1953), pp. 105-28; *idem*, 'Quis Custodiet Custodes: Some Reflections on the Persian Theory of Government', *Studia Islamica*, vol. 5 (1956), pp. 125-48, and vol. 6 (1956), pp. 125-46; and V. Minorsky, *Tadhkirat al-Muluk: A Manual of Safavid Administration* (London, 1943).

2. Traditional Iranian absolutism was akin to the type of Oriental despotism discussed by Marx and Engels. See H. Draper, *Karl Marx's Theory of Revolution, vol. I. State and Bureaucracy* (New York, 1977), pp. 523ff.

3. On the difference between Eastern absolutism and Western feudalism see R. Bendix, *Nation-Building and Citizenship* (New York, 1969), p. 37.

4. For detailed accounts of the system of land-holding and the relationship between the state and the landed class see Lambton, *Landlord and Peasant*; *idem*, 'The Evolution of the Eqta in Medieval Iran', *Journal of the British Institute of Persian Studies* (1967), pp. 41-50; and N.R. Keddie, *Historical Obstacles to Agrarian Change in Iran* (Claremont, California, 1960).

5. On the economic functions of the absolutist state see R. Savory, *Iran under the Safavids* (Cambridge, 1980), pp. 177-202.

6. Semi-feudal land-holdings were established under the Mongol and Tamerlane dynasties; see Lambton, *Landlord and Peasant*, Chapter 4. A number of scholarly studies have attempted to interpret the history of Iran up to the nineteenth century in terms of Marxian modes of production. N. Pigulovskaya *et al.* in *Tarikh-e Iran az Dowreh-ye Bastan ta Payan-e Sedeh-ye Hezhdahom* (*A History of Iran from Ancient Times to the End of the Eighteenth Century*), trans. K. Keshavarz (Tehran, 1346), have studied Iranian history in terms of the four stages of the early communal society, slavery, feudalism and capitalism. The bulk of the history of Islamic Iran, in their view, consists of the rise and demise of feudalism. By contrast, A. Ashraf, in *Nezam-e Feodali ya Nezam-e Asiai* (*Feudal System or Asiatic System*) put emphasis on the despotic-bureaucratic structure of the state in pre-modern Iran (Tehran, 1347). See also R. Shaikholeslami, 'Sale of Offices in Qajar Iran', *Iranian Studies* (Spring 1972).

7. See Lambton, *Landlord and Peasant*, Chapter 5; Savory, *Iran under the Safavids*, pp. 177-202; and A. Ashraf, 'Historical Obstacles to the Development of a Bourgeoisie in Iran' in M.A. Cook (ed.), *Studies in the Economic History of the Middle East* (London, 1970), pp. 308-32.

8. Keddie, *Historical Obstacles*, p. 4; Z. Abdollaev, 'Bourgeoisie and Working Class' in Charles Issawi (ed.), *The Economic History of Iran* (Chicago, 1971), p. 45, discusses the dramatic emergence and growth of the capitalist and landed class between 1880 and 1900.

9. On the growth of Western influence in Iran see F. Kazemzadeh, *Russia and Britain in Persia, 1864-1914: A Study in Imperialism* (London, 1968).

10. Abdollaev, 'Bourgeoisie and Working Class', mentions a dozen of the most powerful Iranian trading houses and merchant families who competed with Western and Russian merchants.

11. The Shiites supported the claim of Ali b. Abitaleb, the cousin and son-in-law

of the Prophet, to the leadership of the Moslem community as the successor to the Prophet. They believed that Mohammad had appointed Ali as Caliph by the order of Allah. For the Shiites, then, the Moslem community is divinely guided through the Imams. See H. Algar, *Religion and State in Iran: 1785-1906, the Role of the Ulama in the Qajar Period* (Berkeley, 1970), Chapter 1; L. Binder, 'Religion and Politics in Iran' in *Arabic and Islamic Studies in Honor of H.A.R. Gibb* (Leiden, 1965), pp. 118-40; and S.H.M. Jafri, *Origins and Early Development of Shia Islam* (London, 1979), pp. 289-312, on the doctrine of Imamate.

12. It was Ulama power reinforced by that of the bazaar which made Naser ed Din Shah cancel the Reuter Concession in 1872, which had sold all the national resources for a very low price. Again in 1891 the Ulama staged a successful mass movement against the British Tobacco Concession; see Kazemzadeh, *Russia and Britain in Persia*, pp. 105ff; N.R. Keddie, *Religion and Rebellion in Iran: The Tobacco Protest of 1891-1892* (London, 1966).

13. Some accounts of Ulama power are given in N.R. Keddie, 'The Roots of the Ulama's Power in Modern Iran', and H. Algar, 'The Oppositional Role of the Ulama in Twentieth-Century Iran', both in N.R. Keddie (ed.), *Scholars, Saints and Sufis: Moslem Religious Institutions in the Middle East since 1500* (Berkeley, 1972).

14. E. Abrahamian in 'Oriental Despotism: The Case of Qajar Iran', *International Journal of Middle East Studies*, vol. 5 (1974), pp. 3-31, shows how the Qajars, despite their absolutist pretensions, lacked effective power and instead had to manipulate local magnates in order to perpetuate their despotic position. On the Qajars see also A.K.S. Lambton, 'Persian Society under the Qajars', *Journal of the Royal Central Asian Society*, vol. 48 (1961), pp. 123-38; and H. Busse (trans.), *History of Persia under Qajar Rule* (New York, 1972).

15. See E.G. Browne, *The Persian Revolution: 1905-9* (Cambridge, 1910); and A. Kasravi, *Tarikh-e Mashruteh-ye Iran* (*A History of the Constitutional Movement in Iran*) (Tehran, 1340).

16. Browne, *Persian Revolution*, p. 355.

17. Z. Shajii, *Nemayandegan-e Majles-e Shura-ye Melli dar Bist-o Yek Dowreh-ye Qanungozari* (*Members of Parliament in Twenty-One Sessions of the Majles*) (Tehran, 1345), pp. 137ff.

18. Keddie, *Historical Obstacles*, p. 7; M.S. Ivanov, *Tarikh-e Iran-e Novin* (*Contemporary History of Iran*), trans. H. Tizabi and H. Qaemnia (Tehran, n.d.), p. 34.

19. Shajii, *Nemayandegan-e Majles-e*, p. 173.

20. M.T. Bahar, *Tarikh-e Mokhtasar-e Ahzab-e Siyasi-ye Iran* (*A Short History of Political Parties in Iran*) (Tehran, 1322).

21. Fedaiyan-e Khalq Organisation, *Rural Research Series*, no. 1 (n.d.), pp. 1-15; see also *The Cambridge History of Iran*, vol. 1 (1968), p. 687; according to M. Soudagar, *Barresi-ye Eslahat-e Arzi: 1340-50* (*An Analysis of the Land Reforms: 1961-71*) (Tehran, 1351), p. 76, 40% of all villages belonged to 12% of the landowners and 55% of cultivable land was owned by 1% of the population.

22. A list of major oligarchic families can be found in the appendix to Shajii, *Nemayandegan-e Majles-e*. A. Qassemi has carried out research on a number of interrelated aristocratic families: *Oligarshi ya Khanedan-haye Hokumatgar-e Iran* (*Oligarchy or the Ruling Families of Iran*) (4 vols., Tehran, 1354, 1355, 1356, 1357). On the domination of the legislative process by the oligarchy see: 'Jami', *Gozashteh Cherag-e Rah-e Ayandeh ast* (*The History of Iran between Two Coups d'état*) (Tehran, n.d.), p. 223.

23. On such factions see, e.g., E. Abrahamian, 'Factionalism in Iran: Political Groups in the 14th Parliament', *Middle Eastern Studies*, vol. 14 (1978), pp. 22-55.

24. An account of the party is given in L. Binder, *Iran: Political Development*

in a Changing Society (Berkeley, 1962), pp. 206-8; and E. Abrahamian, 'The Social Bases of Iranian Politics: The Tudeh Party, 1941-53', unpublished PhD thesis, Columbia University, 1969.

25. Qassemi, *Oligarshi*, vol. 1, *passim*.

26. R. Cottam, *Nationalism in Iran* (Pittsburgh, 1964), p. 44.

27. For instance, in the town of Borujerd in the west of the country, shop-keepers usually wear the clerical garb, and some of them perform the mullah's job of *rouzeh-khani* (preaching in the mosque).

28. The 1919 Treaty, which was negotiated in secrecy between the British and the British-backed government in Tehran, would lead to British domination of Iran's army, economy and administration. In the face of strong domestic opposition, it was never put into effect; see G. Lenczowski, *Russia and the West in Iran, 1918-1948: A Study in Big Power Rivalry* (Ithaca, 1949), pp. 45-7.

29. B. Jazani, *Tarikh-e Si Saleh-ye* (*A Thirty-Year History*) (Tehran, n.d.), p. 141; the party proposed the establishment of two houses of parliament: a house of Mujtaheds and a house of people: *Khalq* (the party organ), no. 7, 1 Mordad 1344.

30. Figures calculated from The Plan and Budget Organisation, *National Census of Population: 1966* (Tehran, 1968); and Statistical Centre of Iran, *General Census of Population and Households: 1976* (Tehran, 1976).

31. Cottam, *Nationalism*, p. 265; some account of the party is also given in R. Cottam, 'Political Party Development in Iran', *Iranian Studies* (Summer 1968), pp. 82-96.

32. Calculated from the censuses of 1956 and 1976.

33. Ministry of Agriculture, *Agricultural Statistics* (1339), vol. 15, p. 9.

34. Soudagar, *Survey of Land Reforms*, pp. 81ff.

35. K. Khosrovi, *Jamei-ye Dehgani dar Iran* (*The Peasant Community in Iran*) (Tehran, 1357), p. 124, explains: 'The townspeople in their interactions with the peasants have found them a "polite", "calm" and "peaceful" people. There is no doubt that the fear of the landlord has resulted in such behavioural appearances.' However, a number of conflicts occurred between peasants and landlords in the 1956-8 period as reported by Ivanov, *Tarikh-e Iran-e Novin*, p. 209.

36. Sazeman-e Enghelabi, *Nehzat-haye Kargari pas az 1320* (*The Working Class Movement after 1941*) (Tehran, 1350), p. 23.

37. Ibid., p. 54.

38. For a full account of the history of the party see S. Zabih, *The Communist Movement in Iran* (Berkeley, 1966); for the social and communal bases of the party see Abrahamian, 'The Social Bases of Iranian Politics'.

39. Of the founding members of the organisation, 11 were students, 5 were teachers, 8 engineers, 12 workers, 1 civil servant and 1 army officer: from a list of the 'martyrs of the Fedaiyan-e Khalq' published in various issues of *Kayhan* (Farvardin and Ordibehesht, 1358).

40. Shajii, *Nemayandegan-e Majles-e*, pp. 173ff.

41. J. Bharier, *Economic Development in Iran, 1900-1970* (London, 1971), pp. 84-6.

42. P. Avery, *Modern Iran* (London, 1965), p. 451.

43. Iranian Students Association in Europe, *Mosaddeq va Nehzat-e Melli-ye Iran* (*Mosaddeq and the National Movement of Iran*) (Tehran, 1357), pp. 20ff.

44. On the oil nationalisation movement and its politics see L.P. Elwell-Sutton, *Persian Oil: A Study in Power Politics* (London, 1955).

45. Ayatollah Kashani's letter to Dr Mosaddeq, dated 18 August 1953, is reproduced in the *Echo of Islam* (June-July 1981), p. 189.

46. On the US support for the royalists which led to the overthrow of Mosaddeq see K. Roosevelt, *Countercoup: The Struggle for the Control of Iran* (New

York, 1980); and A. Tully, *CIA: The Inside Story* (New York, 1962), pp. 88-99.

47. In the 1950s US economic loans and grants to Iran totalled $520 million; of this $195 million was in loans and $327 million in grants. In the same period US military loans and grants to Iran totalled $400 million (US AID Mission, *Economic Assistance Activities in Iran, 1950-65* (Tehran, 1966), quoted by Bharier, *Economic Development*, p. 119).

48. US investment in the 1962-7 period amounted to 54% of all foreign investment in Iran, or $230 million: Bank Markazi, *Annual Report* (1968); it was to increase to $560 million in the early 1970s.

49. Cf. A. Westwood, 'Elections and Politics in Iran', *Middle East Journal*, vol. 15 (1960), pp. 397-415.

50. After the fall of Reza Shah religious rituals were resumed and the ban on the pilgrimage to Mecca was lifted. The government itself put emphasis on religious ceremonies (see Avery, *Modern Iran*, p. 481).

51. This was in spite of the Mosaddeq agrarian reforms according to which out of a 20% deduction from the landlord's share 10% would be returned to the peasant and the other 10% would be earmarked for rural development. Although Mosaddeq's reforms did not touch the tenurial system, with his fall most of the reforms were written off. See A.K.S. Lambton, *The Persian Land Reforms: 1962-1966* (Oxford, 1969), pp. 39-40.

52. On this process see G.A. O'Donnell, 'Corporatism and the Question of the State' in J. Malloy (ed.), *Authoritarianism and Corporatism in Latin America* (Pittsburgh, 1977), pp. 47-87.

53. See R. Pfau, 'The Legal Status of American Forces in Iran', *Middle East Journal*, vol. 28 (1974), pp. 141-53 at p. 148.

54. Ivanov, *Tarikh-e Iran-e*, pp. 207-9.

55. Of the nominees 37 were doctors, 45 landowners, 5 engineers, 3 merchants, 4 lawyers, 8 journalists and 3 retired army officers: *Kayhan*, 27 Teer 1339, quoted by Westwood, 'Elections and Politics'.

56. Thus out of 176 deputies elected for the 20th Majles, 96 were landed magnates; see Shajii, *Nemayandegan-e Majles-e*.

57. *Ettelaat*, 24 Aban 1340.

58. By 1964 some 9,000 whole or parts of villages had been distributed among *nasaqdār* families. See Lambton, *Land Reforms*, p. 91; and H. Mahdavi, 'The Coming Crisis in Iran', *Foreign Affairs*, vol. 44 (1965), pp. 134-46 at p. 138.

59. On the relationship between the emergence of authoritarianism and economic crisis, see, e.g., J. Malloy (ed.), *Authoritarianism and Corporatism in Latin America* (Pittsburgh, 1977), pp. 149ff.

60. Lambton, *Land Reforms*, p. 41.

61. *Ettelaat*, 29 Esfand 1342, surveyed the pressures of new taxes and other measures of the reform cabinet on the bazaar.

62. *Iran Almanac*, 1343.

63. Ibid., p. 433.

64. The regime itself named the following as opponents of land reforms: Ayatollahs Behbehani, Golpaygani, Marashi, Shirazi and Khorasani, *Iran Almanac*, pp. 432ff. Ayatollah Khomeini's opposition was for the first time expressed against the electoral bill of September 1962. There are no statements in which Ayatollahs Khomeini, Taleqani or Shariatmadari express opposition to the land reforms.

65. The emergence and intensification of this indigenous religious nationalism as the major platform of an important segment of the Ulama since the closing decades of the nineteenth century is the subject of Chapter 3.

2 THE OLD REGIME: THE RULE OF THE MONARCHY

The emergence of the authoritarian regime under the Shah in the early 1960s led to important changes within the power bloc. The old power bloc, which had been composed of the landed class, and the national commercial bourgeoisie had been in a process of disintegration. The landed class was in dissolution due to the country's transformation from a predominantly agrarian to a semi-industrial society. On the other hand the middle classes were divided. All this contributed to the handing back of political power to the Shah, and to the emergence of a new power bloc. As a result of the economic development and industrialisation programme which aimed at property concentration in industry and a change in the productive structure, the power bloc became dominated by a grand industrial and financial bourgeoisie which had tenuous local and strong international ties. The royal family itself replaced its Crown lands with vast industrial and financial holdings and encouraged the expansion of the upper bourgeoisie. However, the authoritarian regime of the Shah was not a direct class rule, but as a bureaucratic regime it sought to maintain a degree of autonomy from the dominant class interests.[1] Thus it established a corporatist political structure in order to encompass and control major class interests. The Shah reached out to the peasantry, the industrial bourgeoisie and the working class for political support. He sought to create a 'rural bourgeoisie' benefiting from the land reforms. By promoting industrialisation, the regime encouraged the emergence of the upper bourgeoisie which prospered in a hot-house fashion. At the same time, it also attempted to create a 'labour aristocracy'. To subordinate these diverse classes, the Shah turned the New Iran Party (NIP) into a corporatist political organisation seeking to control all classes. The Shah's authoritarian regime was based on five foundations: (a) state control of large financial resources made available through the massive oil billions; (b) the success of the economic stabilisation and growth programme and the intervention of the Shah in the economy to ensure economic stability; (c) intermittent attempts at mass mobilisation and the creation of an equilibrium of classes through their economic control and intervention in the economy; (d) the establishment of patron-client relations with the upper bourgeoisie and the Shah's control of private enterprise through participation in entrepreneurial activities; and (e) the expansion of the coercive forces of the state, and reliance on Western and especially US support.

The Shah's Party

The NIP was the Shah's political organisation built to carry out his reforms and to control government and parliament. It was the first successful court party to dominate parliament and government and was the first of its kind to emerge in Iran.[2] The party functioned as a channelling agency devised to bring the main interest groupings under the mantle of the state. It was generated from the reform movement and court ideology which was presented not as a class ideology but as the state ideology allegedly representing diverse class interests.[3] Thus the party extended its control to all employers' associations, trade unions, bazaar guilds, civil service associations and rural cooperatives established in connection with the land reforms. The party brought the major employers' associations under government control and sought to define and restrict the fields of commerce. Among these associations were the Syndicate of the Owners of Textile Industries, the Syndicate of Metallic Industries, the Syndicate of Iranian Industries and the Chamber of Industries and Mines.[4] In addition there was the Chamber of Commerce encompassing all the registered commercial companies and large trading houses. Formed under the Chamber were 25 commercial federations administered by commissions of large businessmen in various fields of trade.[5] In March 1964 the new regime organised an economic conference between the government under the control of the NIP and the Chamber and other associations in which the grievances and demands of the industrialists and businessmen regarding the reduction of income tax, credit facilities and customs exemptions were put forward. In response the government promised to meet their demands.[6]

In addition, under the new regime a serious attempt was made at organising labour unions. Previous governments had been unwilling to organise labour. Following the establishment of the Ministry of Labour in 1946 to outmanoeuvre the Tudeh Party's trade unions, by setting up an official trade union, government interest in labour affairs subsided and in the decade after the 1953 *coup* even government trade unions were discouraged. However, the new regime brought all registered trade unions under control and party slogans put stress on the workers' professional rights. The NIP functioned as a mediator between workers and employers in their disputes. For instance, in 1971 it mediated a series of wage disputes between the Workers' Organisation and the general Syndicate of Employers, both affiliated to the party.[7]

The party also attempted to bring under government control the traditional bazaar guilds. The guilds lost their power after the fall of the National Front government under which they had been politically active. The Guilds Law of 1957 in particular stripped them of their independence and power. According to this, the guilds were only to be formed with the permission of the government, and the High Council of Guilds would operate under the supervision of city governors.[8] In 1971 the guilds were brought under close party control. A new Guilds Code dissolved the High Council of Guilds and instead established the Chamber of Guilds with full supervisory power over all guilds. The Chamber, composed of party members, provided the NIP with an effective instrument in implementing the guild regulations concerning the issue of trade permits, price fixing, working hours and so on. Since the guilds covered all large and small shops (with an overall membership of 500,000) the bazaars came to feel the weight of the ruling party.[9]

Associations of civil servants had sprung up under the National Front government. There were the associations of teachers, engineers, doctors, lawyers and so on. Since most of these had been linked with various National Front parties, they were all suppressed after the fall of Mosaddeq.[10] In place of the old associations, the NIP established its own organisations to represent professional groups.

Of great interest to the regime were the rural cooperatives. After the land reforms the Central Organisation of Rural Cooperatives, an independent company, was formed to supervise the cooperatives. Later the government brought the cooperative movement under its control by incorporating the organisation into the Ministry of Land Reforms. Local party cells established links with the cooperatives and put a few peasants on party councils. Almost all of the 8,000 cooperatives had affiliated to the party.[11]

The most significant political aspect of the NIP was that it signalled the end of open conflict for control of parliament that had marked the years since the accession of the Shah. Thus candidates for elections had to join the court party which carried out all the necessary screening of candidates. The process of the nomination of candidates was carried out through an extensive hierarchy of organisations. The party convention nominated legislative candidates, invited delegates from towns and villages and announced party platforms. As it appears from its parliamentary slates, the party nominated candidates from diverse classes indicating the regime's attempt at recruiting a dependent clientele. It put particular emphasis on a symbolic representation of the lower classes. In the 21st Majles, the first which was held under the new regime, of the deputies 95 were civil servants, 32 professionals, 24 cultivators, 9 workers, 8 traders, 7 landlords, 11 employees of the private sector and 4 were from the bazaar guilds.[12] In the last Majles convened under the NIP, of the deputies 121 were engineers, judges, lawyers and journalists, 46 were civil servants, 23 were farmers, 22 were industrialists and businessmen, 21 were teachers and 15 were workers.[13]

By controlling government and the entry into parliament, the NIP provided the court with an effective instrument for controlling legislation through the High Economic Council. This was a weekly session held at the court between the cabinet and the Shah to discuss (especially) economic matters and was the major source of proposals for legislation. The council included ministers in economic and developmental affairs, the governor of the Central Bank, the director of the Plan Organisation and the chairman of the Oil Company.[14] The guidelines given by the Shah in the council were translated into proposals for legislation by the ministries and were sent to the NIP's Central Committee for investigation. Then the proposals were sent to the Executive Committee attended by the party's parliamentary group. The Executive Committee finally prepared the bill to be presented to the Majles where the NIP assured its smooth passage.[15] Thus the whole structure of the state, including government, parliament and the ruling party, was subordinated to the court which was at the centre of power.

Despite its organisational strength the NIP remained an instrument in the hands of the Shah. The party conventions were either attended or guided by the Shah and their most important function was to update the party's platform with the latest pronouncements of the court. Since the major function of the party was the mobilisation of support for the court it was finally the Shah's decision that the NIP had failed to mobilise a wide range of interests that led to the eventual dissolution of the party before the revolution of 1979.

The Bases of the *Status Quo* before the Revolution

For more than a decade (1963-76) a combination of factors held the Shah's authoritarian regime together. We will examine each in turn.

Coercive Forces and US Support
Prior to the 1963 mobilisation effort by the Shah, the army had been

his main power base. In the 1940s he had sought to reorganise the military by applying for US military grants; and in the 1950s he had constantly used the army to keep down the population and to suppress the National Front and the Tudeh opposition. The modern army had been created by Reza Shah on the British model. The court had patrimonial authority over the army, which, as a new institution having few links with the oligarchy, became closely identified with the Shah. It was the separation of the military from the landed class that enabled the Shah to curb the power of that class and of the tribal nobility. It was also control over the military that enabled the Shah to extend his powers beyond and above the Constitution. He recruited a loyal officer corps and purged the older military elite which had tended to develop a power base within the army. Thus in 1962 when he was consolidating his power, several army officers considered political rivals were arrested and 33 generals and 270 colonels were retired.[16] From the time of his accession to the throne the Shah sought to rebuild the army which had disintegrated after the Allied invasion of Iran. By the mid-1970s, he had created a most formidable military structure through increasing the defence budget, seeking military aid from abroad and expanding the forces. The army was enlarged from 120,000 in 1941 to 400,000 in 1977.[17] Annual military expenditure rose from $70 million in 1960, to $3,500 million in 1973, and to $9,000 million in 1977. On average, it formed 30 per cent of the annual budget. The army was increasingly equipped with modern weaponry made available through military aid and grants, provided especially by the US. Between 1953 and 1970, US military and economic grants to Iran amounted to $2.3 billion.[18] Of this more than $1 billion were in military aid and grants. With the advent of the oil billions, especially in the early 1970s, the military was expanded unprecedentedly. Between 1975 and 1979 the regime purchased $6.6 billion worth of US arms. Thus in 1976 Iran obtained 160 F-16 fighter planes at the price of $3.4 billion.[19] US military sales to Iran increased from $10 million in 1950, to $100 million in 1970, and to $3.9 billion in 1974.[20]

Constitutionally the Shah was the supreme commander of the army. Prior to his consolidation of power, powerful prime ministers had sought to wrest the control of the army from the Shah. One of the issues which led to direct confrontation between the Shah and Mosaddeq had been control over the military. To ensure the loyalty of the army the Shah controlled military recruitment and the organisation and size of the armed forces. Important promotions needed his personal approval. From the beginning the maintenance of such a loyal army required considerable liquid assets on the part of the Shah to ensure adequate subsistence. Reza Shah had given land to his officers. Under his son, US military grants and the oil billions provided a dependable financial resource, making possible the maintenance of a privileged class of officer corps. Also, the recruitment of foreign military advisers and personnel made the army more dependable because they had little contact with the subject population. This was not unlike past practices of the absolutist kings whose select military force consisted of aliens who were considered more reliable than local recruits.

While the army remained the mainstay of the monarchy, the regime used the political police to eliminate opposition. The repressive apparatus included the Imperial Special Bureau and the Imperial Inspectorate, which had supervision over all other repressive organisations and ensured order within the army; the Military Intelligence Agency; and the State Information and Security Organisation, SAVAK, which dealt directly with civil opposition. SAVAK had been organised in 1957 with active assistance from the US government.[21] The US also had an intelligence mission with SAVAK. Numbering tens of thousands, SAVAK penetrated all government institutions, trade unions, universities, bazaar guilds, the press, factories, rural cooperatives, and so on.[22] Its members enjoyed arbitrary powers in security matters and used extensive methods of interrogation, trial, torture and physical elimination.[23]

The Shah's military power had from the beginning been determined by his dependence on the US. Thus indirectly American support for the Shah constituted a major power base of his regime, in terms of military build-up, political support and economic interdependence. To be sure, in the 1962-79 period Iran-US relations assumed new dimensions and went beyond Iran's sheer political dependence on the US.[24] Previously, in the wake of the war the Shah had to reformulate Iran's foreign policy orientations after the fall of the pro-German Reza Shah regime. He did so in line with an old foreign policy stance of seeking a 'third power' in order to ward off pressures from the two major powers, Britain and Russia. Thus US support was actively sought for putting pressure on the Red Army to evacuate the provinces of Azarbayjan and Kurdestan which it had occupied during the war. Later even Dr Mosaddeq had to seek US support in his dispute with Britain over the oil issue.[25] However, up to the 1953 *coup d'état*, US support for Iran was confined mainly to the assignment of advisory military missions to the Shah's army. Thus total US economic and military loans and grants to Iran before 1953 did not exceed $59 million. It was after the *coup d'état* that the US became committed to the stability of the Shah's regime. In the 1953-7 period US economic and military loans and grants to Iran rose to $500 million.[26] At the same time the US obtained a 40 per cent stake in Iranian oil. US-Iran relations, however, witnessed their lowest ebb under the Kennedy administration, which in the early 1960s cut back military aid to Iran and made its continuation conditional on the adoption of reforms by the regime. With the Johnson administration, the relationship between the two states picked up again. In 1964 the Shah made a visit to the US for a meeting with the President in order to persuade the US to resume and expand its military credit to Iran. The US agreed to grant Iran $200 million in military credit. Under the Nixon administration, Iran's alliance with and dependence on the US were further deepened. Considering Iran as a 'developed' country, the US ended its aid programme to Iran in 1967. In May 1972 Nixon visited the Shah in Tehran and agreed to sell Iran 'any conventional weapons systems it wanted'. This signalled the emergence of more complex relations between the two states. In the early 1970s, the Iranian regime with its increasing oil revenues and importance emerged as a mainstay of Western economic stability and political influence.[27] It aligned itself with the shift in US foreign policy in 1969 (known as the Nixon Doctrine) from a direct American involvement in areas of political interest to the US to one of creating 'regional powers'. It was a combination of this and Iran's increasing oil revenues that enabled the Shah to expand and equip his army phenomenally. Even prior to this, due to the new international situation after the Cold War and the diversification of Iran's foreign relations, the regime had sought to adopt a new foreign policy stance *vis-à-vis* its outright dependence on the US in the previous decades. Thus in 1966 it declared a 'national independent foreign policy', meaning a realignment in Iran's foreign relations on the basis of its direct national interests. This led to establishing trade relations with Soviet Russia and the adoption of a policy of regional security in the Persian Gulf in order to safeguard Iranian/Western interests in the region.[28]

In spite of the changes in the regime's foreign policy in the 1966-78 period, US support formed a basis of its power, not only in the sense of international security but also in terms of domestic power – if only on account of the 1953 precedent of US active support for the Shah. Iran's political, economic and military dependence on the US had taken root during the Cold War era, and the more recent diversification in Iran-US relations did not eliminate Iran's basic need for security which lay behind those relations. The Shah himself counted on US support for his regime. In 1976 he said: 'The United States understands us better for the simple reason that it has so many interests in Iran. Economic and therefore direct interests, political and therefore indirect interests.'[29] The US was deeply involved in the industrial and military build-up of Iran, which obviously required the stability of the regime. US private investment in Iran reached $1 billion in 1975.[30] Still, the Shah called on US businessmen to 'be more aggressive' in seeking contracts in Iran.[31] There were some 400 US firms with stakes in Iran's economy, and some 44,000 Americans were resident in Iran in connection with the arms industry and other businesses. In 1975 an agreement for economic co-operation was signed between the two countries; it was to cover $15 billion worth of trade excluding oil.[32] In the 1970s Iran was the largest client of US arms; it planned to purchase $10 billion worth of US arms between 1975 and 1980. Certainly, US involvement in Iran formed a major basis of the Shah's power so far as any opposition to him had to reckon with the US support for the regime. We shall see that during the 1979 revolution, a major segment of the opposition had to approach the US Embassy and officials, in order to undermine the regime's external support.

Oil and Economic Stability

The inflow of the 'oil billions' formed the cornerstone of the autonomy of the state by providing it with an independent source of revenue.[33] Having little to do with domestic economic processes the oil revenues were not unlike 'external rents' given to a state which was dependent on their receipts on a regular basis.[34] Yet these revenues enabled the regime to enlarge public expenditure without the need to extract the necessary resources from the domestic economy through high taxation. Financially the oil revenues, constituting the major source of government income, enabled the regime to expand regular governmental expenditures. The share of the oil revenues in total government revenues increased from 11 per cent in 1954, to 45 per cent in 1963, to 56 per cent in 1971, and to 77 per cent in 1977. In the 1963-73 period the oil earnings provided between 60 and 79 per cent of the state's foreign exchange income and formed an average of 50 per cent of government revenues. By way of contrast, in the same period the share of direct taxes in government revenues did not change substantially and constituted no more than an average of 7 per cent of those revenues. Neither did the relative share of indirect taxes increase; they formed an average of 19 per cent of total government revenues.[35]

The oil revenues thus provided the regime with a regular source of funds without the need to resort to fiscal and monetary measures to curtail public consumption in order to finance large governmental expenditure. Thus while taxes were kept low government expenditure did not affect private consumption. In fact, through an expansion in liquidity and credit availability private consumption and investment increased. Between 1962 and 1972 private consumption expenditure increased from 252 to 572 billion rials and private investment from 45 to 92 billion rials. The dependence of the state on oil revenues consequently tended to prevent the development of a regular and efficient taxation system for the mobilisation of resources from within. Tax regulations remained arbitrary and subject to change at the discretion of the government. In the case of the bazaar guilds the amount of taxation was open to lengthy negotiation but the government could demand prompt payment.[36]

As a result of the substantial increase in the amount of oil revenues — from 29 billion rials in 1963 to 182 billion rials in 1972 — the government could accomplish more than ever before. Between 1962 and 1972 current expenditure by the government increased from 35 to 189 billion rials. Previously the oil sector contribution had been low. It was only from 1964 onwards, coinciding with the ascendancy of royal power, that oil's contribution began to accelerate. This enabled the regime to make attempts at comprehensive planning. The earlier plans had been no more than allocation of public revenues by the government. Oil revenues constituted the major source for financing the comprehensive development plans which followed.[37] Thus, relying on the oil revenues, the public sector was able to carry out its industrialisation, electrification and communications schemes.

The stabilisation policy adopted in 1962 was to prove successful. With the application of orthodox policies, the 1963-73 period, in contrast to the preceding and subsequent periods, was marked by economic stability in prices, wages, employment and taxes. Following the period of economic crisis (1957-62) which prompted the emergence of the authoritarian reform regime under court hegemony, the government adopted a growth policy, imposed credit and trade restrictions and cut down on imports. Increasing oil revenues enabled the regime to keep prices down by imposing trade restrictions and by using government monopolies and extensive subsidisation. Thus in the period between 1963 and 1972 prices rose by an average of 3 per cent. There was also stability with regard to the increase in wages; those of industrial workers increased by an average of 7 per cent and those of non-industrial workers by an average of 4 per cent, as shown in Table 2.1.

Table 2.1: Consumer Price Index and Wages, 1963-72

Year	1963	1964	1965	1966	1967	1968	1969	1970	1971	1972
Prices	89.4	93.3	93.5	94.3	95.1	96.6	100	101.5	107.1	113.8
Industrial wages	77	81	83	96	100	108	116	122	130	147
Non-industrial wages	33	36	37	37	40	44	51	52	54	63

Prices: 1969 = 100.   Industrial Wages: 1967 = 100.
Non-industrial Wages: 1974 = 100.
Source: The Central Bank, *The National Income of Iran* (Tehran, 1338-50).

In this period tax regulations were somewhat relaxed. From 1950 income tax laws had been subject to a process of regular revision. A law in 1955 had reduced direct taxation by introducing exemptions and allowances as well as lower rates. In 1956 the progressive tax system established according to the first comprehensive progressive income tax law of 1930 was in the main abolished, leading to substantial tax reductions. Further, the general income tax law of 1967 raised the exemption level still further and many concessions were given, especially to new firms.[38] Indirect taxes were not charged on necessities and essential commodities. With the exception of customs revenues, half of the indirect taxes consisted of taxes on fuel for cars, 15 per cent were excise taxes and the remainder were taxes on exchange duties and cars.[39]

As a result of this success in economic stabilisation, the regime was able to pursue a growth policy. In the period being considered, the gross national product increased from 340 to 979 billion rials, or by a compound rate of 10 per cent at *current prices*. But since there was little price increase, the gross national product increased at a compound rate of 8.5 per cent in *constant prices*. As a result of such growth the rapid increase in national and *per capita* income in the period led to a rise in total private consumption (13 per cent in urban areas and 5 per cent in rural areas annually).[40] On the whole the regime proved able to combine stabilisation with the continuation of sustained growth.

The political significance of this factor is evident against the background of the social tension exacerbated by the preceding economic crisis which coincided with political conflicts in the power bloc and which contributed significantly to the hegemony of the royal power. In turn the relative success of the stabilisation policy was due to the emergence of the authoritarian regime. The maintenance of economic stability was to be a major foundation of royal power. Hence, under the authoritarian regime the state began to play a dominant role in the economy. In 1964 it adopted a comprehensive budget policy. Previously, budgets were no more than a record of revenues and expenditures based on the financial laws of 1911, which had been adopted from the French laws of classical liberal economy advocating government non-intervention.[41] The new budgets expanded the role of the public sector. Under the authoritarian regime the court had an active role in economic decision making through the High Economic Council which discussed the budget, development plans and the state of the economy, especially the price situation. The government was especially concerned with the provision of basic commodities. Because the consumption of bread was a major item in the family budget (17 and 30 per cent of the budget of urban and rural families respectively) the government kept its price stable by marketing and distributing subsidised flour among the bakeries. In this period the price index of bread rose from 111.7 to 121; the wholesale price declined by 38 per cent between 1965 and 1969. The government also set up its own stores to provide commodities at subsidised prices for special groups such as teachers.

On the whole the stabilisation policy succeeded in terms of price behaviour while the vast financial resources enabled the regime to lift the credit restrictions initially imposed to achieve stabilisation.

Class Support and Control

In his endeavours to maintain the stability of the regime the Shah sought to create a socio-economic equilibrium by granting concessions to the main social classes.[42] In this the court was aided by the state's access to huge financial resources. But the concessions granted were intermittent and in the case of the lower classes were more nominal than substantial. The measures adopted were essentially political rather than socio-economic in purpose, in that they aimed at mobilising political support for the regime.

The Industrial Bourgeoisie. In the regime's industrialisation drive private initiative was strongly encouraged. This prepared the ground for the development of a modern industrial bourgeoisie emerging under the tutelage of the court. The new regime imposed trade restrictions and high tariff rates in order to prevent the growth of the commercial bourgeoisie and to encourage domestic production. In this connection it adopted policies of fiscal concession, tariff protection, easy loans and credits, subsidies, industrial grants, tax exemption and monopoly concessions. Between 1961 and 1975 the Industrial Credit Bank's loans to the private sector increased from 20 million to 20,000 million rials.[43] The restriction of foreign trade also ensured high prices, especially for local monopoly industries. The encouragement of foreign investment further stimulated the growth of the industrial bourgeoisie and some two hundred foreign companies participated in joint ventures with local partners. To further promote private enterprise the government established a Stock Exchange in 1967.

Thus with state encouragement, a large industrial bourgeoisie began to emerge. The number of industrial establishments increased from less than 1,000 in 1957 to 6,200 in 1974, producing 75 per cent of the industrial products in the latter year.[44] The upper bourgeoisie was composed of some 150 families, mostly from a bazaar background, who owned 67 per cent of all industries and financial institutions. Its members sat on more than 1,000 boards. Out of the 473 largest private industries 370 were owned by ten families. The upper bourgeois families were also closely knit together through joint investment in industrial, commercial and financial enterprises.[45]

Among the more prominent entrepreneurial families were:

— The Farmanfarmaian family, an old landed aristocratic family with extensive interests in the economy. Its industries and companies included the Shahriar Industrial Group, consisting of five large steel-rolling factories, the Shahra, Shahpur, Shahab and Shahbaz companies and several construction companies; it also had large shares in the Iran-National Car Manufacturing Company, paper industries and cement industries, as well as extensive shares in several of the private banks.

— The Rezai family owned eight large units of steel production in the Shahriar Industrial Group, the Ahvaz steel-rolling industry, the Arak machine tools factory, copper and lead mines and the Shahriar Bank, as well as holding shares in several other banks. The Rezai family rose from the bazaar trading background.

— The Khayami family also came from a trading background and established the largest private enterprise in the country, the Iran-National car manufacturing industry and owned chain stores, agribusiness enterprises, textile factories and insurance companies, and had large shares in several banks, especially the Industrial Bank.

— The Sabet family, another *nouveau riche* family, owned a whole empire of industries and companies in all branches of business. The family owned 41 large enterprises, including the General Motors Industry, the Jeep factory, television factories and the Daryush Bank. According to *Newsweek*, 10 per cent of everything in Iran belonged to the Sabet family (14 October 1974).

— The Lajevardi family, another family of bazaar origins, owned the Behshahr Industrial Group, comprising 22 large companies, the Behpak food industries and the Kashan velvet factories as well as holding shares in more than 45 other companies and banks.

— The Barkhordar family, again from a merchant background, owned electrical industries, cement factories and carpet factories, and held large shares in many other industries and banks.

— The Irvani family, from a traditional handicraft background, established the extensive Melli Industrial Group, originally a shoe-making industry but comprising food industries, transport companies and so on.

— The Elqanian Jewish family owned the extensive plastic industries, engaged in manufacturing and retailing and held shares in many other businesses.

— The Khosrowshahi family owned food industries, medicine industries and had shares in other enterprises and banks, especially the Industrial and Mining Development Bank.

— The Vahabzadeh family owned car industries, machine-tool industries and also had large land-holdings in urban centres as well as shares in foreign banks.

— There were other equally large business families such as the Akhavans, owners of large stores and tile factories, the Fooladis, owners of the tyre factories, the Bushehris who owned various industries, the Behbehanis, owners of glass factories, the Hedayats, owners of sugar factories, the Azod family, owners of paper factories, the Nemazi family who owned large textile factories, the Rastegar family, owners of many mining industries, the Yazdani family who owned large land-holdings and real estate, the Laleh, Arjomand, Ebtehaj, Tajadod, Qasemiyeh families, and many others.

The court maintained close links with the business community and encouraged, or ordered, entrepreneurs to invest in its favourite enterprises and invited successful businessmen to work within the scope of the regime's development schemes. The royal family itself had large commercial and industrial holdings (see below) in partnership with large industrialists. As the *credit mobilier* the court provided protection and access to capital for entrepreneurs. As A. Rezai, an industrial magnate, acknowledged, 'without the Shahanshah's help and support I could never attain my present position'. 'This was because 70% of the capital of Rezai and his partners came from low-interest government loans. His companies were exempt from taxes, for five years in Tehran and for twelve years in the provinces. According to him, some of his companies yielded 50 to 80 percent net profit.'[46] Another large industrialist, A. Khayami, also benefited from the Shah's support and established his manufacturing industries by order of the Shah.[47] Thus under the authoritarian regime government-business relations were distributory, i.e. the regime distributed resources among the entrepreneurs in the form of easy loans, tax exemption and monopoly concessions. The entrepreneurs also sought to influence government policies in order to increase the benefits they received from the regime. The employers' syndicates, affiliated with the NIP, held frequent conferences with government ministries and thus influenced government policies concerning taxes and credits.[48] Large industrialists disliked the public sector in general and demanded that the government abolish all state monopolies and transfer state-owned industries to the private sector.[49] Partly due to the growing influence of the upper bourgeoisie, in 1970 the government reorganised the structure of business associations. Thus a law was passed for the integration of all the Chambers of Commerce and the Chamber of Industries and Mines in Tehran and in the provinces to form the single Chamber of Commerce, Industries and Mines. This was to operate in close cooperation with the Ministry of Economy and the aim was to align the activities of the industrialists with state economic policies and make possible the implementation of public-sector schemes through private investment. The government further defined its preferred fields of industry, putting emphasis on production in the export sector.[50] Thus from 1970 government-business relations began to move from distribution towards the regulation of the type of business by the government.[51] In spite of closer regulation there were indications, from 1972, of the regime's dissatisfaction with the speedy growth of the upper bourgeoisie. As an official source wrote: 'For some time, the Government gave one hundred per cent support to this ["bourgeois"] class through legislation and other protection. Over the years, over-protectionism led to complacency among some industries, so much so that they stopped improving their quality or raising their efficiency or lowering their prices. There were murmurs that "industrial feudalism" was replacing landed feudalism.'[52] From distribution and regulation the court policy began to move towards redistribution of industrial wealth and control of the size of ownership. In May 1972 the Shah ordered the holding of a High Social Council with great fanfare in order to deliberate on how 'to narrow the gap between the rich and the other classes'.[53] The Shah's major order concerned the sale of shares in private-sector industrial establishments to their workers and the public. The Council ordered the 5,100 large private enterprises affected to sell 33 per cent of their shares to workers within three years. The decision, however, was not to be carried out until 1975[54] when, as will be seen, its extension and implementation at a time of economic crisis were to prove disruptive to the *status quo*.

On the whole the regime, through its corporatist organisation, sought to enlist the support of the upper bourgeoisie while at the same time seeking to control it. In his decrees in this connection the Shah claimed to aim at creating a social balance of classes. The relations between the regime and the upper bourgeoisie, however, went beyond corporatist control (see below: 'Clientelism').

The Working Class. The regime sought to structure relationships with the lower classes from above without politically activating them. The industrial working class was the principal object of state corporatist control, by imposing upon it official organisations.[55] At the same time it tried to enlist its support by providing such symbolic benefits as profit-sharing in industry, the setting of a minimum wage, intervention in labour-employer conflict and, later, share participation. The court ideology thus put emphasis on working-class protectionism. The Shah presided over the annually held National Congress of Labour and set the framework for labour policy. The policies adopted by the Congress regarding wages, insurance and the formation of syndicates were implemented by the Chamber of Commerce and the government. Symbolically the Shah was the bearer of the first account number in the state-owned Workers' Welfare Bank. However, the measures adopted by the regime for the benefit of the working class affected only a small portion of that class in large industries. Among these measures was the profit-sharing scheme to distribute 20 per cent of the profits among the workers in factories with more than ten workers. According to official figures, by 1975, 6,000 factories with 295,000 workers had been affected. At that time there were 235,000 factories employing 2,140,000 workers; thus only 2.4 per cent of factories and 13.8 per cent of the workers had been brought into the scheme.[56]

The corporatist labour structure was laid down in the Labour Law of 1959 and its 1964 amendment. Existing unions were disbanded and the main characteristic of the new structure which had important implications for the control of the working class were that only individual syndicates were allowed and no federation of unions was permitted. The official function of the syndicates was to conclude profit-sharing agreements and set up cooperative societies. Although the law granted union members the right to collective bargaining, in practice it was the government which arbitrated in the disputes.

The corporatist control of the working class occurred mainly through wage policy. The High Council of Labour set and adjusted the minimum wage at regular periods. The major demand of the strikes which occurred during the economic crisis of the late 1950s had been for higher wages. In the period between 1963 and 1975, due to the success of the economic stabilisation policy, the minimum wage issue was defused. Thus changes of the minimum wage were not due to labour protest; rather the government itself continued to adjust the minimum wage. Large industries in particular were supervised by the regime in order to carry out wage increases. On the whole, the regime controlled the working class politically through corporate organisations and sought to enlist its support through the distribution of some benefits.

The Peasantry. By instituting land reforms the Shah expected to reap political support in the countryside. In the beginning the distribution of land among some peasants and the raising of the expectations of others brought about some definite support for the Shah. The general feelings of the peasants were often expressed in sentences such as: 'from serf we have become master', 'so far we had laboured under oppression', 'we had not been human beings', 'we are freed', 'our eyes have been opened' and so on.[57] The peasant support, however, was by no means universal, for the implementation of the reforms remained partial and a large segment of the rural population was excluded. One of the major features of the reforms was that land redistribution was carried out on the basis of the existing village layouts. Thus on the one hand they did not affect the existing land allotments and only transferred the title deeds to the sitting peasants, and hence the existing disparities in peasant holdings remained unchanged. And on the other hand, since land redistribution was on the basis of the existing *nasaq*s, the agricultural labourers received no land at all.

Prior to the reforms there were great differences in the size of the *nasaq*s. Out of 3.2 million rural families in 1960, 1.9 million were *nasaqdār*. Some 56 per cent of the *nasaqdār* families had holdings between 0.5 and 4 hectares, 38 per cent worked holdings between 4 and 20 hectares and the remaining 6 per cent had holdings of between 20 and 500 hectares. On the other hand, out of the 3.2 million peasant families (15 million people), 1.3 million families had no *nasaq*s and thus remained landless.[58]

The actual results of the reforms which were carried out in three phases have been a matter of some dispute. According to official figures, altogether 1.3 million peasant families obtained some land.[59] The picture which emerged after the implementation of the reforms was a reflection of the pre-existing disparities in peasant holdings. For instance, in East Azarbayjan 11 per cent of the beneficiaries received plots of land less than 1 hectare, 30 per cent obtained land up to 5 hectares, 27 per cent received between 5 and 10 hectares, 25 per cent obtained between 10 and 20 hectares, and 7 per cent obtained more than 20 hectares. In Khuzestan the disparity was even greater: while 13 per cent of the beneficiaries owned only 1 per cent of the land distributed, 5 per cent of the families obtained 20 per cent of the land. The pattern of land redistribution was no different in other provinces.[60] According to one account summing up the end results of the reforms, in 1974, of the total rural population, 33 per cent had no land, 39 per cent owned an average of 2 hectares, 12 per cent owned an average of 7 hectares, 14 per cent owned an average of 18 hectares and 0.5 per cent owned an average of 190 hectares.[61]

In spite of the land reforms, the remnants of the landlord class continued to possess large holdings as a result of the many legal exemptions. In 1971 there were 62,000 large land-holders from the landlord class; in the main their lands were worked by wage labourers but in some areas the crop-sharing system was still in operation.[62] As a direct outcome of the reforms, however, a rural middle class began to emerge, benefiting both from the reforms and other government measures. In fact the Shah's explicit policy was not an egalitarian land redistribution. He declared: 'Our aims are not to destroy small landlords. What we are doing is a means of making it possible to become small landlords. Those who become owners of land today, we hope, will become small landlords in the future.'[63] According to one account rural middle-class families numbered 570,000, each owning an average of 20 hectares and comprising about 15 per cent of the peasant families in 1971.[64] The rural cooperatives were run by the better-off farmers. In the Central Organisation of the Cooperatives, a state-financed institution, the peasants were not represented but 'the local managers of that Organization were usually selected from the better-off farmers assisting government officials in the village'.[65] The major function of the cooperatives was to make loans to their members. Only the *nasaqdaran* (who had become small-holders after the reforms) could join the cooperatives; the landless peasants were not entitled to do so.

Thus while a rural middle class emerged as a result of the reforms and became the target of the regime's corporatist mobilisation, the rural lower class remained unaffected and bypassed by the regime. The regime sought to enlist the support of the peasants through controlled organisations and distribution of benefits among them. Peasant cooperatives were vertically tied to the state bureaucracy and the peasantry became subject to economic and political control. By promoting small-holding the regime sought to create a rural base of support. Some peasant support for the regime was to appear during and after the 1979 revolution.

Clientelism. On the surface the regime structured a corporate framework in order to channel diverse interests through state organisations. In practice the real business of politics went on behind the back of the formal organisations. In other words the representation of interests was based on clientelism. Clientelism consisted of relationships between the regime, which was capable of dispensing resources, and private interests with channels of access to public institutions attempting to influence public policy and extract resources. It was thus a more informal process based on individual relations between private interests and state institutions. Here some of these relations involving business interests, bureaucrats and public agencies will be touched upon as one of the bases of the *status quo*.[66]

Clientelistic relationships were concentrated within the decentralised agencies of the government of which the Oil Company was the central financial institution. It was independent from the ministries and its chairman, one of the most important posts, was appointed by the Shah and was directly responsible to him alone. The accounts of the company were not exposed to public scrutiny and were the concern of its directorate. The company acted as an informal source of finance circumventing the constitutional distinction between state funds and the court's private wealth. A frequent considerable discrepancy was reported between the company's statement of its sales and the foreign exchange earnings as reported in the balance of payments by the Central Bank. This discrepancy has been accounted for by the informal links which existed between the company and the court's Pahlavi Foundation due to a regular transfer of funds from the company to the Foundation.[67] The Foundation itself, formally a charity organisation financed by the Shah's wealth, was the largest industrial and commercial group with extensive interests in all major economic fields and played a regulatory role in government-business relations in the sense of giving incentives or withholding favours.[68]

Under the bureaucratic regime the Majles lost its importance in representing private interests on an organised basis. Instead the private sector circulated around the executive institutions in order to exert influence on the implementation of policies. As already noted, government-business relations were based on a distribution-regulation pattern, and this created an environment of clientelism, discretionary policies and pressure to influence public policy.[69] Of the public agencies the Plan Organisation was the central institution around which business interests circulated. It had considerable financial and administrative powers and was in a position to deal directly with business interests. The organisation contained a large number of financial, planning and regulatory agencies functioning as lobbies for businessmen and contractors. Although development goals were specified in the Economic Plan, the organisation enjoyed considerable discretionary powers in the implementation of policies. This enabled business interests to exert their petitionary influence.[70] Relations between public and private sectors were informal. Benefits were granted to industrial groups on an irregular basis. These included import licences, tariff concessions, tax exemptions, easy access to bank loans and guarantees against competition and loss. As a portion of the development budget was allocated to the private sector, the Plan Organisation influenced business interests through regulation and distribution. Development banks were also important in implementing discretionary policies through the use of credit to direct investment in priority economic areas broadly determined by the court through the High Economic Council.[71] Because the public and private sectors in the field of banking were not clearly separated, the private sector had an influential position in that field. This was the case especially in the Industrial and Mining Development Bank and the Bank of Development and Investment, which were mixed public-private banks and had representatives of the private sector on their boards. Different agencies had different clienteles. For instance in the field of agriculture the Ministry of Agriculture and the Ministry of Cooperatives were engaged in rivalry over the beneficiaries of agricultural policy. The clientele of the Ministry of Agriculture were large land-holders and farming enterprises and the Ministry advocated large agricultural schemes. By contrast, the Ministry of Cooperatives advocated policies in the interest of small-holders and the grant of credits and subsidies to the cooperatives. Finally the conflict was resolved with the dissolution of the latter Ministry due to the 'more powerful supportive interests' of the Ministry of Agriculture.[72]

The influence of business interests, however, was limited to the way policies were implemented. For all practical purposes economic policy making originated in the court which was also the centre of clientelistic relations. Such relations were fostered by the court's favourite policy of relying on certain priority areas of private enterprise for economic development. Thus if clientelistic relations are to be viewed as 'corruption' and 'traditional behaviour', they stemmed from the court. The royal family was closely intertwined with the upper bourgeoisie through the holding of large shares in all major industries. The royal family owned 80 per cent of the cement industry, 35 per cent of the car industry, 62 per cent of banks and insurance companies, 40 per cent of the textile industry, 42 per cent of the construction industry, 70 per cent of the hotel industry and 55 per cent of the steel industry.[73] Courtiers and financial advisers of the Shah acted as brokers and held shares in large industries and companies on his behalf. Industrialists also preferred to offer the court a few shares in their industries in order to benefit from the discretionary powers of the royal family, such as the provision of credits and tax exemption.[74]

Clientelistic relations were, however, partial in their effect in that they were confined mainly to the modern industrial bourgeoisie and did not include the traditional petty bourgeoisie which remained a marginal sector of the society. This was a reflection of the economic policy of the court which put emphasis on large modern industry. The traditional bazaar petty bourgeoisie included some 219,000 handicraft industries and workshops which employed 600,000 people. Economically they were not part of the modern industrial edifice and its clientelistic relations. Thus there was no tariff protection, government subsidies, tax exemption or credit provision policy for the petty bourgeoisie.[75] Consequently, while the modern bourgeoisie, despite its tenuous local links, occupied a monopolistic position and relied on informal relations with the regime, the traditional petty bourgeoisie remained self-sufficient.

The political function of clientelism both within the court and the bureaucracy was to create a dependent relationship between the bourgeoisie and the state. Consequently, the bourgeoisie was subordinated and integrated into the government, a fact which ensured the security of established interests and formed one of the bases of the *status quo*.

In the 1963-75 period the authoritarian regime was held together on the basis of the five foundations discussed above. From 1975 the changing situation was to affect the regime's financial capacity, economic stability, the established clientelistic relations, the model of class control and mobilisation and finally even the coercive capacity of the regime and its relations with the US. Concurrently, a new revolutionary ideology challenging the dependent authoritarian regime of the Shah emerged and attracted a large section of the population.

Notes

1. For a discussion of the relative autonomy of the bureaucratic state from the dominant classes see H. Draper, *Karl Marx's Theory of Revolution, vol. I. State and Bureaucracy* (New York, 1977), pp. 410ff, 478; Poulantzas, *Political Power and Social Classes*, pp. 255-62; J. Rex, *Key Problems in Sociological Theory* (London, 1961), pp. 124-30; and E. Trimberger, *Revolution from Above: Military Bureaucrats and Development in Japan, Turkey, Egypt and Peru* (New Brunswick, 1978). Trimberger's argument is also applicable to the case of the Shah's 'white revolution'. According to her, revolution from above is generated through the autonomy of the state rulers from the landed and merchant class in response to international political and economic pressures.

2. Under Reza Shah, his Court Minister, Teimoortash, founded a New Iran Party in order to establish a party government. Subsequently three more parties emerged. But the Shah banned all party activity in September 1927. See D. Wilber, *Reza Shah Pahlavi: The Resurrection and Reconstitution of Iran* (New York, 1975), p. 122.

3. Hassan Mansur, the founder of the party, also claimed, at the time of the establishment of the party, that 'The party is composed of people with similar background to my own' and that 'the doors of the party will be open to all classes': see *Iran Almanac* (1965).

4. The emergence of the employers' associations after the fall of Reza Shah is discussed in 'Safari', *Vaze Konuni-ye Eqtesad-e Iran* (*The Present Conditions of the Iranian Economy*) (Tehran, 1356).

5. A full account of the Chamber and its Federations is given in L. Binder, *Iran: Political Development in a Changing Society* (Berkeley, 1962).

6. *Tehran Economist*, Aban 1345.

7. On this and other functions of the NIP see M. Weinbaum, 'Iran Finds a Party System: The Institutionalisation of the Iran-e Novin Party', *Middle East Journal*, vol. 27 (1973), pp. 439-55.

8. Binder, *Iran*.

9. *Iran Almanac* (1972), p. 583.

10. Binder, *Iran*.

11. A.K.S. Lambton, 'Land Reforms and the Rural Cooperative Societies' in E. Yar-Shater (ed.), *Iran Faces the Seventies* (New York, 1971).

12. Z. Shajii, *Nemayandegan-e Majles-e Shura-ye Melli dar Bist-o Yek Dowreh-ye Qanungozari* (*Members of Parliament in Twenty-One Sessions of the Majles*) (Tehran, 1345), p. 192.

13. *The Echo of Iran*, 6 December 1971.

14. See E. Bayne, *Persian Kingship in Transition: Conversations with a Monarch Whose Office is Traditional and Whose Goal is Modernization* (New York, 1968), p. 1.

15. Weinbaum, 'Iran Finds a Party System', pp. 450-2.

16. *Iran Almanac* (1964).

17. The air force in particular was greatly expanded in the 1970s (in 1976 it numbered around 81,500). The new officer corps of air force cadets (Homafaran) were recruited mainly from school-leavers who could not get a place in the universities because of an excess of applicants (in 1976 there were 300,000 applicants for 30,000 university places). The air force cadets, however, were to play a major role in the 1979 revolution.

18. R. Ramazani, 'Iran and the United States: An Experiment in Enduring Friendship', *Middle East Journal*, vol. 30 (1976), pp. 322-34 at p. 327.

19. US ACDA, *World Military Expenditures and Arms Transfers* (1970-9); *New York Times*, 27 August 1976.

20. L. Pryor, 'Arms and the Shah', *Foreign Policy*, vol. 31 (1978), pp. 56-71.

21. The Shah himself in his autobiography, written after the revolution remarks: 'Many Savak officials went to be trained by the CIA at Langby. They also went to other Western countries to observe the methods used there': *The Shah's Story* (London, 1980), p. 175.

22. *Newsweek*, 14 October 1974, estimated the number as up to 600,000.

23. In 1976 the International Commission of Jurists found 'abundant evidence showing the systematic use of impermissible methods of torture of political prisoners': *New York Times*, 28 May 1976.

24. See S. Chubin, 'Iran's Foreign Policy, 1960-1976' in H. Amirsadeghi and R. Ferrier (eds.), *Twentieth-Century Iran* (London, 1977), pp. 211-16.

25. The US did appear as a 'third power' at first: it objected to the 1919 Anglo-Iranian Treaty; Reza Shah asked the US to prevent the Anglo-Russian invasion of Iran; the US played an active part in the Tehran Treaty which ensured Iran's territorial integrity during the war.

26. J. Bharier, *Economic Development in Iran, 1900-1970* (London, 1971), p. 119.

27. This was despite the emergence of some differences between Iran and the West over the oil price policy, which will be discussed in Chapter 4, in connection with the disintegration of the Shah's foreign support immediately before the revolution.

28. See R. Ramazani, 'Iran's Search for Regional Cooperation', *Middle East Journal*, vol. 30 (1976), pp. 173-85.

29. O. Fallaci, *Interview with History* (New York, 1976), p. 280.

30. According to a 1955 economic agreement between the two countries US investment in Iran was protected against nationalisation; Ramazani, 'Iran and the United States'.

31. *New York Times*, 21 December 1974.

32. The main financial and monetary channel between the two countries was the banking link which integrated the Iranian economy into the American financial network. Major US banks such as Chase Manhattan, First National Bank of Chicago and Citibank maintained credits or invested in major Iranian banks such as the Industrial Credit and the Industrial and Mining Development Banks. An account of this is given in B. Jazani, *Tarh-e Jameishenasi va Mabani-ye Jonbesh-e Enghelabi-ye Iran (A Sociological Sketch of the Revolutionary Movement)* (Tehran, 1355).

33. The oil industry was operated by a consortium of Western oil companies which had reached an agreement with the government in 1954 on a 50/50 basis of profit-sharing. The consortium controlled production, marketing and pricing and thus in fact the oil nationalisation law remained a dead letter. The consortium consisted of BP 40%, US companies 40%, Dutch Shell 14% and the French oil company 6%.

34. See H. Mahdavi, 'The Patterns of Economic Development in the Rentier States: The Case of Iran' in M.A. Cook (ed.), *Studies in the Economic History of the Middle East* (London, 1970).

35. Figures are taken from the Central Bank, *Bank Markazi Annual Report and Balance Sheet* (Tehran, 1960-78); idem, *National Income of Iran* (Tehran, 1959-71); and The Plan Organization, *The Main Economic Indicators* (Third Report, Tehran, 1976).

36. The procedure of taxing the guilds is elaborated in N. Jacobs, *The Sociology of Development: Iran as an Asian Case Study* (New York, 1966), pp. 89-92.

37. They financed 66% of the expenditure of the Third Plan (1962-7, with a total expenditure of rls. 230 billion); 63% of that of the Fourth Plan (1968-72, with a total expenditure of rls. 810 billion) and 80% of that of the Fifth Plan 1973-8, with a total expenditure of rls. 4,698 billion).

38. G.H. Ashrafi, *Majmueh-ye Qavanin-e Maliyati* (*A Collection of Fiscal Laws*) (Tehran, 1351); Bharier, *Economic Development*, pp. 76-7.

39. F. Firoozi, 'The Iranian Budgets: 1964-70', *International Journal of Middle East Studies*, vol. 5 (1974), pp. 328-43 at pp. 330-4.

40. Bank Markazi, *National Income*, p. 63.

41. Firoozi, 'The Iranian Budgets', pp. 328-40.

42. F. Firoozi has traced the source of the Shah's idea of 'greater distribution of income and wealth' to Leon Walras, the nineteenth-century Swiss economist. The idea was of course a major tenet of nineteenth-century corporatist social thought. The impact of Walrasian thought on the Shah may have been due to his education in Switzerland. See F. Firoozi, 'Income Distribution and Taxation Laws of Iran', *International Journal of Middle East Studies*, vol. 9 (1978), pp. 73-87.

43. *Iran Almanac* (1975), p. 287.

44. *Tehran Economist*, 22 Azar 1354; Ministry of Economy, *Statistics of Large Industries* (Tehran, 1353), p. 4.

45. This information is based on Rah-e Kargar, 'Social Classes', *Fashizm*, no. 1, (Tehran, 1358), pp. 4-5; and *Tehran Economist*, 28 Farvardin 1355.

46. *Le Monde*, 5 October 1973.

47. Reported by R. Graham, *Iran: The Illusion of Power* (London, 1978), p. 48.

48. For instance, *Tehran Economist*, 10 Aban 1345.

49. See ibid., 23 Khordad 1345.

50. Ministry of Information, *Iran* (Tehran, 1971), pp. 247-8.

51. In general three patterns may obtain in government-business interactions: distribution of resources by the state; regulation of the type of business; and redistribution of wealth through control over the size of ownership of property; see T.H. Lowi, 'American Business, Public Policy: Case Studies and Political Theory', *World Politics*, vol. 16 (1964), pp. 677-715.

52. *Iran Almanac* (1972), pp. 514-15.

53. Ibid., pp. 512ff.

54. Only 11 major private companies sold the required shares to the public in that year: *Keyhan International*, 28 October 1972.

55. Between 1960 and 1980 the industrial labour force grew from 23% to 34% of the total labour force while the agricultural labour force declined from 54% to 39% of the labour force: World Bank, *World Development Report: 1982* (Oxford, 1982), p. 147.

56. *Tehran Economist*, 10 Khordad 1345; Ministry of Industries, *Industrial Statistics* (Tehran, 1975).

57. As reported by A.K.S. Lambton, *The Persian Land Reforms: 1962-1966* (Oxford, 1969), pp. 186-7, 190.

58. M. Soudagar, *Barresi-ye Eslahat-e Arzi* (*An Analysis of the Land Reforms*) (Tehran, 1351), Ch. 2.

59. There were 760,000 families (21% of the rural population) in the first phase; 210,000 families in the second phase; and 330,000 families in the third phase: *Iran Almanac* (1974). According to N. Keddie, 'Iranian Village Before and After Land Reforms' in H. Bernstein (ed.), *Development and Underdevelopment* (London, 1973), p. 170, up to 1969 only 15% of the peasants (some 480,000 families) had been affected by the reforms.

60. *Majalleh-ye Tahqiqat-e Eqtesadi*, no. 9-10, p. 189; no. 13-14, p. 149; and no. 17-18, p. 70.

61. Mobarezin-e Rah-e Kargar, *Tahlili az Sharayet-e Jamei-ye Rustai* (*An Analysis of the Rural Conditions*) (Tehran, 1357), pp. 61-2.

62. Ibid.

63. Quoted by Keddie, 'Iranian Village', p. 171.

64. Soudagar, *Barresi-ye Eslahat-e Arzi*, pp. 38-40.

65. Ibid., pp. 82-3.

66. Most of the following general observations are based on my interviews with a number of commissions in the Plan Organisation and the Ministry of Economy in March 1980.

67. As reported by Graham, *The Illusion of Power*, pp. 154-5.

68. The Foundation exerted control over industrial and business enterprises through the Development and Industrial Bank of Iran and the Omran Bank by giving loans, licences and grants. It held shares in these banks and other commercial and industrial ventures (for a long list of its assets see ibid., pp. 214-17). The Development and Industrial Bank provided loans and grants to medium-sized firms while the Omran Bank invested in construction and commercial activities.

69. This situation was mainly due to the government policy of encouraging private initiative in development affairs. On the assumption of a favourable industrial environment, a substantial group of businessmen became involved in development activities with government participation and encouragement. This was because private businessmen were not willing to invest in large-scale ventures on their own. In this category were the Iran National, the Behshahr Group and other large private groups which emerged in the 1970s. See P. Richardson, 'Understanding Business Policy in Iran', *Journal of General Management*, vol. 4, no. 3 (1979), pp. 42-53.

70. This was because of the pervasive regulatory powers of the government. It regulated most activities of the private sector, like the location of the plants which needed government permission, and the kind of policies adopted by the private sector which had to be beneficial to the state. 'Government bureaucracy has really slowed the pace of business. The private sector is required to obtain the approval of the state bureaucracy even for most of its minor decisions.' See P. Wright, 'Corporate Strategy at Admiram Manufacturing Company: An Iranian Case Study', *Long Range Planning*, vol. 13, no. 3 (1980), pp. 115-24.

71. For instance the Industrial and Mining Development Bank provided extensive credits and loans for the Arj and the Pars electric companies which became two of the biggest ventures in the country. Also Lajevardi, the owner of the Kashan velvet company, received a substantial investment loan to develop his company.

72. M. Weinbaum, 'Agricultural Policy and Development Politics in Iran', *Middle East Journal*, vol. 31 (1977), pp. 434-50 at p. 444.

73. This was taken from a report in the magazine *8 Days*, 8 December 1979, p. 6.

74. A detailed documentary report in *Enghelab-e Islami*, 22 Azar 1358, describes the relationships between the royal family, the Pahlavi Foundation and the industrialists.

75. Iran's small businesses have not required the massive assistance from the state that the new infant industries in the modern sector have obtained. There is no infant industry tariff protection for the craft industries, yet for modern textile plants the rate of effective protection can be as high as 74 per cent, while for the car assembly it is 86.6 percent . . . the workshop owners have to borrow, either from the private banks at commercial rates, or from the traditional moneylenders, who demand extremely high interest charges. (R. Wilson, *The Economies of the Middle East* (London, 1979), pp. 10-11)

V. Costello, 'The Industrial Structure of a Traditional Iranian City', *JESG (Journal of Economic and Social Geography)*, vol. 64, no. 2 (1973), pp. 108-20, analyses the shift of the labour force from working in a large number of small workshops in the bazaar to working in a small number of large factories in the city of Kashan.

3 THE RISE OF A REVOLUTIONARY IDEOLOGY: RESURGENCE OF ISLAMIC NATIONALISM

> ... the word 'revolution' meant originally restoration. The revolutions of the seventeenth and eighteenth centuries, which to us appear to show all evidence of a new spirit, the spirit of the modern age, were intended to be restorations ... [They] were played in their initial stages by men who were firmly convinced that they would do no more than restore an old order of things that had been disturbed and violated by the despotism of absolute monarchy ... They pleaded in all sincerity that they wanted to revolve back to old times when things had been as they ought to be. (Hannah Arendt, *On Revolution*, pp. 43-4)

In a decade or so before the 1979 revolution, a new, revolutionary ideological trend emerged and changed the climate of opinion among a segment of the intelligentsia. In order to account for this development, which constitutes the ideological cause of the 1979 revolution, we have to make more explicit some of the assumptions underlying the discussion in Chapter 1.

As a consequence of the expansion of the capitalist world market and the incorporation of Iran into the Western economic exchange system the internal social structure underwent important changes in the second half of the nineteenth century. It led to the increasing dependence of the local economy, the decline of native manufacture, and the emergence of a dependent mercantile bourgeoisie. From then on capitalism began to emerge dominant in the social formation and to subordinate local petty commodity production. The expansion of the capitalist exchange system to Iran had two interrelated effects. First, it resulted in a partial 'structural convergence' between the Iranian social structure and Western capitalism. This was manifested in the consolidation of landed private property, in the political arrangement of the new social formation, i.e. Western constitutional government, and in an emerging modern intelligentsia. Secondly, it resulted in a 'partial divergence' (at the superstructural level), i.e. a reaction against this development in the form of nationalism expressed in terms of the dominant cultural form, the religion of Islam.[1] The increasing competition of foreign interests undermined the traditional petty commodity production

centred in the bazaars.[2] As a result the traditional petty bourgeoisie
emerged as the social basis of resistance to Western economic, political
and cultural influence and as the stronghold of nationalism.[3] The constitutional movement which was highly nationalistic, like the tobacco
movement of 1891, was strongly defended by the craft guilds.[4] It was
from this conjuncture of interactions between Iranian and Western economies that early Iranian nationalism emerged as a protest movement.
It was also the nature of this conjuncture that gave Iranian nationalism
its particular characteristics: nationalism was expressed in terms of
Islam and Islam was expressed in terms of nationalism.[5] The expansion
of Western capitalism and its political and cultural consequences created
not only economic but also religious reactions. The reassertion of the
Ulama who were alarmed by increasing Western influence accompanied
the reaction of the bazaar to Western economic penetration. Thus the
reassertion of Islam in this conjuncture was also an eruption of nationalism. The Ulama defended the traditional culture and assumed an
important position of power as the result of this conjuncture of interactions. On the whole, early Iranian nationalism emerged at a time of
rapid social change induced by the expansion of world capitalism. Soci-
ally, it was founded on the petty commodity mode of production which
was being subordinated by Western economic penetration. Culturally,
it was upheld by the religious institution which thus assumed a new
power position. The result was the strengthening of local culture and
national consciousness formulated in terms of Islam.

It was the combination of these economic and ideological forces that
led to the constitutional movement. The resulting document curbed the
absolute power of the Shah — who was blamed for much of the Western
political and economic penetration — and gave parliament binding
powers in all financial matters, especially the granting of concessions
to foreign powers, the recruitment of foreign officials and the raising of
foreign loans. The authority of the Ulama and the supremacy of the laws
of Islam were also recognised. As a consequence the Ulama emerged as
the representatives of the indigenous nationalist movement.

It was the nationalistic issue which formed the Ulama's major oppositional platform, rather than any doctrinal dispute, although theoretically the Shiite doctrine of Imamate posed a potential threat to the state
authority.[6] According to this doctrine, legitimate rule belonged to the
Imams who were descendants of Ali, the successor of the Prophet and
the first Shiite Imam. The Shiites believed in the continuation of divine
guidance through the Imams whom they considered as both political and
religious leaders.[7] With the Occultation of the last Imam, Mohammad

Mahdi in AD 874, there began a period of 'specific agency' in which the Hidden Imam was represented by four deputies. After the death of the fourth, there began the era of 'general agency' (*velayat-e ammeh*) in which the Ulama, as the vicars of the Imam, had the right to guide the community of believers. In practice, the Shiite Imams and the Ulama accepted the existence of temporal power and the doctrine of Imamate was confined to the religious sphere. Shiite doctors of theology such as al-Mofid, al-Mortaza and al-Tusi regarded the Imamate mainly as religious authority over the community.[8] In fact, the theory of Occultation combined with the practice of *taqiyyeh* (both by the Imams and the Ulama) signified the impossibility of theocratic rule and the separation of temporal power from religious authority.[9]

Historically, despite the existing tension between religious authority and political power, in the main the Ulama cooperated with the rulers and legitimised their power. In other words the Persian tradition of kingship based on the concept of divine right prevailed over the Shiite notion of authority, obviously because the Shahs were more powerful than the Ulama. The Safavids (1501-1737), who were the first Shiite rulers of Iran, declared themselves kings as well as descendants of the Imams; hence the Ulama did not even enjoy a monopoly of claim to divine legitimacy. Although

> the clergy, and all the holy men of Iran, consider that rule by laymen was established by force and usurpation, . . . the more generally held opinion is that royalty, albeit in the hands of laymen, derives its institution and its authority from God; that the King takes the place of God and the prophets in the government of the people; that the *sadr*, and all other practitioners of the religious law, should not interfere with the political institution; that their authority is subject to that of the King, *even in matters of religion*.[10]

Unlike the Safavids who thus combined political and religious authority, the Qajars (1796-1925) had no claim to direct religious authority, and under their rule, due to a functional differentiation of the authority structure, religious and political powers became separated. Thus the great Shiite doctors of the Qajar period, Mohaqqeq-e Qumi and Seyyed Jafar Kashfi, legitimised the temporal power of the monarchical state from the viewpoint of Shiite jurisprudence.[11] We can thus conclude that the rift which arose between the Ulama and the state towards the end of Qajar rule was not a doctrinal but a 'civil', nationalist opposition in reaction to Western influence and the increasing incorporation of Iran into the Western political and economic structure.[12]

As a result of their conflict with the Shahs over the latter's arbitrary
policies of encouraging foreign influence in the country, the majority
of the Ulama who participated in the Constitutional Revolution in
effect withdrew their legitimisation of absolutism. But constitutionalism
was not the Ulama's ideological movement; it was rather a modernist
Western-influenced movement launched by the modern intelligentsia.
The Ulama did not originally propose a Majles and a Constitution;[13]
rather they later accepted constitutionalism as a necessary device to
limit the power of the Shah. On the whole, the Ulama's original opposition was nationalistic rather than doctrinal or constitutional. In this
light, they also opposed Western-style reforms by the government which
threatened the Ulama's prerogatives.

The Ulama's opposition to the state, however, paved the way for
doctrinal rethinking. Withdrawing their legitimisation of the absolutist
Shahs, the majority of the Ulama endorsed limited monarchy. That the
king was to be limited by the law, however, raised the further question
of which law should be adopted. While the majority of the high-ranking
Ulama and especially the Najaf school of the Shiite Ulama accepted the
constitutional arrangement, which allowed for the implementation of a
combination of *Shariat* and parliamentary legislation, a minority of the
Ulama called for the implementation of *Shariat* alone. From among the
constitutionalist Ulama, Sheikh Mohammad Hossein Naini (1860-1936),
while rejecting the absolutist theory of kingship, sought to legitimise
limited monarchy and constitutional democracy from the viewpoint of
Shiite jurisprudence. Naini's basic premiss in his important book on
constitutional government is that temporal government is basically illegitimate and usurpation (*qasbiyat-e asl-e tasaddi*).[14] And although he
states that minimally *velayat-e ammeh* (the authority of the Ulama) is
restricted to personal affairs such as care for the insane and orphans, he
clearly implies that it also includes governance over the community.[15]
In his attempt to find the type of government which is closest to *velayat* and Imamate, he divides actual government into two major types:
tyranny based on absolute personal authority and serving personal
interests; and legally restricted government serving the public weal.
Considering the latter type the only alternative (*qadr-e maqdur*) in the
absence of the infallible Imam, Naini states:

> The first form of government [tyranny] is both usurpation of divine
> right and injustice to the unity of God and usurpation of the posi-
> tion of *velayat* and injustice to the sacred domain of *Imamat*, and

injustice to the worshippers, whereas the second form [of government] is only usurpation of and injustice to the sacred status of *Imamat* and is bereft of the other two injustices.[16]

The power of the constitutional government is like the intervention of an administrator not lawfully appointed to endowments with the intention of protecting them; with the issue of legal permission this intervention can be made legitimate. Similarly with the Ulama's issue of permission to the ruler, whence the injustice inflicted upon the office of Imamate will be removed. By contrast, tyranny is like expropriation of endowments and cannot be legitimised.[17] Constitutional government is justified because, given the absence of the Imam, the Ulama can do no more than impose limits on the power of the monarch through the establishment of a 'consultative foundation' or parliament.[18] Regarding the doctrine of *velayat*, he contends that it is difficult to prove who the deputy of the Imam is among the Ulama and hence the only option available is to turn to constitutional government, based on 'freedom', 'equality', 'popular elections' and 'the majority principle'.[19] The constitution, however, cannot abrogate the *Shariat*, which is 'the fixed law' of the state; and the government can be removed if it deviates from the constitution and the *Shariat*.[20] Finally, Naini contends that tyranny has been responsible for the decline of Moslems and that the adoption of a constitutional government is necessary to save them from domination by the Christian West.[21]

Only a minority of the Ulama objected to constitutionalism and called for the adoption of the *Shariat* as the law limiting the power of the Shah. This position was not different from that of the previous Qajar Ulama who had legitimised absolutist kings and demanded the observance of the *Shariat*. Typical of the Qajar Ulama, Sheikh Fazollah Nuri, the religious leader who tenaciously supported the Shah during the Constitutional Revolution and was finally executed by the constitutionalists, opposed the adoption of a Constitution based on Western laws, the establishment of a parliament, popular representation and equality before the law.[22]

On the whole the Ulama considered absolutism illegitimate, and maintained that the Shah's power should be limited by a constitution. The Ulama also found the adoption of a constitution necessary to safeguard Islam against foreign encroachments.[23] It was the Ulama's nationalist opposition to the threat from the West that led to their doctrinal reconsideration of the legitimacy of the ruler. On the other hand, although it was not based on the *Shariat* — as the Ulama might

have expected[24] – the Constitution of 1906 institutionalised the relationship between temporal and religious authority, and thus the religious
power of the Ulama was incorporated into the new political arrangement.

The Constitutional Revolution, however, as a secular-modernist
movement, in fact marked the beginning of the secularisation of the
state and society.[25] Beset by mounting international encroachments and
pressures, the state was forced to mobilise its resources and strengthen
itself through military-bureaucratic reorganisation, and administrative,
legal, economic and educational reforms on the Western model. Although
Reza Shah did not live up to the liberal ideology of the Constitutional
Revolution, his reforms were in fact the expression of the secular-
modernist ideology of that revolution. The Pahlavis adopted integral
nationalism which was itself a Western idea.[26] The aim was to consolidate state power on the basis of military and bureaucratic organisations
in order to mobilise the resources necessary for economic development.
The Pahlavis were determined to imitate closely the Western model in
creating a new state and economic structure. The bureaucratic, educational and legal systems were reorganised on the Western model. Furthermore, with increasing Western economic influence and the expansion
of the public sector to promote industrialisation, the trade guilds were
broken up and local manufacture declined (see below). The industrialisation policy led to further incorporation of the Iranian economy into
the Western economies. The Pahlavi monarchs subordinated the Constitution to their absolute power, suppressed the religious institution and
bypassed the constitutional power of the Ulama. Their mass mobilisation efforts included such policies as the break-up of landed estates,
female enfranchisement and control of endowments, which was aimed
at eliminating the influence of the clergy. Furthermore, after the Second
World War, as a result of a reorientation in the state's foreign policy,
foreign influence was encouraged, and in particular the US began to
obtain increasing footholds in Iran, in the form of economic, political
and military influence, the capitulations agreement of 1964 and other
economic and military agreements.

Generally speaking, as a result of the above developments following
the Constitutional Revolution, the influence of the Ulama was reduced.
In a sense, the Constitution's Christian overtones of the separation of
Church and state came to be realised in practice, although in principle
it had recognised the Ulama's political influence. The Ulama and the
traditional corporate organisation became increasingly subordinate
to the new bureaucracy. The early Islamic nationalism which was the

movement of the Ulama and the bazaar was further antagonised due to the advent of more Western economic and political influence. In sum, the Ulama's opposition to the state had two major dimensions: (a) Islamic nationalistic reassertion against foreign influence since the mid-nineteenth century; (b) opposition to Western-style reform, which took place in the context of increasing Western influence in Iran, and which threatened the Ulama's prerogatives. The vehemence of Ulama opposition in the early 1960s (as described in Chapter 1) was due to a coincidence of these two dimensions. After a short period of cooperation between the two (1941-60), the state began to undermine the influence of the religious institution through reforms detrimental to the Ulama's position. At the same time, foreign influence in the country acquired new dimensions. The conflict was basically over the relationship between political and religious power, and the extent to which the Ulama could have influence in political matters, especially in legislation affecting the Ulama and the *Shariat* as well as the general policies of the state.[27] As we have seen, the nationalist opposition of the Ulama in the late nineteenth century had led to doctrinal developments in the form of withdrawing religious legitimisation from absolutism and imparting it to limited monarchy. Now, the experiences of the Ulama during the constitutional period, the rise of authoritarianism and so on, prepared the ground for further doctrinal developments which we shall now study in more detail.

The major clerical figure who emerged from among the Ulama in 1963 and voiced the opposition of the clerics and the bazaar was Ayatollah Ruhollah Khomeini of Qum. Born in 1902 into a clerical merchant family and having achieved the degree of *ejtehad* in 1936, Ayatollah Khomeini had long been active against anti-clerical trends and Western influence in Iran. He had published his first book in 1945 in which he attacked the Pakdini movement of Ahmad Kasravi, the leading anti-clerical intellectual, as well as Reza Shah's autocracy. He insisted that in Islam legislation is a divine affair and called for the establishment of a government closely guided by the *Shariat*. But although he criticised Reza Shah for his 'attempt to uproot Islam and cooperation with the colonialists', he did not attack the institution of monarchy as such; in fact he referred to the historical cooperation between the Shahs and the Ulama.[28] As a constitutionalist, he called for the Shah's power to be limited by the law and the *Shariat*. During the National Front government he supported Ayatollah Kashani and the oil nationalisation movement, and condemned Mosaddeq's appeal to the US for financial aid. In the 1953-61 period when the Shah paid lip-service to the Ulama and Islam, Khomeini remained politically silent, as did his mentor, Ayatollah Borujerdi.[29] After the Shah's suppression of the Constitution and the Majles, Ayatollah Khomeini voiced his opposition, insisting that legislation (especially that affecting the *Shariat*, as was the case with the Electoral Law) would be valid only if passed by parliament and approved by the Ulama according to the Constitution. He declared 'our forbears have bought the Constitution with their blood; we will not permit the government to suppress the Constitution. All we want is the implementation of the existing laws.'[30] The majority of the Ulama also focused their opposition to the issue of the Constitution. Thus 27 members of the Ulama issued a statement which in part read:

> As you know the state of Iran is a constitutional state; the closure of parliament is thus a great sin ... The Ulama are opposed to the change from constitutional and collective government to personal rule. The establishment of constitutional government is possible only through free elections ... The Majles and Government which are not based on the Constitutional Laws will not be legitimate.[31]

Along with the other Ulama, Ayatollah Khomeini initially stood for the Constitution. But increasingly he came to believe that Islam and nationalism were under greater danger from 'colonialism', and thus shifted his emphasis from the Constitution to Islam. He made this distinction clearly in 1962 when he stated:

> We speak to the regime 'in its own accepted terms' – not that the Constitution is, in our view, perfect. Rather, if the Ulama speak in terms of the Constitution, it is because Article 2 of the Supplementary Fundamental Laws does not recognize any legislation opposed to the Quran as law; other than that the only accepted law is the law of Islam and the Traditions of the Prophet and the Imams. Whatever is in accord with the law of Islam we shall accept and whatever is opposed to Islam, even if it is the Constitution, we shall oppose.[32]

Even before the conclusion of the 1964 capitulations agreement (which Ayatollah Khomeini opposed vehemently and was consequently sent into exile), everywhere in his sermons and speeches he referred to Iran and Islam and the threat to them from Western colonialism. Thus he declared:

> all the problems facing Iran and other Moslem nations are the work

of America. Until recently, the British enslaved the Moslem nations; now they are under American bondage . . . The Americans appoint Majles deputies; and attempt to eliminate Islam and the Quran because they find the Ulama to be a hindrance to colonialism.[33]

Khomeini was the hero of the bazaar petty bourgeoisie and the bazaar was the stronghold of opposition to the Shah. His Islamic nationalism was cut from the same fabric as the nineteenth-century Islamic nationalist movement which had been generated from the reaction of the bazaar petty bourgeoisie to the expansion of world capitalism in Iran. Thus he complained that:

Large capitalists from America are pouring into Iran to enslave our people in the name of the largest foreign investment . . . This is the result of the political and economic exploitation by the West on the one hand . . . and the submission of the regime to colonialism on the other. The regime wants to put our agriculture, manufacture, mines and even the domestic distribution of commodities under their control, thus to enserf our people by the capitalists . . . Now all the resources of our nation are in the hands of the colonialists, and respectable merchants are becoming bankrupt one after another . . . The regime is bent on destroying Islam and its sacred laws. Only Islam and the Ulama can prevent the onslaught of colonialism. In recent times the salvation of Iran from collapse has been due to the endeavours of the Ulama and the *Marjaa Taqlid* of the time, Mirza Shirazi [reference to the tobacco movement]. In the present time we are confronted with the ever increasing blows upon Islam, the enserfment of the nation by the imperialists and their control of the bazaars and all military, political and commercial aspects of life. The bazaar is no more controlled by the Iranians, and traders and cultivators are faced with bankruptcy and deprivation.[34]

Ayatollah Khomeini's banishment and isolation in exile radicalised him even further. No more posing his challenge in terms of constitutionalism, and radically disillusioned with the increasing power of the Shah and Western influence in Iran, he began to rethink the relationship between politics and religion.[35] Seizing upon the original Shiite political doctrine of Imamate, he rejected the Shiite political theory which had evolved after the constitutional movement (i.e. legitimisation of royal power limited by a constitution). Instead, he reverted back to the concept of the Shiite divine state and the rule of the Imams and the 'general agency'. He thus declared monarchy as being against the law of Islam and illegitimate; and called for the incorporation of the political state into the religious institution according to the doctrine of Imamate. This was a novel idea both in terms of historical precedence (i.e. the practice of the Ulama since 1500) and Imamite traditions.[36] Thus in his treatise entitled *The Rule of the Jurisprudent*, Ayatollah Khomeini put forward the idea that only a theologian with the knowledge of the Divine Law could be the legitimate ruler. Accordingly:

> Islamic government is not any of the existing types and systems of government. For instance it is not dictatorial government in which the power of the head of state is arbitrary, allowing him to interfere with the lives and properties of the people, to grant assignments to whomever he chose and to give away people's property as he wished. The Prophet and the Imams had no such powers. Islamic government is not dictatorial or absolutist but limited and conditioned. Of course, not constitutional in its present ordinary sense in which legislation is based on the views of the individuals and the majority. It is constitutional [limited] in the sense that the rulers are bound by a collection of conditions defined by the Quran and the Traditions of the Prophet. The conditions are those rules and laws of Islam which must be observed. Thus, Islamic government is the rule by the Divine Law of the people . . . No one has the right to legislate and no such legislation can be put into execution. Whereas in the constitutional monarchies and republics the majority of those who represent the majority of the people can impose their legislation on the people, Islamic government is the government of Divine Law. In this system of government sovereignty originates in God, and Law is the word of God. In this regard the ruler must have two characteristics: knowledge of the Law and justice. He must have knowledge of the Law because Islamic government is the rule of law and not the arbitrary rule of persons. In this sense only the theologian [*Faghih*] can be the righteous ruler.[37]

Ayatollah Khomeini's central thesis in the treatise is that in Islam there is (should be) no distinction between temporal and religious powers. He rejects the prevalent notion that the jurists' task should be limited to understanding and interpreting the *Shariat*. They are not the mere collectors of Traditions; rather it is also part of their duty to implement the law.[38] Ayatollah Khomeini contends that the most important aspect of Islam does not concern private religion and individual salvation but the political life of the state. According to him, putting the greater emphasis on the individual faith is a direct consequence of the machinations of Western imperialism in order to strip Islam of its political dimension.[39] The fact of the Imam's Occultation does not imply that the world of Islam should remain leaderless. But as was the case also during the Lesser Occultation, the Imam should be represented by a *Faghih*, as the sole holder of legitimate authority.[40] In an Islamic government, the ruler-jurist would hold the same powers and position as the Prophet and the Imams had held, i.e. a position of trusteeship over the community of believers.[41] The ruler-jurist does not legislate, but only implements divine laws as embodied in the Quran and the Traditions. Ayatollah Khomeini thus implicitly refutes the constitution-alist Ulama such as Naini, who had accepted the existence of temporal power embodied in a limited monarchy. Naini had argued that it is difficult to find the deputy of the Hidden Imam among the general agency. Replying to this type of criticism Ayatollah Khomeini writes: 'If God has not appointed a specific person to govern during the era of Occultation, He has nevertheless set the general characteristics [of that person].' And 'despite the absence of a directive regarding the choice of an individual jurist to rule in the absence of the Imam, the presence of the qualities of the Imam in any jurist would be sufficient to qualify him to rule the community'.[42] Like Naini, however, Ayatollah Khomeini ends his treatise with a reference to the 'colonialist threat', maintaining that the establishment of an Islamic government by the Ulama is necessary in order to stop the imperialist onslaught.

The rethinking of the relationship between temporal and religious authority was not confined to the ideas of Ayatollah Khomeini. Following the death in 1960 of Ayatollah Borujerdi, the highest religious leader (*Marjaa Taqlid*) who had been known for his political quietism, there were signs of increasing thinking and activity among the Ulama. To be sure, a revival of attention to Islam had begun immediately after the fall of Reza Shah in the form of the re-establishment of those religious practices previously banned, and the publication of a large number of books on Islam.[43] In 1943 the Association of Islamic Propaganda (Anjoman-e Tabliqat-e Islami) had been established in order to propagate Islam and publish Islamic literature. By 1957, the membership of the association had reached 10,000.[44] But in the 1941-57 period, the religious revival had been apolitical and had concerned mainly matters of faith and theology. By contrast, in the early 1960s the Ulama, faced with increasing political authoritarianism, became highly politicised. The choice of Borujerdi's successor was a major issue contributing to this.

Although there were a number of qualified candidates for the position in Iran (Ayatollahs Milani, Shariatmadari, Khonsari and Khomeini), the Shah by sending a telegram to Ayatollah Hakim in Najaf in Iraq tried to designate him as the *Marjaa* and thus to interfere with internal issues of the religious institution.[45] In reaction to this and other issues a number of clerics, concerned about the increasing threats to the religious institution, advocated a more politically active role for the succeeding *Marjaa*.

A major advocate of this was the religious-minded layman, engineer Mehdi Bazargan, the leader of the Freedom Movement. Bazargan called for the strengthening of the office of the *Marjaa* as a place of refuge from the tyranny of the state. According to him, the reason for the decline of Islam was the Ulama's failure to guide government and the administration of social affairs. He contended that it was the state which was interfering in the religious domain rather than the other way round; and 'if religion does not take control of politics, politics will destroy religion'.[46] He blamed the Ulama for 'retiring into their shell' and pas-sively waiting for the Second Coming, whereas 'the emergence of Shiism and the hostility of Sunnism [towards it] had no other root than taking charge of government and politics'.[47] Citing a number of Traditions of the Prophet and the Imams, Bazargan supports his view that Shiism is all about political administration.[48] As a constitutionalist, however, advocating the supervision of politics by religion, he stops short at call-ing for a take-over of the state by the religious institution. Accordingly, the clergy should not 'enter into details of politics' or interfere with political appointments. After all, there should remain a borderland be-tween religion and politics, in the sense that the political and spiritual offices should be separate.[49]

Also in the early 1960s, a group of Ulama including Ayatollahs Mohammad Beheshti, Mortaza Motahhari, and Mahmud Taleqani organ-ised a monthly discussion session in order to define Shiite political theory in general and the procedures for the emergence of the *Marjaa* in particular.[50] Traditionally, the highest religious authority 'emerged' from among the most learned Ulama and was acknowledged as such by the community. The discussants of the monthly session maintained that the state in the past had exerted influence over the emergence of the *Marjaa*, and sought to pin down concretely that process to certain pro-cedures. Ayatollah Taleqani in particular proposed that a council of the Ulama should replace the office of the *Marjaa* in order to strengthen that office *vis-à-vis* the state. Its duty would be to organise councils of the provincial Ulama and to deliberate on current issues. In order to strengthen the religious office further, its finances should be reorganised through the registration of the religious taxes and donations. Another discussant, Allameh Mohammad Tabatabai, argued that Islam has a governmental system of its own, and that *velayat* also includes political administration on the basis of the Divine Law. Hence Islamic government is by nature different from constitutional democracy, which is based on the will of the people. Besides, constitutionalism in Iran originated in Western imperialism, and since it has not functioned in Iran, the only way out of the tyranny of the state would be the establishment of an Islamic state. On the other hand, the mere absence of the Imam does not imply that *velayat* should remain suspended. Rather a major aspect of Shiism is the administration of society by the 'general agency' in the absence of the Imam. Thus, according to Tabatabai, temporal government is all usurpation and cannot be legitimised by the *Shariat*. Ayatollah Beheshti went further and argued that if the government deviated from religious law, it would be incumbent upon the believers either to force the rulers to observe the *Shariat* or to overthrow the government and establish one based on the law. Thus during the Occultation all the believers have the duty to help bring about a just order based on the *Shariat*.

On the whole, the politically articulate among the Ulama in the 1960s were concerned about such issues as the nature of the relationship between temporal and religious power, the proper role of the *Marjaa* in public life, the weakness of the religious office and the practical implications of the doctrine of Imamate. Although some like Bazargan called for a closer supervision of politics by religion within the constitutional framework of the separation of the political and religious offices, while others like Tabatabai rejected the institutional separation of the two powers, they all stopped short of legitimising temporal power as completely divorced from religion (i.e. the existing situation). The revival of the early Shiite political theory of Imamate and the idea of a state based on this religious doctrine was tantamount to a total withdrawal of religious legitimisation from temporal power. This was a significant and novel development because it was a break both from the constitutional theory and the practice of the Ulama of the absolutist era. It was thus the first revolutionary ideology to emerge in the post-constitutional period in which all active political forces had called for the implementation of the ideology of the Constitutional Revolution and had thus posed no revolutionary challenge to what the revolution had theoretically established. It was also a revolutionary ideology in the original sense of the term which signified a movement of revolving back to a predestined point.[51]

To be sure, this ideological development, despite its religio-historical overtones, was not a 'Utopian possibility' in the sense of being the image of a possible world not based on the existing socio-economic system and lacking any congruence with the existing modality of production. Rather it was based on an 'objective possibility' corresponding to the objective interests of a class and its particular position in the socio-economic system.[52] It corresponded to the particular position of the petty bourgeoisie of the bazaar which had historically been the social basis of indigenous Islamic nationalism and the ally of the Ulama. In the 1962-79 period, the petty bourgeoisie was politically suppressed and economically excluded from the clientelistic relations of the regime. Faced with a process of disintegration and subordination to the modern industrial edifice, the bazaar resisted the regime economically and poli-tically. The decline of the traditional petty bourgeosie (especially its manufacturing segment) had been long under way as a result of the emergence of state capitalism promoting Western economic penetration and the emergence of modern economic and financial systems.[53] Under the policy of import-substitution adopted by the regime from 1963, an attempt was made to prevent the growth of mercantile capital and to promote 'internal' production through the import of capital and machinery. As a result, the public sector put emphasis on 'the modern and the industrial', leading to the emergence of an upper monopoly bourgeoisie dependent on foreign capital and imports at the expense of traditional manufacture.[54] In 1976 the traditional industries numbered 219,000 and produced only 24 per cent of industrial products, whereas the 6,626 modern industries produced 76 per cent of total industrial production.[55] In addition bazaar manufactories did not benefit from tariff protection and subsidies provided for the modern industrialists. Petty commodity production thus suffered further disintegration. According to an official account: 'Since large industries are established with the participation of banks and foreign companies they benefit from state support whereas small manufactories are run by traditional people lacking necessary capital and management. The banks are only interested in granting large loans.'[56] An indication of the decline of the bazaar is the rate of import-export. The ratio of exports to imports de-creased from 30 per cent in 1950 to 22 per cent in 1960, 19 per cent in 1970 and 5 per cent in 1975. Justifying the decline of manufactures, the same official source wrote. 'In our country, like the Western countries in their process of industrialization, small manufactures gradually become uneconomical and either disappear or are absorbed in large industries. And this is in the interest of the country.'[57] As early as 1966 an observer described the process of the disintegration of the petty bourgeoisie thus:

> But today, the bazaar, which has survived the vicissitudes of invaders, is dying. It is dying even though the volume of retail trade has increased within the bazaar, for retail trade outside the bazaar has increased at an even greater rate . . . In the last few years, the bazaar as a way of life has come under attack. Cheap mass-produced goods of every description to meet every need – needs that the bazaar can no longer meet – flood the market. New ideas proclaim the baths, restaurants and shops of the bazaar merchants as unclean and unsuitable; new beliefs call his religious behaviour decadent and superstitious; new business ethics condemn his codes as archaic and provincial; new business methods outside the bazaar jeopardize his profits; and new banking procedures have broken down his system of finance.[58]

Yet despite this economic decline the organisational structure of the bazaar had changed little, a fact that accounted for its ability to counterattack.[59] In the early 1970s a group of bazaar merchants and clerics established the Mahdiyeh financial, charity and religious organisation, a nation-wide private organisation independent of the government. It established 'Islamic banks' which gave small interest-free loans to small businessmen at a time when private commercial and state development banks were interested only in giving loans and credits to large modern industries. The Mahdiyeh institution also established hospitals and built mosques and held regular religious sermons. In addition the bazaaris in Tehran acted together to prevent the Saderat Bank (which had branches in all bazaars) from falling under the domination of an industrial magnate and associate of the regime (and a Bahai) H. Yazdani, by threatening to withdraw their accounts from the bank. Earlier the bazaaris in Tehran had established the Sanaye Bank in reaction to the dominant private banks. However, another bank owned by the bazaaris, the Asnaf (Guilds) Bank became bankrupt in the face of competition from more successful large private (Iranian and foreign) banks.

The 1960s, coinciding with the rise of the authoritarian regime and the suppression of the petty bourgeoisie, also witnessed increasing political resistance by the bazaar against the regime. It was in this period that the Fedaiyan-e Islam re-emerged and several other fundamentalist Islamic groups based in the bazaar were organised. The Fedaiyan reorganised themselves and held secret meetings in the Ironmongers Guild and in 1964 – after the granting of capitulatory rights to the Americans in Iran – planned and executed the assassination of H.A. Mansur, the first Prime Minister appointed by the Shah after the suppression of the Constitution. In this connection twelve bazaar merchants, shopkeepers and religious students were imprisoned. Another fundamentalist party, the Party of the Islamic Nations which originated in the bazaar's theological college in the early 1960s, set out to assassinate many associates of the regime, taught its members the tactics of guerrilla warfare and aimed at destroying Western influence and setting up an Islamic state.[60]

As traditionalist-religious groups these parties were mostly confined to the bazaar and had little influence outside. From the late 1960s the grievances of the bazaar began to surface in a new ideological trend which aimed at a radical alteration of the *status quo*. This was the development and spread of political Islam as a revolutionary ideology among a segment of the modern intelligentsia. The early Iranian intelligentsia had advocated extreme nationalism, democracy and socialism, but Islam as a political ideology had had very little appeal for them. From the late 1960s, however, the spread of political Islam and the revival of interest in Islamic themes among the intellectuals turned into an influential political ideology. We will first describe the new intellectual trend and its main exponents before attempting to explain the new development and its meaning.

This trend was extremely novel in that the older Iranian intelligentsia (since its emergence from the late sixteenth century) had been known for its irreligious or even anti-religious outlook. As in France, where the word 'intellectual' first gained currency, in nineteenth-century Iran its equivalent, *'roushanfekr'*, had a clear anti-clerical implication. The origins of the modern intelligentsia go back to the reformist statesmen of the Qajar state which sought to reform the army and the administrative and educational systems on the Western model in order to catch up with strong Western powers. Taking their lead from state reformers, the early modern intelligentsia sought to Westernise society. Thus Mirza Malkam Khan (1833-1908), a Western-educated intellectual, established the first Freemason society in Iran in order to spread the idea of constitutionalism. Mirza Aga Khan Kermani, another influential anti-clerical intellectual who had earlier been a member of the clergy, was among the founders of secular nationalism, identifying Iran with its pre-Islamic past. Other intellectuals before and after the Constitutional Revolution such as Talebzadeh, Akhondzadeh, Taqizadeh, Iraj Mirza, Mirzadeh Eshqi, Aref Qazvini, Kasravi and Bahar went so far as to curse the Ulama and Islam for all the ills and backwardness of the country. Influenced by Western liberal constitutionalism, they in effect turned their backs on the indigenous culture. Not unexpectedly, with increasing anti-clericalism and secularism under the Pahlavi state, a segment of the conservative intelligentsia identified themselves with it and in fact had a major role in propounding its integral nationalist ideology.

The main objective of the modern intelligentsia was the building of a new nation-state on the Western model, and for this they relied on reforms from above rather than populist mobilisation. One of the most ardent advocates of this was Seyyed Hasan Taqizadeh (1878-1970), who in 1920 explicitly called for the adoption of Western civilisation in all its political, social and cultural aspects as the foundation for building a new nation-state in Iran.[61] Born into a clerical family in Tabriz, Taqizadeh began his studies in the traditional religious schools, but soon left religious studies for a modern education. He had a major role in drafting the Constitution of 1906 (which was adopted from the 1930 Belgian Constitution), and after the constitutional movement led the Democrats' Party in the Majles, which called for industrialisation and the creation of a new administrative system. In 1911, accused of having planned the assassination of Ayatollah Behbehani, the religious leader of the Constitutional Revolution, he left Iran for exile in the West, but later obtained high positions under the modernising regime of Reza Shah. In particular, he was anti-clerical and denounced the 'ignorant and fanatic self-seeking religious leaders' as a hindrance to development.[62] He advocated the separation of politics and religion and had opposed the granting of veto powers over parliamentary legislation to the Ulama, embodied in Article 2 of the Constitution. Clearly, Taqizadeh's main concern was the creation of a new national identity in which Islam would not form the major foundation. Although he later modified some of his views concerning a total adoption of Western civilisation,[63] this attitude typified the modern intelligentsia early in this century.

In the same vein Ahmad Kasravi (1890-1946) called for the building of a new nation-state on the basis of modern, rational values. He was a historian and a jurist and, like Taqizadeh, received a traditional religious education early in life. At twenty he joined the clergy but soon resigned from this because of the hostility of his teachers to his novel views. As a rationalist he questioned the worth of Iran's religion and culture, and launched the most vehement onslaught yet on Shiism and the Ulama. For instance, he challenged the historical authenticity of the existence of the Hidden Imam.[64] He attacked the Ulama for using the story of the Hidden Imam for meddling in politics in order to establish an anti-democratic theocracy:

Today in Iran we are witness to the idea based on ignorance that, among the Shiites, government belongs to the hidden Imam and in his absence, to the Mujtaheds. This ignorance is the foundation of Shiite religion . . . The ignorance of the Islamic world stems from the ignorance of the chiefs of Al-Azhar and the Ulama of Najaf . . . who oppose ideas of freedom emanating from the West . . . The ignorant Ulama, on the basis of lies rule the people without having a crown.[65]

Instead, Kasravi viewed constitutional democracy as the best system of government, and considered the Constitutional Revolution as the watershed marking the separation of religion and politics in Iran for the first time.[66] Kasravi's anti-religious views caused much uproar in religious circles and in the government and he was finally assassinated by a member of the fundamentalist Fedaiyan-e Islam.

On the whole the early intelligentsia were anti-tradition and anti-clerical.[67] This observation can be extended even to the case of the famous Pan-Islamist of the nineteenth century, Jamal ed-Din 'al-Afghani' (1838-97). He had sought to mobilise Moslem peoples against Western imperialism on the basis of Islam. Hence he obtained his reputation as a Pan-Islamic revivalist. Yet in his more private moments he denounced religion as a hindrance to change.[68] Thus although he had to cloak his anti-imperialism in the guise of Islam his thought had been greatly affected by the secularist trends of the time.

By contrast, the young intelligentsia of the 1970s turned to Islam and presented it as a revolutionary ideology by putting selective emphasis upon it. Although partly anti-clerical, the new intellectuals sought to restore the political role of religion. They were in search of a new political community in which Islam would constitute the principal foundation. The main features of this new ideology were hostility to the West and an emphasis on the local economy and culture. The major exponent of this was Dr Ali Shariati (1933-77) and his Ershad group. He was born into a clerical family and studied sociology in Paris. In 1964 he lectured in the University of Mashhad for a short while before being dismissed for his political activism. Between 1969 and 1973 he lectured at the religious centre of Ershad in Tehran, where he drew a large audience of students and youth.

Shariati sought to lay the ideological foundation for the creation of a new nation-state in Iran on the basis of Islam as a political ideology, counter to the attempts of the secular intelligentsia. Despite his call for a return to early Islam, he did not seek to revert society back to the pristine simplicity of the first Islamic century. Rather, Islam for him existed to provide the ideals and values for establishing a new order.[69] Thus, in his attempt to create a new community, he sought to reformulate some of the traditional concepts of Shiism. His new political community would be built around a charismatic authority of the early Shiite type particularly identified with Imam Ali. He was searching for a 'spiritual element' as the pivot of the new nation-state. In this he was trying to do away with the traditional notion that until the Second Coming of the Mahdi, one must accept secular, unjust government.[70] Shiism has had three stages: prophecy; Imamate; and Occultation. But the era of Occultation is not a period of passive waiting; rather it is a time of human freedom in which man is left to himself and responsible for paving the way for the reappearance of the Imam and realisation of absolute justice.[71] In this period, the Imam is represented by 'knowledge' which is embodied in charismatic leadership. As the people are, according to the Quran, the vicars of God on earth, and responsible during the Long Occultation, it is their duty to choose from among themselves the leader and impart to him the status of Imamate.[72] Shariati in effect rejected the traditional idea that in the absence of the Imam, the Ulama, as His general agency, have the exclusive right to rule and guide the community.[73]

The essence of Shariati's thought was hence that although the 'establishment' Ulama, like the priesthood, had historically formed a segment of the ruling class and had been the bastion of conservatism, Shiite Islam had always been the movement of the oppressed. Citing Prophetic Traditions, he deplored the fact that while the Ulama should have acted as the 'heirs of the prophets' they had cut themselves off from the community.[74] In this connection he distinguished between 'Safavi Shiism' and 'Alavi Shiism'; the former being the official religion of the state and the conservative Ulama, and the latter the original messianic of the early Shiite martyrs.[75] Perhaps borrowing his concepts from Talcott Parsons,[76] he described Alavi Shiism as a 'movement' and Safavi Shiism as an 'institution'. Islam was a revolutionary ideology as long as it was a 'movement', but as soon as it turned into an 'institution', it became reified like all institutions become.[77]

Shariati's overall theme was a search for national identity and a return to the self; hence his recurrent discussion of 'alienation' referring to one 'who has cut himself from his own roots, is alien to himself'.[78] This is the typical Iranian intellectual who has been a byproduct of Western imperialism. He thus attacks Western cultural domination and calls for a return to the indigenous culture. The content of Shariati's Islam is nationalism. He states: 'I support religion in a way that even a

non-religious intellectual can join me.'[79] Thus although his Islam was
to form the ethos of his ideal political community, it was not quite
clear how much Islam would actually reshape social, political and legal
institutions.

Of equal influence to Shariati was Jalal Al-e Ahmad (1923-69) in
directing the climate of intellectual opinion towards Islamic nationalism. He too was born into a clerical family, and was a teacher, scholar
and novelist. Early in life, like many intellectuals of his time he was a
member of the Tudeh Party, but by the time of the conflict between
the Ulama and the Shah, he had developed an appreciation of Islam as a
political ideology.[80] Al-e Ahmad's main theme was opposition to Western economic and political influence in Iran. In his celebrated book,
Gharbzedegi, he analysed Iran's failure to industrialise and develop
alongside Western countries in the eighteenth and nineteenth centuries,
and attributed the cause of its backwardness mainly to the devastating
effects of imperialism.[81] He strongly attacked the Westernised intelligentsia of the constitutional period and after for spreading the influence
of the West and turning their backs on Islam. He deplored that being
an intellectual in Iran has come to mean one 'who is Western in his
habits, is irreligious or pretends to be so, is alien to his own local environment . . . and in the name of a scientific attitude has a colonialistic
attitude'.[82] Like Shariati's, the Islam of Al-e Ahmad was highly symbolic
and nationalistic. He thus regarded the Hidden Imam more as a symbol
of resistance and search for justice.[83] And although he criticises the
conservative clergy he admits that 'the Shiite Ulama in their defence of
tradition, have been a resisting power in the face of colonialist aggres-
sion'.[84] Al-e Ahmad admired both Ayatollah Khomeini and Shariati for
putting up resistance against the West.

Of less influence was Abolhasan Bani-Sadr (b. 1933), an exile in
France, who articulated his Islamic views mainly in economic terms. He
was born into a landowning clerical family and studied economics in
Paris. Bani-Sadr's main theme is also a struggle against imperialism, and
he considers religion as the main instrument for this struggle. He puts
forward the concept of 'Islamic economics' as an alternative to Western
capitalism. He contends that the capitalist path of development adopted
by countries like Iran leads only to economic domination and oppression, because capitalism is based on the concept of absolute private
ownership. 'Absolute property is a characteristic of Western laws which
are based on disbelief and individualism. In Islam there is only the right
to ownership of labour and its product and this right is relative.'[85] In
Islam absolute ownership belongs to God alone, and private ownership

is subordinate to communal/divine ownership. In an Islamic state there would be no accumulation of wealth and no class economic domination; imperialist economic control would be ended and domestic production and distribution would be put back into their proper Islamic order. 'Islamic monotheism requires the absence of any economic, political and intellectual centre of power accumulation.'[86] Thus the state must have minimal powers because, according to Bani-Sadr, authority relations like economic relations are a major source of class domination and oppression in the society. Thus in the Islamic state power is not concentrated in one group or individual; contrary to the traditional notion, Imamate is not the personal authority of the 'traditional guardians of faith'. 'The Islamic society will materialise when everybody is a Mujtahed, and when no one needs to ask anyone about his duty because this will lead to religious dictatorship.'[87] Thus the whole people are the vicars of God on earth and the Imam organises the relationship between the individual and the community. The Islamic state also regulates its relations with the 'world centres of domination' on the basis of a policy of 'negative balancing'.[88]

The ideology of Islamic nationalism was represented also on an organised basis by a number of political groups which began to emerge from the mid-1960s. Radical Islamic organisations such as the Mojahedin-e Khalq, the National Freedom Movement led by Dr Habibollah Payman, the Revolutionary Movement of the Moslem People led by Dr Kazem Sami, the Islamic Movement of Councils and other groupings emerged from among urban educated youth, predominantly from a bazaari background. They were all opposed to Western capitalism and imperialism and offered a radical interpretation of Islam bordering on socialism. They advocated the establishment of an Islamic order based on popular councils, which they considered to be the main form of government in Islam. For instance Dr Payman, an associate of Dr Shariati, offered arguments similar to that of Bani-Sadr about the communal nature of property in Islam.[89]

The most important of these radical groups was the Mojahedin-e Khalq Organisation which was formed in 1965 by a group of radical intellectuals and students. The founders of the organisation had defected mostly from the Freedom Movement in order to engage in active armed opposition to the regime. As an underground guerrilla group, the Mojahedin assassinated a number of American military officials in Iran, and in response were mostly arrested and executed by SAVAK. They were opposed to Western capitalism and imperialism and called for the establishment of a 'classless monotheistic society'. The Mojahedin put emphasis on the 'qualitative difference between the Islam of the Organisation and the Islam of the society'.[90] As Islamic socialists, they were opposed to the concentration of wealth and rejected the absolute right of private property. According to Ahmad Rezai, one of the founders of the organisation:

> Islam is by no means similar to capitalism or separate from the state. It has nothing in common with Western democracy either. Rather, it calls for the exercise of collective power and leadership. Thus a group of pious and knowledgeable men will take over the leadership and power and will move the society towards Islam. This group will emerge from the toiling class.[91]

Thus the Mojahedin's opposition to Western influence and its call for economic freedom from the West led it to reject the system of capitalism and to present a radical interpretation of Islam.[92] This was also true of the radical Islamic nationalist movement as a whole. The Mojahedin were active in establishing 'Islamic libraries' and 'Islamic societies'. The former were small lending libraries established from the early 1970s in all university faculties by 'Islamic students'. Islamic societies were formed, especially in provincial towns, for the purpose of Islamic teaching and propaganda, and were attended mainly by high-school students and teachers.[93]

Undoubtedly the climate of opinion among a segment of the intelligentsia was altering. But why did a large segment of the intelligentsia, in contrast to the early Iranian intellectuals, increasingly turn to Islam as a political ideology? The causes of this development are undoubtedly complex; the explanation offered here can be only partial. Similar ideological shifts and intellectual trends in other societies have been explained from diverse viewpoints. A popular theme in the literature on the intelligentsia sees them as 'free-floating', changing positions and turning to diverse ideologies.[94] A variation on this theme is Edward Shils' discussion of the intellectual evolution of the intelligentsia in the Third World and the 'phases' through which they go in terms of their political outlook. According to Shils, in the first phase, that of constitutional liberalism from its beginning up to the First World War, the intellectuals were fascinated by Western constitutionalism and sought to implant it in their own countries. In the second phase, that of 'moral renewal', 'constitutional liberalism seemed to disappear or to be confined in a very narrow space [while] the movement of moral and religious reform was taken up and developed into a passionate nationalism'.[95] Such explanations either rely on a world politics perspective or treat ideological shifts among the intelligentsia as irrational reactions and thus ignore the social background to the evolution of the intelligentsia and their social basis.[96] From the latter point of view we can understand and explain the emergence of political Islam as a revolutionary ideology among a segment of the intelligentsia on two grounds: first, the social basis of these intellectuals and, secondly, the class-ideological position of the new intellectual trend.

The intellectuals of the 1970s who turned to Islam were the product of their own time, i.e. of the spread of modern education, and were mainly of the younger generation. The early intelligentsia, who had been liberal-constitutionalist, had emerged mainly from the old aristocracy at a time when modern education was the prerogative of an elite. The spread of modern education, especially in the 1960s, and the decline of the bazaar transferred more children of the petty bourgeoisie who previously would have become apprentices in the bazaar to institutions of higher education, in pursuit of prestigious positions in the government bureaucracy. As a result, the educated stratum expanded fast. Adult literacy rates increased from 16 per cent in 1960 to 50 per cent in 1980.[97] Thus it would not be surprising to see the young educated carry with them their family and corporate allegiances to the modern institutions of education.[98] In terms of social origin the intellectuals who turned to Islam and formed Islamic radical organisations rose from a clerical-bazaar petty bourgeois milieu. Shariati, Al-c Ahmad and Bani-Sadr were all sons of provincial clerics closely associated with the bazaar. Shariati's Ershad centre was financed by a group of bazaar merchants who had originally built the modern and imposing Ershad religious centre and mosque. These intellectuals only expressed Islam in a new guise in the light of their modern Western education.[99] They were not 'free-thinkers', but their analysis was essentially shaped by the frameworks of religious concepts and categories. The Mojahedin were also mainly sons of clerics and bazaaris and were all 'born into religious families'. Among them were sons of merchants and high clerics.[100] Therefore it may be said that they were all the new intellectuals of the traditional petty bourgeoisie, whose emergence seemed natural at a time when the Ulama and the mosque were not only suppressed but also were incapable of speaking in terms of modern ideologies and communicating with a new generation brought up with modern education.[101]

In terms of class ideology, the position of the radical Islamic intellectuals, like that of the fundamentalist clerical parties, was an appropriate and rational response to the typical position of the petty bourgeoisie in the process of production. In its essentials the new ideological trend was the same as the Islamic nationalism of the late nineteenth century which had been generated from the position of petty commodity production and its reaction to Western economic and political penetration. It was intensely anti-imperialist and its nationalism was expressed in terms of Islam. One of the major themes of the intellectuals discussed above and of the Mojahedin was that the bazaar economy was being destroyed by the encroachment of big dependent capital. They all condemned the accumulation of wealth and capital, invoking various verses of the Quran which proscribe the concentration of wealth. The intellectuals mentioned above all portray a society made up of small producers, with little or no wage-labour, in which the right to property belongs to small God-fearing individuals. They all call for domestic economic production and distribution to be put back into the old proper order. They attack both capitalism and socialism and call for 'Islamic economics' based on small capital. Theirs is the revolt of a petty bourgeoisie caught in the clutches of Western economic domination and appropriately they put their nationalism in terms of Islam. And in view of the decline of the bazaar their view is not Utopian but corresponds to the objective interests of a class and its particular position in the socio-economic system.[102]

On the whole, we can conclude that the establishment of a Western-style state structure affecting the social position of the Ulama, and increasing Western economic and political influence under the Pahlavis' authoritarian rule, led to the revival of Islamic nationalism, especially in the 1960s. A clear rift arose between the state and the Ulama, and at the same time a spirit of radical revolutionary Islam spread amongst a large section of the intelligentsia. As a rising tide of nationalism, the political ideology of Islam was the continuation of the nineteenth-century Shiite nationalism which had originated in the reaction of the petty bourgeoisie to the expansion of Western capitalism in Iran. This emerging nationalism prepared the ground for new doctrinal developments which provided a religious justification for revolt. The political doctrine of Shiism as it had existed since the Constitutional Revolution (or since the establishment of Twelver Shiism as a state religion for that matter) could not justify a fundamental political change. In 1963 the Ulama had only called for the observance of the Constitution. Theoretically, in order for a religion to stop supporting the *status quo* and to become revolutionary there must arise some doctrinal developments within it to justify revolt. For this to happen, the original religious doctrine must be open to reinterpretation, and the new version propounded must point to a Golden Age either in the past or in the future.[103] In Shiism the doctrine of Imamate has been a highly flexible and manipulable doctrine; but for a long time the theologians of Iran had interpreted it in a politically quietistic manner. The established popular and theological notion was that during the Occultation the existence of a divinely sanctified and just government is not possible. The new doctrinal interpretations – both those offered by the clerics as well as those of the intellectuals – were thus breaking fresh ground. They were making the necessary doctrinal changes to prepare religion for spurring a revolt and for reshaping the bases of the state. As the doctrinal 'cause' of the revolution this new ideology remained in the background until the advent of the revolutionary conjuncture. Revolutions are not of course due only to the emergence of a new ideology. They are caused by a combination of factors, including interests and ideologies. It is to these economic interests that we now turn.

Notes

1. The following works explain the rise of nationalism and national movements during the nineteenth century as being a reaction against the expansion of world capitalism: M. Hechter, *Internal Colonialism: The Celtic Fringe in British National Development, 1536-1966* (Berkeley, 1975); S. Amin, *Unequal Development: An Essay on the Social Formations of Peripheral Capitalism* (Hassocks, 1976); E. Mandel, 'The Laws of Uneven Development', *New Left Review*, no. 59 (1969); T. Nairn, *The Break-up of Britain* (London, 1975); *idem*, 'The Modern Janus', *New Left Review*, no. 94 (1975); and A. Orridge, 'Uneven Development and Nationalism', *Political Studies*, vol. 29 (1981), pp. 1-15 and 181-90.

2. Late in the nineteenth century 'Iran was exporting a volume of raw materials five times larger than the volume of finished goods it was importing and was paying three times more for its imports than it received for its exports': N.R. Keddie, *The Impact of the West on Iran* (Berkeley, 1955), p. 60. From 1880 as a result of competition by goods imported from Manchester the textile industry began to decline: G. Curzon, *Persia and the Persian Question* (London, 1892), pp. 245-50, 270-3.

3. For instance, a group of clerics and bazaaris in Esfahan organised an 'Islamic Company' in order to boycott imported goods. The clergy in Esfahan also led a protest movement against the British Imperial Bank and forced foreign firms to reduce their prices. They also offered protection to bazaar merchants facing legal action for their debts to foreigners: S. Bakhash, *Iran: Monarchy, Bureaucracy and Reform under the Qajars: 1858-1896* (London, 1978), p. 291.

4. As described by A.K.S. Lambton, 'The Impact of the West on Persia', *International Affairs*, vol. 33 (1957), pp. 12-25.

5. The identity of Islam with nationalism in Iran created no problems of the sort which emerged in other Islamic countries between Islam and nationalism (see M. Khadduri, *Political Trends in the Arab World: The Role of Ideas and Ideals in Politics* (Baltimore, 1970), for Shiism was a national religion exclusive to Iran. In fact it was this combination of Islam and nationalism which signified a major

development in national consciousness. In terms of ideology and 'nation-building' two periods have been formative in the history of Islamic Iran: first the Safavid era when Iran adopted Shiism as a national religion and became once again a political-ideological unit; second the end of Qajar rule at the turn of the century. The former led to the emergence of the nation; the latter to that of nationalism as a protest movement. On the former development see V. Minorsky, 'Iran: Opposition, Martyrdom and Revolt' in G. Grunebaum (ed.), *Unity and Variety in Moslem Civilisation* (Chicago, 1955); and C. Gallagher, *Contemporary Islam: The Plateau of Particularism: Problems of Religion and Nationalism in Iran* (American Universities Field Staff Reports, vol. 15, no. 2, 1966).

6. No doubt as we shall go on to show in this chapter the Ulama's increasing power at the end of the Qajar rule and their nationalist reassertion prepared the ground for doctrinal developments, mainly in the form of a liberal-democratic reading of Islamic political theory presented by Naini. However this doctrinal readjustment took place later; originally the Ulama's opposition was mainly nationalistic. Cf. 'any wish to reshape definitely the norms of political life and the bases of the state was foreign to the Ulama in Qajar Iran': H. Algar, *Religion and State in Iran* (Berkeley, 1970), p. 260.

7. In addition to Unity of God, prophecy and final judgement, which are the religious tenets in Sunnism, in Shiism there are two more principles of faith: justice and Imamate.

8. For a full discussion of this see S.A. Arjomand, 'The Shiite Hierocracy and the State in Pre-Modern Iran: 1785-1890', *European Journal of Sociology*, vol. 22 (1981), pp. 40-78; and H. Enayat, *Modern Islamic Political Thought* (Austin, 1982), pp. 173ff.

9. See Algar, *Religion and State*, p. 3.

10. R. Savory's translation of J. Chardin, *Voyages du Chevalier Chardin* (Amsterdam, 1711), vol. 6, pp. 249-50 in R. Savory, 'The Problem of Sovereignty in an Ithna Ashari ("Twelver") Shii State', *Middle East Review*, vol. 11, no. 4 (1979).

11. See Arjomand, 'The Shiite Hierocracy', pp. 51-6; and A.K.S. Lambton, 'Some New Trends in Islamic Political Thought in Late Eighteenth and Early Nineteenth Century Persia', *Studia Islamica*, vol. 11 (1974).

12. Related to the Ulama's nationalist opposition was their opposition to some administrative and legal reforms adopted by the government in order to strengthen the state *vis-à-vis* foreign powers. See, e.g., Bakhash, *Iran*, p. 166. From the start Western-style reforms by the state were considered by the Ulama as part of Western influence.

13. See Algar, *Religion and State*, pp. 247 and 253, notes 61, 65.

14. M.H. Naini, *Tanbih-ol Mella va Tanzih-ol Omma: Dar Asas va Osul-e Mashrutiyat (Concerning the Foundations and Principles of Constitutional Government)*, intr. by Seyyed M. Taleqani, 5th edn (Tehran, 1358), p. 49.

15. Ibid., pp. 49-50.

16. Ibid., p. 47.

17. Ibid., p. 48.

18. Ibid., pp. 56-7.

19. In this connection he describes his 'true dream' in which he had met the Mujtahed Mirza Hossein Tehrani who tells Naini on behalf of the Hidden Imam that 'constitutionalism is a new name; its content is old', thus approving of the constitutional system (ibid., p. 48).

20. Ibid., p. 106.

21. Ibid., p. 50.

22. See Shaykh Fazl Allah Nuri, 'Refutation of the Idea of Constitutionalism', trans. A.H. Hairi, *Middle East Studies*, vol. 13 (1977), pp. 327-39.

23. Cf. '[The constitutionalist view] has established itself as the dominant one

among the Iranian *Ulama* and continues to inform their attitudes in contemporary Iran': H. Algar, 'The Oppositional Role of the Ulama in Twentieth-Century Iran' in N.R. Keddie (ed.), *Scholars, Saints and Sufis* (Berkeley, 1972), p. 238.

24. H. Algar, *Religion and State in Iran: 1785-1906* (Berkeley, 1970), p. 253.

25. In fact the insertion of Article 2 of the Supplementary Fundamental Law regarding the Ulama's supervision of legislation was their last resort to prevent the total secularisation of the state: F. Adamiyat, *Maqalat-e Tarikhi (Historical Essays)* (Tehran, 1352), p. 113.

26. On this see C. Hayes, *The Historical Evolution of Modern Nationalism* (New York, 1931); and L. Snyder, *The New Nationalism* (Ithaca, 1968).

27. The more conservative Ulama such as Ayatollahs Borujerdi, Behbehani and Khonsari opposed the measures directly affecting the religious institution, whereas Ayatollahs Khomeini, Milani and Shariatmadari directed their opposition to the general policies, especially foreign policy of the state. Ayatollah Motahhari lists the following as the Ulama's major grievances: absolute despotism; new colonial influence in the country; separating politics from religion; suppressing Islamic culture and law; and close ties with the West: in his *Islamic Movements in the Twentieth Century*, English trans. (Tehran, 1979), pp. 55ff.

28. Ayatollah Khomeini, *Kashf-al-Asrar (Revealing the Secrets)* (n.p., 1324).

29. However it has been said that once, when the Shah was visiting Ayatollah Borujerdi at his home in Qum, Ayatollah Khomeini, who was already there, left the room upon the Shah's arrival, as a sign of opposition.

30. Houzeh-ye Elmiyeh, *Zendeginameh-ye Imam Khomeini (A Biography of Imam Khomeini)* (Tehran, n.d.), p. 46.

31. Statement by 27 of the Ulama of Iran, 31 Khordad 1342 in ibid., pp. 80-1.

32. Ibid., p. 95.

33. Ayatollah Khomeini's 1964 Statement on the US-Iran agreement in ibid.

34. Ayatollah Khomeini, *Khomeini va Jonbesh: Majmueh-ye Nameh-ha va Sokhanraniha (A Collection of Khomeini's Letters and Speeches)* (Tehran, 1352), pp. 58-60, 68-9.

35. It was during his exile years that Ayatollah Khomeini turned from a constitutionalist into a revolutionary calling monarchy illegal and offering a theological justification for a revolution. During those years he sent messages to the clergy and merchants in Tehran and Persian students abroad to condemn the regime. For an account of the impact of political exile on the emergence of a revolutionary ideology see M. Walzer, 'Revolutionary Ideology: The Case of the Marian Exiles', *American Political Science Review*, vol. 57, no. 2 (1963), pp. 643-54.

36. He seeks to establish the legitimacy of the rule of the Ulama by resort to both reason and traditions of the Imams. This is of course in line with the Usuli school of jurisprudence adhered to by the Ulama. In contrast to the Akhbari school which had been predominant in the early Qajar period and which maintained that all binding regulations are embodied in the Traditions of the Prophet and the Imams, the Usulis hold that the Ulama have the authority to deduce laws from the principles of Islam (see Algar, *Religion and State*, pp. 33ff). Thus in his treatise *Velayat-e Faghih, 'Hokumat-e Islami' (The Rule of the Jurisprudent, 'Islamic Government')*, new edn (Tehran, 1357), Ayatollah Khomeini seeks to re-interpret some of the Traditions in order to legitimise political rule by the *Faghih*: pp. 74-80. He also rejects the established Shiite practice of Taqiyeh (dissimulation of belief in time of danger *vis-à-vis* hostile governments), ibid., pp. 201-2.

37. Ibid., pp. 52-4, 58-60.

38. Ibid., pp. 28, 39-40, 77-9.

39. Ibid., pp. 195ff.

40. Ibid., p. 21.

41. Ibid., pp. 64-5.

42. Ibid., pp. 63, 20.

43. As described in Y. Armajani, 'Islamic Literature in Post-War Iran' in J. Kritzeck and R. Winder (eds.), *The World of Islam: Studies in Honour of Philip K. Hitti* (London, 1959).

44. Ibid., pp. 279-80.

45. Because Hakim was an Arab and a resident of Najaf in Iraq, this choice was meant to diminish the influence of the Qum Ulama. See Algar, 'The Oppositional Role of the Ulama'.

46. M. Bazargan, *Marz bein-e Din va Siyasat* (*The Boundary between Religion and Politics*), a speech delivered at the Second Congress of the Islamic Associations in 1960, p. 12.

47. Ibid., pp. 17-25.

48. Ibid., pp. 33-5.

49. Ibid., pp. 47-51.

50. The discussions were later published as a collection of essays entitled *Bahsi dar bareh-ye Marjaiyat va Ruhaniyat* (*A Discussion about the Highest Religious Authority and the Clergy*) (Tehran, 1341). A detailed summary of this collection is given in A.K.S. Lambton, 'A Reconsideration of the Position of the *Marja-al-Taqlid*', *Studia Islamica*, vol. 20 (1964), pp. 114-35. Our discussion of the clerics' views is based on Lambton; for a full discussion see S. Akhavi, *Religion and Politics in Contemporary Iran: Clergy–State Relations in the Pahlavi Period* (New York, 1980).

51. For the original meaning of revolution as a 'recurrent movement in space or time' see R. Williams, *Keywords* (London, 1976); and H. Arendt, *On Revolution* (Harmondsworth, 1965), pp. 42ff. Cf. 'We must prepare the ground for the re-establishment of the Islamic state which was in existence unfortunately only for a few years during the time of the Prophet and the very short rule of Ali' (*Khomeini va Jonbesh*, pp. 96-7). On the logic of the kinship of reversion and revolution on the grounds that 'The advantages of a new society are hypothetical until realised; the ideals of reaction have a more powerful appeal,' see F.G. Hutchins, 'On Winning and Losing by Revolution', *Public Policy*, vol. 18 (1969), p. 21.

52. These concepts are G. Lukács'. Lukács examines ideologies as representations of historical objective possibilities. Every historical situation contains a prefiguration of a range of potential future situations. Class ideology is thus a reflection of the reality of historical possibilities and consists of the rational reactions corresponding to a particular position in the process of production. A Utopian possibility is not thus an objective possibility: G. Lukács, *History and Class Consciousness* (London, 1971), pp. 75-80.

53. V. Costello, 'The Industrial Structure of a Traditional Iranian City', *JESG*, vol. 64, no. 2 (1973), pp. 108-20, has shown this process of the decline of traditional manufacture in the case of Kashan, itself a major centre of traditional crafts. He shows that between 1956 and 1966 'The guilds, representing the traditional self-employed craftsmen trades all continued to wane in power, with the exception of those in the carpet trade' (p. 109). He reports a decline of employment in many crafts as a result of competition from factory goods, and a decrease in the number of textile workshops from 869 to 624 between 1963 and 1966 (pp. 110-11). 'Economic trends were strongly against small units. Some 3,591 miscellaneous industrial enterprises disappeared between 1956 and 1966' (p. 119).

54. See N. Jacobs, *The Sociology of Development* (New York, 1966), Ch. 1.

55. Ministry of Economy, Bureau of Statistics, *Industrial Statistics*, pp. 4ff.

56. *Tehran Economist*, 1 Aban 1355.

57. Ibid., 18 Bahman 1354.

58. G. Miller, 'Political Organisation in Iran', *Middle East Journal*, vol. 23 (1969), pp. 162-3.

59. Cf. 'But despite the fluctuations in economic and social conditions, the bazaar's traditional organizational patterns have changed relatively little': H.J. Rotblat, 'Social Organization and Development in a Provincial Iranian Bazaar', *Economic Development and Cultural Change*, vol. 23 (1974-5), pp. 292-305. Dr David Pool of the University of Manchester related to this author that the persistence of the bazaar guild system in Iran is remarkable by Middle Eastern standards.

60. An account of these parties and their activities in the 1960s is given in *Asnadi az Jamiyat-haye Motalefe-ye Islami, Jama va Hezb-e Melal-e Islami (Documents on the Coalition Groups, Jama and the Party of Islamic Nations)* (Tehran, 1350).

61. He thus remarked: 'We are indebted to the western civilisation and we must surrender to it': I. Afshar (ed.), *Maqalat-e Taqizadeh*, vol. 9 (Tehran, 1977), p. 305.

62. Ibid., vol. 4, p. 196.

63. Ibid., p. 185.

64. A. Kasravi, *Dar Piramun-e Kherad (On Reason)*, 4th edn (Tehran, 1347), p. 33.

65. A. Kasravi, *Dar Piramun-e Islam (On Islam)*, 5th edn (Tehran, 1348), pp. 14-15, 38.

66. A. Kasravi, *Mashruteh Behtarin Shekl-e Hokumat (Constitutionalism, Best System of Government)* (Tehran, 1335), pp. 15-20; *idem, Dar Rah-e Siyasat (On Politics)* (Tehran, 1340), pp. 6-7.

67. Anti-religious ideas were also expressed in many literary works, for instance those by Sadeq Hedayat, Mohammad Masud and Mohammadali Jamalzadeh.

68. As it is evident in his reply to Ernest Renan; see Albert Hourani, *Arabic Thought in the Liberal Age: 1798-1939* (London, 1970), pp. 120-2. See also N.R. Keddie, *An Islamic Response to Imperialism: Sayyid Jamal ad-Din 'Al-Afghani'* (Berkeley, 1968).

69. Ali Shariati, *Ummat va Imamat (Community and Leadership)* (Tehran, 1349), p. 2; *Mazhab alayhe Mazhab (Religion against Religion)* (Tehran, 1356), p. 50.

70. A. Shariati, *Entezar, Mazhab-e Eteraz (Expectation, the Religion of Protest)* (Tehran, 1350), pp. 25, 43-5.

71. A. Shariati, *Shia*, collection of works, no. 7 (Tehran, 1358), pp. 248-9, 168.

72. Ibid., p. 167. For a critique of Shariati's use of Quranic words such as 'people' in an antagonistic sense see S. Zubaida, 'The Ideological Conditions for Khomeini's Doctrine of Government', *Economy and Society*, vol. 11 (1982), pp. 138-72.

73. *Entezar*, p. 27. In *Ummat va Imamat* he tries to resolve the contradiction between the people's choice and Imamate in favour of the former.

74. *Shia*, p. 213.

75. *Tashayo-e Alavi va Tashayo-e Safavi (Alavi Shiism and Safavi Shiism)* (Tehran, 1351).

76. See T. Parsons, *The Social System* (New York, 1964), p. 529.

77. Many clerics, notably Ayatollahs Milani and Mokarem, were opposed to Shariati and his ideas and declared them anti-Islamic; see Islamic Students in Europe, *Vizhehnameh-ye Shariati* (n.p., 1977), pp. 208-9.

78. *Bazgasht*, collection of works (Tehran, 1358), p. 100.

79. *Bazgasht be Khishtan*, p. 17.

80. Thus in 1964 he made a pilgrimage to Mecca and kept a diary which was later published as *Khasi dar Miqat (Dust in the Desert)* (Tehran, 1348). For a discussion of a similar shift of attitude among the Egyptian intelligentsia see

C. Smith, 'The Crisis of Orientation: The Shift of Egyptian Intelligentsia to Islamic Subjects in the 1930s', *International Journal of Middle East Studies*, vol. 4 (1973), pp. 382-410.

81. J. Al-e Ahmad, *Gharbzedegi (The Western Affliction)* (Tehran, 1358).

82. *Dar Khedmat va Khianat-e Roushanfekran (On the Services and Disservices of Intellectuals)* (Tehran, 1357), pp. 48-50.

83. Thus in an interview with Ahvaz University students in 1969, in reply to the question whether he believed in the Hidden Imam, he said: 'there is a hidden Imam in each of us'.

84. *Dar Khedmat*, p. 255.

85. *Osule Payeh va Zabete-ye Hokumat-e Islami (The Basic Principles of Islamic Government)* (n.p., 1354), p. 29.

86. Ibid., p. 24.

87. Ibid., p. 12.

88. *Bayaniye-ye Jomhuri-ye Islami (The Manifesto of the Islamic Republic)* (Tehran, 1358), pp. 90-2.

89. For more details on these parties see below, Chapter 6.

90. Mojahedin-e Khalq, *Amuzesh-ha*, no. 1 (Tehran, 1357), p. 30.

91. A. Rezai, *Nehzat-e Hosseini (Hossein's Movement)* (n.p., 1354), pp. 6-7.

92. In 1975 the organisation split into a Marxist and an Islamic faction. Later the Marxist faction formed the Paykar Organisation.

93. Especially in Tehran there were a great number of religious associations and informal groupings taking their names after the Shiite martyrs, such as Hosseiniyeh, Zeinabiyeh, Akbariyeh, Asgariyeh and others. The Mahdiyeh was the largest of these associations.

94. In particular Mannheim maintained that intellectuals constitute a 'relatively classless stratum which is not too firmly situated in the social order'. Although they come from diverse classes, their original class position does not influence their ideas. See *Ideology and Utopia* (London, 1955), pp. 154-6.

95. E. Shils, 'Intellectuals in the Political Development of the New States' in J. Kautsky (ed.), *Political Change in Underdeveloped Countries* (New York, 1964), p. 225. See also M. Matossian, 'Ideologies of Delayed Industrialisation' in ibid.

96. Cf. 'The shifting social ties of intellectuals should be taken into consideration in accounting for the shifts in their ideologies': R. Brym, *Intellectuals and Politics* (London, 1980), especially Ch. 4.

97. World Bank, *World Development Report, 1982* (Oxford, 1982), p. 155.

98. The audience of Shariati, mostly undergraduates of Tehran University, came mainly from the townships as a result of the massive expansion of higher education.

99. Paradoxically, the modern intelligentsia had all had modern/foreign education, whereas the older intelligentsia such as Kasravi, Taqizadeh and Kermani had started with religious education.

100. 'Many Mujahidin were sons of religious-minded merchants, bazaar traders, clergymen, and other members of the traditional middle class.' Of the nine founding members of the group, three were from clerical families, five from bazaari middle-class families and one from a working-class family: E. Abrahamian, 'The Guerrilla Movement in Iran, 1963-1977', *MERIP Reports*, no. 86 (March-April 1980), pp. 3-15.

101. Cf. N. Cohn, *The Pursuit of Millennium* (London, 1978), pp. 307-19. Cohn argues that revolutionary millenarianism in medieval Europe emerged when the Church could no longer lead the way.

102. Cf. 'The intellectual who is a member of a declining class may go through a complex evolution which ultimately results in the development of a reactionary

ideology': Mannheim quoted by Brym, *Intellectuals and Politics*, p. 58.
    103. On this see G. Lewy, *Religion and Revolution* (New York, 1974), Ch. 22.

4 THE CRISIS OF THE ECONOMY AND THE CRISIS OF THE DICTATORSHIP

In this and the next chapters we will seek to explain the economic and political causes and precipitants of the 1979 revolution. These causes were: the generation of economic discontent on a mass scale; the emergence of some conflict of interest between the state and the upper class; the revolutionary mobilisation of the masses; the occurrence of a political alliance between diverse forces of opposition; and the wavering of the regime's foreign support.

Following the 1963-73 period of relative economic stability, important economic upheavals occurred between 1973 and 1978. These upheavals not only affected the capacity of the regime in terms of its financial resources but also severely affected the conditions of the lower classes and generated mass discontent and grievances. As far as the question of the genesis of grievances on a mass scale is concerned, there exists some theoretical controversy concerning what kind of economic situation prompts a population into a revolutionary situation. In Iran during the 1973-8 period there were both economic growth and decline. How did all this affect various classes? The theoretical views on the matter fall into two groups. On the one hand some consider general economic prosperity as a factor precipitating revolutionary upheavals. The origins of such a viewpoint stretch back to ancient times. According to Aristotle:

> In order to secure his power a tyrant must keep the population in poverty so that the preoccupation with daily bread leaves them no leisure to conspire against the tyrant; he must multiply taxes and engage in great investment projects.[1]

Alexis de Tocqueville, the historian of the French Revolution, attributing that revolution to the growing prosperity of the French people, also wrote:

> It is a singular fact that this steadily increasing prosperity, far from tranquilizing the population, everywhere promoted a spirit of unrest. The general public became more and more hostile to every ancient institution, more and more discontented; indeed it was increasingly obvious that the nation was heading for a revolution.[2]

On the other hand, an opposite postulate based on an abstract generalisation derived from the work of Karl Marx holds that increasing misery precipitates revolutionary upheavals by causing discontent. Combining the two views in his classical article, James Davies has suggested that: 'Revolutions are most likely to occur when a prolonged period of objective economic and social development is followed by a short period of sharp reversal.'[3] In his view, it is neither constant misery nor constant improvement but combined rapid economic growth and decline which drive the population into a revolutionary 'state of mind'.

Looking at the situation in Iran in the light of the above-mentioned theories, it seems that the 1973-8 period preceding the revolution fits the Davies theory, with rapid economic growth being followed by a sharp decline.[4] Thus we will show how for a short while an increase in economic resources raised the expectations of the lower classes and how in the following period of crisis, while expectations continued to rise, the regime's capability of meeting these began to decline. In sum, in this chapter we will cover both how the five foundations of the regime (discussed in Chapter 2) crumbled and the effects of the economic upheavals on the predisposition of the masses to revolutionary mobilisation and action.

The Period of Economic Prosperity

The period between 1963 and 1973 had been one of relative economic stability in prices, wages and in the inflow of government revenues. This had been a result of the adoption of an economic stabilisation programme and the lack of fluctuations in the international economy. The increase in the inflow of oil revenues from 1973 marked the end of that period.

What the oil nationalisation movement of 1951-3 had failed to achieve came to be gradually realised in the early 1970s. Due to the rise in the importance of the oil-producing countries and their international organisation (OPEC), from 1970 the Iranian government came to exert a measure of control over the foreign operating companies both in production and in pricing. At the Conference of Tehran, held under the Shah in 1971, the operators' control over prices was in effect ended and the government obtained one-quarter of the companies' shares. In May 1973 a new agreement was concluded according to which the industry came under full Iranian control.[5] From then on the Shah pressed for higher prices and he gained ground when the 1973 Middle East War broke out. That war prompted the first significant rise in oil prices. In 1973, the Conference of Tehran announced a fourfold increase in prices. Consequently Iran's annual oil revenues increased from $5 billion to $20 billion. This sudden and new financial wealth altered the course and the pace of development of the economy in Iran.

The three years following the price rises witnessed an unprecedented economic upsurge. To begin with, the Fifth Economic Plan which had started a year previously was drastically revised to double the development budget from the original $36 billion to $69 billion. Total expenditure during the Plan was put at $120 billion of which $100 billion were to be received from oil. Some $50 billion were allocated only for current expenditure. The significance of these figures becomes evident when compared with the Fourth Plan's expenditure of $10 billion. The decision to revise the Plan was dictated by the Shah despite reservations on the part of economists; even the guidelines of the IMF were ignored.[6] New policies were adopted. Education was made free from school to university. Government food subsidies were increased; essential provisions, especially wheat, were subsidised by the government. For example, the subsidised price of sugar was 25 rials a kilogram whereas the price of imported sugar was 100 rials. The government also promised comprehensive health programmes, housing and full employment.

Current expenditure showed an increase of 125 per cent only in 1974, and the budget was expanded by 250 per cent, an unprecedented rise. As a consequence the money supply was enlarged. In the ten-year period between 1962 and 1972 the money supply had increased threefold. Between 1972 and 1975 alone, the volume of money increased by 580 per cent. *Per capita* income rose from $500 in 1973 to $820 in 1974 and to $1,600 by 1976.[7] Unemployment almost disappeared, standing at 1 per cent. With an increase in demand, the government had to subsidise increasing imports of food. In 1972 it imported 770,000 tons of wheat; in 1974 this had increased to 1,430,000 tons. The import of meat increased from 7,000 to 53,000 tons between 1972 and 1975.[8] Higher incomes meant more consumption: for example, the annual *per capita* consumption of meat had been 28 kg. before 1973 and had increased to 47 kg. in 1975. Civil service salaries were increased. Between 1971 and 1975 the expense of the bureaucracy increased from 99 to 730 billion rials. Government employees were also granted tax reductions; the share of taxes in government revenues declined from 32.9 per cent in 1972 to 11 per cent in 1974.[9] In the period between 1963 and 1972 there had been a trend towards a more unequal distribution of incomes in the urban areas. According to one account, the Gini Index for

the distribution of expenditure in the urban areas had increased from
0.4552 in 1959 to 0.5051 in 1971.[10] From 1972, however, according
to an economist:

> There seems to be a tendency for the expenditure distribution to
> stabilize or even improve slightly over the two years 1972-3 and
> 1973-4. The expenditure share of the bottom 10 per cent of house-
> holds [which had] decreased uniformly from 1.77 per cent in 1959-
> 60 to 1.34 per cent in 1971-2 . . . increased slightly to 1.37 per cent.
> Similarly, the share of the top 10 per cent of households [which
> had] increased from 35.4 per cent in 1959-60 to the very high level
> of 39.5 per cent in 1971-72 declined sharply to 36.95 per cent in
> 1972-73.[11]

Also according to another analysis the Gini Index declined from 0.5051
in 1971-2 to 0.4946 in 1973-4.[12] The impact of the economic upheaval
must be examined in relation to the conditions of the major social
classes, the upper bourgeoisie and the working class.

The Upper Bourgeoisie

A direct outcome of the expansion in financial wealth was that the
regime adopted an even more liberal policy towards industrialists in
order to encourage investment and increase the supply of goods, lifting
all trade restrictions and controls over banking credits. Between 1971
and 1975 alone, loans to the private sector increased by 289 per cent,
with more than half going into trade and imports. The amount of loans
going to industrialists increased 45 per cent annually. Commercial banks
had to expand their capital in order to cope with increasing demand. In
the 1960s the government had imposed trade restrictions and a high-
rate tariff had been in operation. Now restrictions were lifted and tariff
rates were reduced. Exchange controls were also removed in 1974 and
traders were not required to submit depositing guarantees any more.
This trade liberalisation policy remained in operation until 1977. In
the same period the number of commercial banks increased from 24 to
36 and the volume of banking transactions increased sixfold. 'These
banks were established by a few large industrialists and capitalists in
order to provide a direct financial link between their own monopoly
industries and the banks.'[13] The liberal credit policy led to a growth
in urban land dealing. Speculators concentrated on the booming construction sector. In industry an even greater concentration of capital
became possible.[14] In 1974 large private industries forming 3 per cent

of all industries produced 70 per cent of total industrial surplus value. Between 1973 and 1975 the number of private companies in Tehran alone increased from 1,700 to 2,700.[15] In short:

> the government's deliberate policy of extending and supporting the private sector in the form of the sale of state-owned factories, extension of banking credits and concessions to large private enterprises and the removal of customs barriers all contributed to the speedy growth of the private sector in a short period of time.[16]

The Working Class

For a short period following the rise in oil revenues, the working class benefited from the financial affluence. Demands for wage increases were met by the government after the occurrence of a few strikes in 1971-2. An initial 25 per cent increase in wages was granted. In large industries wage demands of 40 per cent were accepted by the government. In May 1974 the High Council of Labour announced new minimum wages, increasing the daily industrial wage from 100 rials to 204 rials.[17] In practice, then, wages increased sharply: in textiles there was a 100 per cent increase in 1973 and a 200 per cent increase in 1975. In the car industry, between 1971 and 1975 wages increased by 400 per cent.[18] Unemployment virtually disappeared, leading to a shortage in the labour force; foreign labour had to be brought in for new jobs. In a short period after 1973, increases in wages were higher than those in the index of consumer goods. Between 1971 and 1974 the consumer index rose by 40 per cent, whereas industrial wages increased by 90 per cent.[19]

The increase in wages accelerated rural migration. Between 1962 and 1971 some 2 million people had migrated from the countryside to the towns. From 1973 onwards every year 8 per cent of the rural population left for the cities.[20] The rate of population growth in Tehran increased from 3 per cent before 1973 to 8 per cent from then on. Between 1967 and 1976 the urban population increased from 37.7 per cent to 46.7 per cent of the total population.[21] The migrants were mostly employed in the burgeoning construction sector. In 1974 alone, the number of housing permits issued by the municipalities increased by 83 per cent. Altogether there were 800,000 people working in construction. Wages of construction workers increased by 77 per cent in 1974-5.[22] Thus although rural migrants were from the beginning faced with the problem of housing, high wages and subsidised prices offered them a better standard of living than they could have hoped for in the depressed and stagnant countryside.

On the whole, in the two years after the rise in oil revenues, the public benefited from an unprecedented financial affluence. Public expectations were deliberately raised, and the general expectation was one of continued ability to satisfy continually rising demands.

Economic Instability

As a result of the government policy of injecting the new-found wealth into the economy through increasing public expenditure, *per capita* income increased in an unprecedented manner, leading to a widening gap between demand and supply. National income increased by an annual average of 35 per cent and in two years *per capita* income trebled. The volume of money increased at an annual rate of 60 per cent.[23] Higher incomes and subsidised prices increased consumption. Whereas the population grew at a 3 per cent rate, demand for consumer goods rose by 12 per cent annually. There was no comparable rise in domestic agricultural production, however. In fact in the past, agricultural production had been always low, in part due to the state's emphasis on industrialisation. The low productivity of agriculture became distinctly clear from 1973, against a background of rising incomes and demands. The accelerated pace of rural migration left many villages deserted. In 1975 the inhabitants of 8,000 villages had all left for the cities. Low production and increasing demands forced the government to import foodstuffs in large quantities and sell them at subsidised prices. As long as the oil revenues ran high, an elevated level of consumption could be maintained. The value of food imports grew more than four times from 1973 to 1976. Thus, because of an increase in imports and current expenditure, the government was left with a deficit of $1.7 billion in 1975, whereas in 1974 it had a surplus of $5.2 billion.

Increasing demands led to a sharp increase in inflation. Imports were slow in reaching the market and were insufficient. Cargo ships had to wait an average of three months before being able to unload. In 1975 there were two hundred ships waiting in the southern ports at any one time. Although the import of meat increased more than four times between 1972 and 1975, because of increasing consumption there were severe meat shortages in 1975 and 1976. From 1974 prices increased sharply. According to official figures the compound rate of inflation between 1973 and 1977 was 93.8 per cent or an annual average of 18 per cent. But according to *Kayhan* the compound rate of inflation between 1973 and 1976 alone was 200 per cent or an annual average of 50 per cent. There was a 500 per cent rise in the price of land and a 400 per cent rise in rents in Tehran, where a third of the population lived in rented rooms.[24]

Gradually price increases surpassed wage increases, leading to a number of strikes from mid-1974 onwards. At least seven important strikes occurred in 1974 and twelve in 1975 for pay rises and the implementation of the profit-sharing law.[25] As a result of inflation, income gaps began to widen. As already mentioned, in the 1972-4 period the Gini Index had shown a decrease in income differences. From 1974, however, there were indications of an increase in inequality. The Gini Index, which had decreased from 0.5051 to 0.4946 in 1973-4, went up to 0.5144 in 1974-5.[26] An official source also wrote: 'although the level of public welfare has risen there are now spectacular inequalities among various social classes'.[27]

On the whole, the economic crisis undermined the economic stability which had marked the previous decade. The emerging signs of labour unrest also indicated the weakness of the regime's apparatuses for the economic and political control of the subordinate classes.

Populist Efforts

The economic crisis of the early 1960s, as already discussed, prompted the emergence of the corporatist authoritarian regime at a time of conflict within the power bloc. In the mid-1970s, although the court was the only hegemonic power, the deeper economic crisis which was affecting the foundations of the regime prompted the emergence of a short-lived fascist phenomenon. This was the second major attempt at mass mobilisation after the mobilisation of the early 1960s. The court attempted to expand the apparatus of class control by the imposition of a new single political party to mobilise the lower classes and by the articulation of an ideology more heavily imbued with populist overtones. As it appears from the pronouncements of the court, the motivating influences were the court's determination to check the growth of 'industrial feudalism' (the upper bourgeoisie); the emerging signs of working-class unrest; and the inadequacy of the existing ruling party to incorporate diverse interests. The court was thus cultivating the image of being autonomous from the social classes. Undertaking a populist mobilisation effort, the court imposed a new political organisation to mobilise the lower classes economically and politically and activate them within, of course, official bounds. Previously the working class had had no political weight in the state ideology; it had been neutralised rather than antagonised. The new party was to increase this political weight and the previous party was denounced for not having given the working class sufficient attention. Thus what emerged was a populist attempt, in the sense of the controlled activation of the lower classes on the basis of economic concessions in the form of some redistributive measures to transfer property from one social class to another. As a result of these populist moves the clientelist relations which had obtained between government and business began to weaken.

In March 1975 the Shah issued a decree instructing the formation of an 'all-embracing' single party, the National Resurgence Party, the sale of shares in industrial enterprises to workers and the adoption of measures to control businessmen through price controls, an anti-profiteering campaign and checks on the wealth of high-ranking officials. The Shah justified his moves in the name of the prevention of 'class exploitation'.[28] The new move was allegedly discretion on the part of the court. The Shah claimed:

> We are always more steps ahead in satisfying the workers and peasants' demands than what they would expect themselves. For this is a revolution that should always be ahead of the events of the future so that no unexpected event and no social or economic change may catch us unawares.[29]

The new move, labelled 'Asr-e Rastakhiz' ('the era of resurgence'), had definite similarities with fascist movements in that it sought to create a one-party political system for the mobilisation of the masses, especially youth; it put an emphasis on a state-directed collectivist social order and was motivated by a drive to catch up with the developed nations; it explicitly rejected Western liberalism and it allegedly aimed at a general defence of all classes in the interest of the nation.[30] The centrepiece of the movement was the single party. The party was to function as 'a means for the political mobilization of numerous groups. Its main function is the publicization of politics and the politicization of the public. It is to open the political space and make the society political all over.' The previous party was denounced as having been unable to articulate the broad interests of the nation. It had been 'the party of power and domination and the gathering place for political profiteers. The party had been content only with the formal existence of front organizations and trade unions and cooperatives.'[31] 'In order to chain the small minority and bring out the large majority' the party became actively engaged in the mobilisation of workers, peasants and students and established 50,000 party cells throughout the country. Party activists were mostly chosen from students, workers and youth. During the 1975 parliamentary elections the party sought to recruit a new clientele through the nomination of new candidates. It rejected more than half of the previous deputies and as a result 80 per cent of the new deputies were new party recruits.[32]

Directly related to the political mobilisation of workers was the court's redistributive policy.[33] In the previous decade the relations between government and business had been based on distribution and regulation. Now in 1975 the court ordered the implementation of a previously adopted policy of share participation. This was the sale of 49 per cent of the holdings of 320 major private manufacturing companies and 99 per cent of the shares of state companies as an immediate measure in order to 'destroy industrial feudalism and the concentration of capital'.[34] According to the Law for the Extension of Industrial Property, between August 1975 and March 1976, 102 of the large enterprises sold 20 per cent of their shares and continued the sale up to 1978, fulfilling the legal target. The other 218 enterprises affected negotiated with the government for a postponement of the legal deadline. In order to enable the workers to buy the shares the government set up a credit organisation to grant them loans. By 1977, some 72,000 workers in large establishments, a small fraction of the industrial working class, had purchased shares.

Another measure adopted by the regime was the policy of price control and an anti-profiteering campaign which began in 1975 as part of the wider anti-business moves. The new party set up a price commission which, in cooperation with the chamber of guilds, launched an extensive campaign against profiteering. Young party recruits, especially students, checked and fixed prices, beat up businessmen and shopkeepers, smashed shops and stores, harassed and bribed and became a major threat to the stability of the bazaar. Price control and anti-profiteering were declared to be a constant policy of the government.

Although these populist policies did not have any notable impact in economic terms, they were important in fomenting the potential for political conflict. These policies did not lead to any change in the ruling elite, however. In fact, in the course of the following years the Shah vacillated between encouraging continued political mobilisation of the working class and making attempts to redress the complaints of business.

Disruption of Clientelistic Relations

The attempt to overcome the economic crisis involved considerable challenge to the vested interests that constituted the regime's main source of support. Thus as a consequence of the court's populist efforts some fundamental conflict of interest began to arise between the upper class and the state.[35] Although these efforts, especially the gestures concerning the economic gratification and political mobilisation of the working class, were half-hearted, they none the less brought about serious political and economic consequences, creating a range of incompatible political commitments for the court. The industrial bourgeoisie had grown in the shadow of state protection and had become a major client and pressure group with which to be reckoned. The court's new mobilisation efforts and redistributive policies struck fear in the upper bourgeoisie. No confiscation of property took place of course, as the industrialists affected by the Law for the Extension of Property were fully compensated. Indeed, the government organisation responsible for the legal transfer of the shares paid the industrialists more than the workers had paid to purchase the shares. The Prime Minister assured the bourgeoisie that 'they will still have the absolute control of their factory and of the majority of the shares. The aim is to create a sense of equality among workers.'[36] The share-holding workers were thus legally barred from participation in management and while the employers could own up to 51 per cent of the shares, the maximum number of shares which one worker could buy was five.

In the previous decade the entrepreneurs had invested in a secure environment and had obtained high profits. Now the Shah claimed that 'we are determined to resolve all class contradictions in Iran'. As a result of the changed situation, there was an increasing flight of capital abroad. Within one year of the introduction of the redistributive scheme, $2 billion worth of private funds were transferred abroad 'for lack of opportunities for investment'.[37] The regime's anti-business drive was further reinforced by the policy of price control, anti-profiteering and wage increases. The government imposed a profit margin of 15 per cent and since the cost of transportation exceeded this, businessmen declined to shift their goods from the customs, contributing to the congestion in ports. During the anti-profiteering campaign a number of businessmen from large companies were arrested. From the upper bourgeoisie M. Vahabzadeh, the owner of car industries, and H. Elqanian, the owner of plastic industries, were arrested, and the latter's business was closed down for good. H. Sabet, the industrial magnate, was accused of profiteering and left his business idle. H. Hamadanian, a wealthy businessman from Esfahan, was imprisoned on profiteering charges. In a number of radio speeches, the Shah said that the richest men in the country were in prison, implying that his regime was not supporting the wealthy class. Other businessmen and large merchants were banished. In the 1975 elections some major industrialists had been elected to the parliament by spending large sums on the election campaign. The Shah warned the 'wealthy deputies' not to 'exceed their limits'. Extraordinary courts were set up to deal with profiteers. Not only the wholesaler but also the petty retailer of the bazaar came under scrutiny by the party committees and 'shock troops'. The prices of 14,000 items were fixed and within a month more than 8,000 shopkeepers and owners of large stores were cast into prison and fined on charges of hoarding and profiteering.[38] The entrepreneurs were blamed as being the major cause of the economic problems. The official newspaper *Kayhan* wrote:

> Most of the private sector enterprises have sought more and more profit-making as their sole objective. Many of these enterprises make 50 to 100 per cent profit. They attempt to produce the maximum profit with the simplest and least costly technique because they are sure of their sales under customs protection.[39]

Furthermore, the High Council of Labour raised the minimum wage and the government put pressure on employers to increase the wages by a set formula. The state's populist gestures meant a more favourable attitude towards the mounting demands for higher wages. Several strikes occurred for pay rises in mid-1975. The regime, through the Ministry of Labour and the security police, exerted pressure on industrialists to raise wages. On one occasion security forces watched striking workers at the Tehran Power Organisation taking to the streets, until the management was forced to concede more favourable terms.[40] Strikes for wage increases continued and in 1976-7 demands for 50 and even 100 per cent wage increases were satisfied. Furthermore, the Central Bank adopted a stabilisation policy and applied control over private banking credits. The minimum reserve requirement of the commercial banks with the Central Bank was also raised and they were barred from foreign borrowing. As a result, the growth rate of banking credit going to the private sector declined from 55 per cent in 1975 to 20 per cent in 1977.

Thus, in order to deal with the economic situation, the regime had to adopt decisions which penalised at least a segment of the upper bourgeoisie. The entrepreneurs soon began to air their complaints about increasing state intervention in the economy. K. Khosrowshahi, a leading industrialist, complained that 'in a free economy the state should interfere only in those fields that are beyond the management capacity of private enterprise whereas now the state increasingly interferes in free enterprise, causing insecurity and low production.'[41] The industrialist Senator Lajevardi, opposing the policy of price control, stated: 'Nowhere in the world is price control for all commodities permanently practised. Price control is logical only for short periods of time and for goods in public demand. The economy will be healthy when profit is high.'[42] Complaining about the mobilisation of the working class, another industrialist said: 'We should be careful not to repeat the mistakes of Western countries. Workers' organizations should not be turned into a power front against the employers in the name of the protection of workers' interests and rights.'[43]

Clearly, there was no agreement between the regime and the bourgeoisie on the policies to control the economic situation. The resulting dissension was reflected on the political level within the Rastakhiz single party. The court had intended to create a united single organisation in order to implement its mobilisation schemes, but soon the differences between the regime and the bourgeoisie surfaced inside the party. Thus within the single party two political 'wings' emerged and in the course of the following years they engaged in conflicts over political office and the economic policy of the state. The 'Progressive Wing' was the dominant bureaucratic fascist-populist wing and closely followed the mobilisation policies of the court after 1975. This wing was dominated by the elite of the previous ruling party, the NIP, and the 'members' of the wing were mostly senior civil servants and members of the cabinet. The Progressive Wing overwhelmingly supported state economic intervention and comprehensive economic planning and, in line with the new populist moves, launched a propaganda campaign against 'monopoly capital'. The 'Constructive Wing', on the other hand, was known for its advocacy of liberal policies, the relaxation of state control of the economy and a more independent role for the private sector. It was led by the businessman and the Minister of Interior, Hushang Ansari, and among its members there were important industrialists and capitalists, associated especially with the Chamber of Commerce. The Constructive Wing emerged as the opposition faction within the single party. In the Party Congress the dominant bureaucratic faction put an emphasis on 'independent nationalist policies' and called for a 'struggle against imperialism'.

The regime was thus seizing on some of the differences which had
since the 1973 oil price rises emerged between the US and the oil-
producing countries. Since 1954 when the US oil companies obtained
a stake in Iranian oil, there had emerged some differences between the
regime and the oil consortium over the amount of production and pricing. Finally the 1973 Agreement between the two transferred the control over production and pricing to the government. Although he later
moderated his position, the Shah in the beginning pressed for higher
prices.[44] On the other hand the US administration warned the oil countries against price rises and on several occasions pressured the Shah into
adopting a more moderate stance.[45] Relying on the oil billions and the
current US foreign policy (the Nixon Doctrine), the Shah embarked
on a course of massive arms purchases, which invited opposition from
various quarters in the US. The arms dispute was intertwined with the
oil issue, because the more the Shah obtained arms from the US, the
more he would need to raise oil prices. From mid-1970s, an increasing
number of criticisms of the Shah's policies appeared in the US press,
Congress (especially by the Democrats) and the State Deparment.[46] The
Congressional criticisms in particular angered the Shah, who continued
to press the administration for more arms.[47] He warned the US that 'we
can hurt you as badly if not more so than you can hurt us'.[48] At the
same time, under the domination of the bureaucratic faction, the foreign
concerns operating in Iran were also somewhat affected by the Law for
the Extension of Industrial Property. Accordingly, foreign participants
in joint ventures could retain up to 25 per cent of the stake, whereas
previously they had been able to own up to 49 per cent. Some foreign
companies affected by the Law reacted against the new moves: for instance, the B.F. Goodrich company sold off its entire stake. Also in 1976
an American business mission to Iran composed of fifty US businessmen, led by David Rockefeller, failed to conclude an agreement on
further US investment in Iran and the creation of an international
money market in Tehran, with the cabinet dominated by the bureaucratic faction.[49] The mission warned the government that in future it
would find it more difficult to encourage further American investment
in Iran. In an address to the mission Premier Hoveida criticised the conduct of foreign companies in Iran.[50] By contrast, the liberal faction of
the party advocated the expansion of foreign investment in order to
raise domestic production.

On the whole, the economic crisis created a friction within the ruling
class and this in turn increased the difficulties of solving the crisis. The
populist attempts by the Shah penalised a segment of the bourgeoisie,

but they were of no consequence in solving the economic crisis. The entrepreneurs were threatened by the populist gestures of the fascist-oriented Rastakhiz Party; thus the regime was losing the support of some of the vested interests that had thus far constituted its main source of support. In the beginning, there were some indications that the Shah would continue to step up mass mobilisation at any price. But due to the intensification of the economic crisis, he finally decided to demobilise and to redress the grievances of the bourgeoisie.

The Economic Crisis Superimposed

The economic crisis and inflation generated from within further worsened with a decline in the government's financial capability, which forced it to rely on a policy of high taxation. Furthermore, the monetary and direct measures to curb inflation contributed to the onset of a period of recession. The fiscal crisis began from mid-1976 when fluctuations in oil exports, after the earlier phenomenal rise in revenues, led to a reduction in the government's earnings from oil. The annual rate of growth in the oil sector had been predicted at 52 per cent, but due to fluctuations it did not exceed 26 per cent. The decline in oil sales and revenues was due to a decline in the world oil market and a reduction in international oil prices.[51] The decline was reflected in the 1976-7 budget in which foreign borrowing was to compensate for a deficit of $2 billion. This was inevitable, as the pace of economic growth and expenditure had been set at 1973 pricing standards. Thus despite the decline in revenues, current expenditure continued to increase. In 1975-6 current expenditure increased by 30 per cent, whereas oil revenues increased by only 7 per cent. By mid-1977 the deficit had risen to $4.5 billion. As a result, several plans and projects and such spin-offs of the oil affluence as huge food subsidies, low taxes and school meals had to be abandoned. Wage increases were also discouraged and public expenditure was cut. From 1976 imports began to decline. Between 1974 and 1976 they had increased by an annual average of 60 per cent; in 1977 the rate of increase declined to 3 per cent. Thus supplies from imports were not sufficient to meet increasing demands. This led to even higher inflation. A 40 per cent inflation rate continued up to mid-1977, when it slowed down due only to the severe recession which set in from mid-1976 as a result of the control over prices, anti-business moves and monetary and fiscal policies in general. Many factories closed down or cut their production. The recession also resulted in a sharp decline in land dealings and construction activities which were responsible for growing unemployment from late 1976. The rate of unemployment increased from 1 per cent in 1974 to 9 per cent at the end of 1977.[52] The policy of tight credit control, higher interest rates (up to 30 per cent in the bazaar) and control over the money supply led to a decline in financial transactions.[53] From early 1977 bankruptcies occurred among merchants and traders. These were the result of heavy financial commitments undertaken in previous years, the decrease in banking credit and high interest rates in the bazaar.[54] As to agriculture, instead of the predicted 7 per cent annual rate of growth, there was a 1 per cent decline due to the increase in the cost of agricultural production, wage increases and a shortage of rainfall in 1977. On the whole, the economic crisis worsened and was further reinforced by a fiscal crisis and recession.

In order to compensate for declining revenues the government resorted to a policy of high taxation from 1976. Receipts from direct taxes especially increased substantially above the predicted amount. The share of taxes in government revenues, which had decreased from 32 per cent to 11 per cent between 1972 and 1974, increased from 1976, reaching more than 30 per cent in 1978. In absolute terms, due to the massive increases in government revenues the rise in taxes was substantial. Total taxes increased from $2.2 billion in 1973 to $5.9 billion in 1977. In 1975 alone, taxes were raised by 71.6 per cent. In 1977 private corporation taxes were increased by 80 per cent. Taxes on salaries were raised by 71 per cent in 1976 and 51 per cent in 1977. Tables 4.1 and 4.2 show the share of taxes in government revenues and the annual increase in the amount of taxes.

Table 4.1: Composition of Government Revenues, 1972-8 (per cent)

Description	1972	1973	1974	1975	1976	1977	1978
Total Revenues	100	100	100	100	100	100	100
(1) Oil	59	67	86	78	76	73	63
(2) Taxes	32	28	11	17	19	22	29
(Direct taxes)	13	11	5	9.5	10	11	17
(Indirect taxes)	19	17	6	7.5	9	11	12
(3) Government services and others	9	5	3	5	5	5	8

Sources: Central Bank, *Bank Markazi Annual Report and Balance Sheet* (Tehran, 1972-8).

Table 4.2: Yearly Increase in Taxes, 1973-8 (Increase in the absolute amount, compared to the preceding year) (per cent)

Description	1973	1974	1975	1976	1977	1978
Private companies	30	38	24.8	47	80.5	1.3
Government companies	50	68	224	7	7.6	35.7
Taxes on imports	33	4.8	45	32	36	−15
Income tax	28	12	48	59	20	1.2
Wealth tax	37	25	21	31	14	−12
Sales and consumption	21	21	19	24	35	19.5
Total annual increase	33	20	71.6	26	29	4.5

Sources: *Bank Markazi Annual Reports and Balance Sheet* (Tehran, 1973-8).

Direct tax increases during the recessionary period after 1976 were among the contributing causes of public discontent and political opposition, as we will show. As Table 4.2 demonstrates, the fiscal crisis reached its climax in 1978, when the government was nearly bankrupt, as the predicted increases in taxes did not materialise because of the economic slump. In that year the government had to resort to domestic borrowing on a large scale.

The Crisis Cabinet: Reversal of the Populist Policies

The regime was confronted with inflation hitting the public, recession affecting business and the fiscal crisis debilitating the government. During the 1975-7 period the regime's populist attempts had alienated a segment of the bourgeoisie and had caused a cleavage in the state as manifested in the factionalisation of the Rastakhiz Party. Yet these attempts did not stabilise the economic situation which further worsened with the onset of the fiscal crisis and recession.

On the whole, there was no agreement on the policies to deal with the economic situation. From 1977 the regime began to change the policies of 1975, aiming to restore relations between government and business. To heal the rifts caused by the populist moves, it sought to give incentives to entrepreneurs in order to increase domestic investment and to ease their dissatisfaction by giving some prominent businessmen cabinet posts and a say in the formulation of government economic policy. Thus, compared to the fascist moves of 1975, a degree of economic liberalisation began to obtain. Yet it soon became clear that the regime was launching a contradictory venture, seeking to fulfil fundamentally incompatible commitments. On the one hand it wanted to

remove controls on free enterprise and to reserve the role of the bourgeoisie in the economy, and on the other it sought to interfere in the
economy to prevent public dissatisfaction. In the end the regime satisfied neither the entrepreneurs nor the lower classes.

The regime's policy reversal brought about a change in government.
In August 1977, the cabinet, dominated by the bureaucratic fascist
faction of the Rastakhiz Party, which had carried out the court's mobilisation policies, was replaced by a new cabinet with leanings towards
the liberal Constructive faction. It was headed by Jamshid Amuzegar
(an economist) and contained a number of industrialists. In particular,
two major industrialists were appointed as ministers of commerce and
of industries.[55] To heal the rifts with business, the new cabinet was to
encourage the private sector, to check the growth of the public sector,
to revise the price control policy, to stop the anti-profiteering campaign,
to extend banking credit to the private sector and to clarify long-term
policies. In particular, a cancellation of wage increases and subsidies
which had been advocated by the previous cabinet was on the new
cabinet's agenda. In the hope of stimulating increases in the production
of consumer goods the new cabinet also planned to sell state-owned
industries. The Shah spoke of judiciously granting the private sector the
gradual advantage of decision making in business matters. At the same
time, the government was to implement the workers' profit-sharing
and share-participation schemes fully, to control prices indirectly, to
ensure 'reasonable' wages and to raise taxes. In particular, the government promised a 'fundamental' campaign against inflation.[56]

The government was thus trying to serve opposing economic interests. In order to encourage the bourgeoisie, the regime had to give incentives such as tax holidays, to lift direct control over prices and to
control wages and abandon the anti-profiteering campaign. At the same
time, the government was committed to curbing inflation and ensuring
high wages, which would affect the policy of free prices for business.
The government policy was thus contradictory; it had to increase profits, prices and wages and to curb inflation at the same time. In actual
fact, the government abandoned the policy of price control (except on
essential goods). It announced a free price policy, provided financial
facilities for entrepreneurs, reduced tariff restrictions, abandoned the
anti-profiteering campaign and dissolved the related committee in the
Chamber of Guilds. The single party declared that its participation in
price control had been 'a mistake'. The government introduced a new
scheme according to which the workers' share of the net profit would
be paid to them on condition that they raised the output and efficiency

of the factory. The government also announced a wage freeze and stabilised the salaries of government employees. But the policy of free prices led to more inflation at a time of stable wages, and hence the government was forced intermittently to control prices or increase wages. In mid-1978 the government had to call for a 50 per cent increase in wages. In particular in 1978, the government was forced to control prices under increasing public pressure — pressure which had been given an opportunity for expression under the liberalisation policy (see below).

The crisis cabinet was thus riven with tensions and contradictions. The bourgeoisie was dissatisfied due to the government's economic intervention and the lower classes were discontented because of inflation, low wages and higher taxes. We will examine the failure of the crisis cabinet in terms of the effects of its policies on the upper bourgeoisie and the general public.

The new cabinet sought to accommodate industrialists through a policy of economic liberalisation and wage stabilisation after two years of price control and the anti-profiteering campaign. It also decreased its intervention on behalf of workers in industrial relations, while some factories cut wages and others ended the workers' shares in profits. Thus the ratio of wage expenditure declined from 22.9 per cent in 1976 to 19.1 per cent in 1977. Mobilisation of workers for party rallies was slowed down. More banking credits were granted to entrepreneurs and initially 14 large agri-business complexes owned by the state were sold to the private sector.

However, the policy of free prices favoured by business and the campaign against inflation were particularly contradictory. Under the pressures of public dissatisfaction and increasing inflation the government was gradually forced to move towards a policy of price control. In the beginning, the government pledged to grant the private sector a say in economic decision making; in practice the Shah frequently bullied the bourgeoisie, saying: 'we are determined to raise production and lead this nation into the prosperity of a great civilization, if necessary by force'.[57] The entrepreneurs at least wanted to have a say in economic policy making concerning wages, prices and profit. The *Tehran Economist* summed up the complaints of the bourgeoisie as being: (a) the state's increasing intervention in the economy; (b) sudden changes in laws and regulations; (c) government interference in domestic trade; and (d) lack of continuity and perspective in government economic programmes.[58] The bourgeoisie demanded:

(1) changes in laws and regulations in the interest of industrialists

and capitalists and the provision of more credit and capital; (2) concentration of all economic policies in one single organization; (3) exemption from taxation up to 10 percent of the net profit; (4) reduction of taxation rates for industrialists and traders in the provinces; (5) reduction in the price of raw materials; (6) reforms in laws regarding income tax on the basis of suggestions from the Chamber of Commerce.[59]

Businessmen also demanded:

a revision of the wage policy in order to stop wage increases; a revision of the regulations of the Central Bank in order to reduce the deposits of the private banks with the Central Bank, and an increase in the grant of credits to the investors.[60]

Industrialists also complained about the court's intervention in the economy. For instance it is reported that Ali Rezai, a member of parliament and a major industrialist, told the Shah: 'You determine the prices, the wages, the profit, the customs duties and so on. It would be better if you would please take charge of the management of industries yourself.'[61] The policy of high taxation, especially on income and private companies, provided another cause for complaint by the entrepreneurs. In 1977 the government started to investigate taxes which had been payable in 1975, but remained unpaid due to irregular tax collection. All past and current tax records were brought under investigation to exact the unpaid taxes. The government announced that a large number of people with high incomes had been identified for tax payment and shortly ordered payment of taxes by 2 million people. After a period of very low taxes or tax immunity, the adoption of a retroactive policy of high taxation caused complaints among employers. The syndicate of machine factories and workshops encompassing 2,000 production units sent a letter to the Prime Minister complaining that in the past it had been deprived of all the privileges provided by the government for other industries and now it had to bear the burden of high taxation and warned that if the government failed to solve tax problems, it would close down its factories.[62] The government also began to control urban land dealing and speculation which in the past few years had become a major field of investment, and set maximum prices for urban land. Land dealers and speculators complained that due to price restrictions imposed by the government, their dealings had drastically declined.[63] Also in order to ease public dissatisfaction with the acute housing problem the Tehran municipality leased many empty houses to applicants without the consent of their owners. These were expensive houses beyond the public's purchasing power. There were complaints about the insecurity of private property and the interference of members of the royal family in business affairs.[64] Flights of capital, which had been already under way, intensified, and an increasing number of companies were closing down in late 1977. On the whole, the regime found it difficult to appease the bourgeoisie in a situation of economic crisis.

From 1975 the petty bourgeoisie of the bazaar had been hit by the anti-profiteering campaign and price control. The bazaaris particularly disliked the Chamber of Guilds, which was the watchdog of the single party in the bazaar. The Chamber had full supervisory powers over all bazaar guilds and imposed the guilds' regulations and fixed prices. Although in 1977 the anti-profiteering campaign was officially abandoned, the Chamber of Guilds continued to fix prices in the bazaars. In the month of April 1977 alone, the government received 600 million rials in fines for profiteering, mostly from the shopkeepers of the bazaar. In the same year, 20,000 shopkeepers and traders were imprisoned and fined. Files on bazaar businessmen pertaining to taxes, fines and anti-profiteering had been compiled in the municipalities and had become a major preoccupation for the courts. In 1978 new regulations were drawn up for taxing the bazaar guilds. The 1977 tax rates were announced to be the base (retroactively) for the five preceding years. The same rates were to become the basis for taxation in the following five years. Retroactive and high taxation led to protests by the bazaar guilds against 'arbitrary regulations'.[65]

The measures which the government adopted to combat inflationary pressures, to end the recession and to solve the fiscal crisis imposed hardships on the public who were now faced with salary freezes, tax increases and rising prices. In the 1976-8 period, in contrast to the preceding 1974-6 period, the sharp increase in the price of consumer goods, a decline in the anti-profiteering campaign, the policy of free prices and the wage-freeze policy increasingly widened the gap between wage increases and the rate of inflation. According to official figures, in 1977 industrial wages increased by 25 per cent while the index of consumer goods showed a 30 per cent rise.[66] The daily *Kayhan*, however, disputed the official figures for inflation in 1977-8 and put the rate of inflation at 85 per cent. According to *Kayhan*, the policy of free prices adopted from early 1977 was responsible for this sharp increase in inflation.[67] The tax increases also hit the lower classes. According to *Kayhan*:

The real reason for tax increases was not a more equitable distribution of income; rather the pressing needs of the government for more revenues dictated the tax policy. Hence from 1975, taxation not only did not bring about a better distribution of income but in fact it worsened the situation.[68]

According to a report, 'the pressures of high taxes and rising prices are the cause of public dissatisfaction. The tax-collecting apparatus has become a means for violence.'[69] In a series of surveys carried out by *Kayhan*, people also complained about the government's abandonment of the anti-profiteering campaign and price control. Obviously, the government's pressing needs to extract unprecedentedly large financial resources from the domestic economy penalised the upper as well as the lower classes.

On the whole, during the 1975-7 period of economic upheaval, which caused large-scale mass grievances, the regime undertook a fascist mobilisation effort which created some important conflicts of interest between the state and the bourgeoisie. It also increased the difficulties of solving economic problems by contributing to the recession. Thus there were no good prospects for the political consolidation of the fascist-populist regime and the political situation remained fluid. Due to these problems, the regime abandoned some of the populist gestures and by instituting a new government it sought to redress the discontent of the bourgeoisie as well as the grievances of the public. Thus it was seeking to fulfil fundamentally incompatible commitments and was launching a contradictory venture. In particular, the free price policy and the campaign against inflation were irreconcilable. Thus the crisis cabinet failed to contain the economic situation, to heal the rifts with the bourgeoisie or to consolidate the political situation. Indeed, it further paved the way for the expression of economic dissatisfaction through a policy of political liberalisation which made the politicisation of economic grievances possible.

Political Liberalisation

The new liberal economic policy which the regime adopted in 1977, in response to the difficulties caused by the populist efforts and the economic recession, was accompanied by a vague and half-hearted programme of political liberalisation which was initially an internal liberalisation effort, leading to the appointment of the liberal faction of the Rastakhiz Party to government.

The political liberalisation policy had external pressures behind it. As we have seen, since 1973 and especially since the establishment of the Rastakhiz Party, some differences had emerged between the regime and the US, especially in the field of oil price policy, arms and, to some extent, business relations. Criticisms of the Shah's style of rule had appeared in the Western press from 1975. Within the US, while the Pentagon and the arms industries in general supported the Shah's policies, the State Department and the oil companies became increasingly critical of US-Iran relations formulated under the Nixon administration. Under the Republican administration Iran had obtained a major role in US foreign policy. The new Democratic administration under Carter initiated policies which affected established US-Iran relations. During the campaign for the 1976 presidential elections, the Democratic Party put emphasis on the policy of 'human rights', and Carter asserted that Iran was one of the countries where human rights were violated. Under the Carter administration, the State Department's Bureau of Human Rights condemned the Shah's regime for its violation of human rights.[70] The US Ambassador in Tehran, William Sullivan, passed on the administration's human rights advice to the regime.[71] The differences between the administration and the Shah's regime were domestically reflected within the Rastakhiz Party and thus had a direct bearing upon domestic politics. While the party congress held under the bureaucratic wing spoke of the 'interferences of imperialism' in national affairs, the liberal faction of the party representing the private sector supported the US human rights policy.

The Carter administration's new foreign policy stance departed from that of the preceding Republican administration. It was underlined clearly in a summit conference of Western countries (at Guadeloupe) which was held in January 1979 to investigate general economic conditions in the West. The conference declared support for the 'national internal forces' and the 'private sector' *vis-à-vis* authoritarian regimes, and put an emphasis on the 'human rights' policy. It also called for an oil price freeze and advocated a reversal of the policy of creating 'regional powers' previously associated with US foreign policy. All these points clearly referred to the case of the authoritarian regime in Iran.

Whatever differences had existed between the US administration and the Shah's regime were intensifying under President Carter until the Shah's visit to Washington in November 1977. During the visit, the President put emphasis on the stability of the Shah's regime, and praised his 'progressive leadership' and promised to consider the sale of more arms to Iran as demanded by the Shah.[72] In return the Shah agreed not to

press for higher oil prices, and although their discussion on the liberalisation policy was not made public, the Shah implicitly agreed to adopt
a more liberal policy. After the visit, the Shah remarked that the 'small
differences' which had existed between the two countries had been
resolved and that his 'heart feels lighter'. The tough rhetoric which the
regime had employed during business relations with the West was also
abandoned. The US-Iran Joint Commission for Economic Cooperation
held its fourth session in Washington in January 1978 'for the expansion of commercial relations' between the two countries; it also praised
Iran's efforts to apply a freeze on oil prices.

On the whole, the Shah, who in the 1973-7 period had sought to
exert a measure of independence of action from the US, once again
harmonised his policies with the US stance. For this he had to pay with
the adoption of the liberalisation policy.

Although the liberalisation programme initially referred to the single
party, its meaning changed as the situation evolved, ultimately leading
to demands for the establishment of a constitutional regime. The vague-
ness of the policy made it even more effective in encouraging the opposition. Liberalisation was supposed to be a sign of the power of the
regime, as had been the case with the slogan of 'mobilisation', but gradually it increasingly indicated its weakness. The policy meant an official
recognition of the existing political repression. The Shah pardoned a
number of political prisoners. International human rights organisations
were allowed to visit prisons and investigate the extent of repression.
Political trials were to be held in civil rather than military courts. The
regime's pretensions to liberalisation further unleashed constitutional
opposition from below. Protests by the intelligentsia were increasingly
expressed in the form of open letters and petitions. In June 1977, the
National Front leaders criticised the regime in an open letter for its
despotism and called for a return to constitutional government. In July,
lawyers called for the abolition of the non-constitutional courts. In
December, a committee was formed for the protection of human rights,
and held a public press conference. The National Front leaders made
contacts with the US Embassy in order to put forward their criticisms
of the regime. At Tehran University, students held demonstrations in
support of US human rights policy. Some factions broke away from
the official single party to form independent groupings. Thus political
groups which had been considered subversive began to re-emerge. Under
the pressure of public dissatisfaction and constitutional opposition the
Shah promised free elections and a free press. The liberalisation programme thus provided an opportunity for the expression of grievances

caused by the economic crisis. It was a major and immediate factor in the regime's disintegration of power. Alexis de Tocqueville has explained the role of liberalisation in precipitating revolution thus:

> It is not always by going from bad to worse that a society falls into revolution. It happens most often that a people, which has supported without complaint, as if they were not felt, the most oppressive laws, violently throws them off as soon as their weight is lightened. The social order destroyed by a revolution is almost always better than that which immediately preceded it, and experience shows that the most dangerous moment for a bad government is generally that in which it sets about to reform. Only great genius can save a prince who undertakes to relieve his subjects after a long repression. The evil, which was suffered patiently as inevitable, seems unendurable as soon as the idea of escaping from it is conceived.[73]

During the 1973-8 period the economic stability, fiscal capacity, class control, clientelism and coercion which had *en bloc* formed the *status quo* for more than a decade and had held the regime together began to falter. The economic crisis undermined the regime's economic basis, while political liberalisation made the politicisation of economic demands possible. At the same time the upper class, growing discontented, could not carry on in the old way. In response, the regime sought to make new alliances through populist gestures and liberalisation, but its manoeuvres further intensified and politicised the ongoing crisis.

As for the general public, the five-year period witnessed great economic upheavals. Early in the period economic growth and expansion in the resources led to a rise in the economic capabilities of the population. But the economic crisis which followed created large-scale mass grievances. Thus a long period of economic stability and growth was followed by a short period of sharp reversal and a grave economic crisis. On the whole, the convergence of several causes weakened the regime and created a revolutionary situation. In the following chapter we will explain the actual disintegration of the regime and its collapse in terms of the more immediate and political factors.

Notes

1. Aristotle, *Politics*, Book V, Ch. 11, quoted by A. Gerschenkron, *Continuity in History and Other Essays* (Harvard, 1968), p. 324.

2. Alexis de Tocqueville, *The Old Regime and the French Revolution* (New York, 1955), p. 175.

3. J. Davies, 'Towards a Theory of Revolution', *American Sociological Review*, vol. 27 (1962), p. 6.

4. It should be clear (see Introduction) that the Davies theory, despite claiming to explain revolution, has nothing to say about a revolution, but in fact is a theory seeking to explain the genesis of grievances in any situation. Here we treat the revolution as a conjuncture and use Davies only to account for the genesis of mass discontent as one element in the conjuncture.

5. According to the 1971 Agreement, Iran in return gave the consortium members a 22% discount for any barrel of Iranian oil they exported. According to the 1973 Agreement, the consortium gave full control of the southern operations to the NIOC in return for a guarantee of receiving 'substantial quantities' of crude oil for twenty years: *Middle East Economic Survey*, 24 May 1973.

6. International Monetary Fund, *Staff Report on Iran* (January 1975).

7. Plan and Budget Organisation, *The Main Economic Indicators* (Third Report, Tehran, 1357), p. 128.

8. Bank Markazi, *Annual Report and Balance Sheet* (hereafter *BMAR*) (Tehran, 1975-6), p. 35.

9. The share of the direct taxes declined from 13% to 5.2% and that of indirect taxes also declined from 19.9% to 6.1%. *BMAR* (Tehran, 1972-5).

10. *Kayhan*, 30 Mehr 1357. The Gini Index is a measure that shows how close a given distribution of income is to absolute equality or inequality. Absolute equality is demonstrated by zero and absolute inequality by one.

11. M. Pesaran, 'Income Distribution and its Major Determinants in Iran' in J. Jaqs (ed.), *Iran: Past, Present and Future* (New York, 1976), p. 268.

12. *Kayhan*, 30 Mehr 1357.

13. *BMAR* (Tehran, 1978), p. 53.

14. Cf. 'Some of the more socially-conscious businessmen were seeking ways of reducing 100% returns on equity'! P. Richardson, 'Understanding Business Policy in Iran', *Journal of General Management*, vol. 4, no. 3 (1979), p. 47.

15. *Tehran Economist*, 22 Azar 1354; *BMAR* (Tehran, 1973), p. 204.

16. *Kayhan*, 14 Teer 1354.

17. *Iran Almanac* (1976), p. 354.

18. *The Economist* (London), 20 December 1975, p. 69.

19. *BMAR* (Tehran, 1974).

20. *The Economist* (London), 28 August 1976.

21. K. Kohli, *Current Trends and Patterns of Urbanisation in Iran: 1956-76* (Plan Organisation, Report No. 1, Tehran, 1977), p. 28.

22. *BMAR* (Tehran, 1974), p. 101; (Tehran, 1975), p. 106.

23. *BMAR* (Tehran, 1976), p. 48.

24. *Kayhan*, 18 Mehr 1357; *Tehran Economist*, 18 Teer 1356.

25. *Mardom*, 22 June, 23 August, 6 September and 23 October 1975.

26. *Kayhan*, 30 Mehr 1357.

27. *BMAR* (Tehran, 1977), p. 68.

28. M.R. Pahlavi, *Be Suye Tamaddon-e Bozorg* (*Towards the Great Civilisation*) (Tehran, n.d. [1977]), pp. 92-3.

29. The text of the Shah's decree published by the Ministry of Information (Tehran, 1975).

30. The common features of fascist movements are analysed in A. James Gregor, *The Fascist Persuasion in Radical Politics* (Princeton, 1974), pp. 175-80.

31. *Ayandegan*, 18 Esfand 1353.

32. The party put emphasis on the symbolic representation of workers. Of the new deputies 25 were doctors, 27 teachers, 7 university professors, 7 lawyers,

11 workers, 34 farmers, 6 directors-general, 4 top officials and 'only a few business-men': *Iran Almanac* (1976), p. 92. Among these businessmen were large indus-trialists such as the Chairman of the Chamber of Commerce and of the Carpet Employers' Union. On their election, the Shah, in line with the new mobilisation policy, warned the industrialists that 'they will be no more allowed to pursue their own interests in order to loot others' (*Ayandegan*, 15 Mordad 1354).

33. In his budget speech of January 1975 Hoveida put emphasis on 'a more equitable distribution of wealth and income through assisting the lower classes as well as taxation' (*Kayhan*, 20 Day 1353). *Tehran Economist*, 17 Farvardin 1353, criticised those who took advantage of the oil boom to pocket huge profits.

34. Pahlavi, *Be Suye Tamaddon-e Bozorg*, p. 128.

35. Cf. Theda Skocpol, *States and Social Revolutions: A Comparative Analysis of France, Russia and China* (Cambridge, 1979). Skocpol demonstrates that great revolutions were initiated as a result of a conflict between the state and the upper class over the extraction of economic resources, especially at times of internal conflict. However, in an article which she wrote on the Iranian revolution in 1982, entitled 'Rentier State and Shia Islam in the Iranian Revolution', *Theory and Society*, vol. 11 (1982), she does not apply her analysis in *States and Social Revolutions* and instead puts emphasis on the ideological aspects in the Iranian revolution, thereby making an exception of the Iranian case.

36. *Kayhan*, 26 Mehr 1354.

37. *Business Week*, no. 17 (1975).

38. *The Economist* (London), 13 December 1975, p. 54; *New York Times*, 4 August 1975.

39. *Kayhan*, 14 Teer 1354.

40. *Mardom*, 22 June 1975.

41. *Tehran Economist*, 1 Azar 1354.

42. Ibid., 28 Farvardin 1355.

43. Ibid., 6 Day 1354.

44. 'We are going to defend ourselves by increasing the price of our oil': the Shah in *Middle East Economic Survey*, 11 April 1975.

45. For instance in *New York Times*, 24 September 1974.

46. *New York Times*, 1 August 1976. In 1975, the Democrat Senator Edward Kennedy had spoken against an 'unregulated flow of arms' to Iran, in his visit to Tehran: *New York Times*, 27 May 1975.

47. Ibid., 6 August 1976; Iran also threatened to cut back arms purchases from the US and to acquire some of its military needs from other sources: ibid., 3 February 1976.

48. Ibid., 14 March 1976.

49. Ibid., 1 March 1976.

50. Ibid., 3 March 1976.

51. The economic crisis was no doubt to some extent due to the world econ-omic crisis which was reflected on the local scene through the interdependence of Iranian and Western economies; see P. Vieille, 'Transformation des rapports sociaux et révolution en Iran', *Peuples mediterranéens*, vol. 8 (1979), pp. 25-58.

52. *BMAR* (Tehran, 1977), p. 117.

53. The dealings of the Stock Exchange declined from a 115% annual rate of growth in 1976 to 16% in 1977 (ibid., p. 80).

54. Cf. 'Most businessmen maximise their opportunities by setting up com-panies with high-equity ratios . . . This financial structure has the effect of maxi-mising returns on equity . . . Its disadvantage is that the firm is burdened with high interest payments when growth declines or a recession arrives' (P. Wright, 'Cor-porate Strategy at Admiram Manufacturing Company: An Iranian Case Study', *Long Range Planning*, vol. 13, no. 3 (1980), p. 117.

55. These were Kazem Khosrowshahi, who had earlier opposed the government's interventionist policies, and Mohammad-Reza Amin.

56. Ministry of Information, 'The Programme of the Government of Dr. Amuzegar' (Mordad 1356).

57. *Kayhan*, 3 Aban 1356.

58. *Tehran Economist*, 29 Mordad 1356.

59. *Kayhan*, 13 Bahman 1356.

60. *Tehran Economist*, 28 Farvardin 1355.

61. 'Then the Shah replied "if you want to close the steel factory, then close the Shahriyar Bank as well, which gives you 900 million in profit". Rezai remains silent': Mojahedin-e Khalq, *Dowreh-ye Zamamdari-ye Karter (The Administration of President Carter)* (Tehran, 1357), p. 52.

62. *Kayhan*, 1 Aban 1357.

63. Ibid., 19 Mordad 1357.

64. Ibid., 24 Mordad 1357.

65. *Ettelaat*, 19 Mordad 1357.

66. *BMAR* (Tehran, 1977), pp. 61, 121.

67. *Kayhan*, 15 Mordad 1357.

68. Ibid., 1 Aban 1357.

69. A report on the economic situation by the 'Group for the Investigation of Iran's Problems', quoted in A. Haj Seyed Javadi, *Daftar-haye Siasi-ye Jonbesh (Political Notebooks of the Movement)* (Tehran, 1357), p. 31.

70. E.g. a report prepared by the State Department on the human rights situation in Iran was made public by a House of Representatives Committee, *New York Times*, 1 January 1977.

71. In his autobiography written after the revolution, the Shah writes that the US Ambassador continued to encourage him towards 'extremes of liberalisation': M.R. Pahlavi, *The Shah's Story* (London, 1980), p. 186.

72. *New York Times*, 16 November 1977.

73. De Tocqueville, *The Old Regime*, p. 178.

5 THE COMING OF THE REVOLUTION

The constitutional opposition to the regime which had been stimulated by the political liberalisation programme consisted of already organised political groups and parties whose emergence was not a novel development. The revolution began with the emergence of a popular mass movement which soon turned into a formidable and uncontrollable force. This popular opposition passed through several phases. Initially it consisted of scattered and spontaneous events such as outbursts of recent rural migrants filled with anger at the demolition of their shanties by the municipal police, of labourers and low-paid government employees faced with the inflationary spiral, and of students and intellectuals haunted by the fear of SAVAK, which under the cover of official liberalisation harassed and tortured dissidents. The public was faced with shortages of food, increasing rents, prices and taxes and an acute housing problem. The massive migration of the previous years had caused overpopulation in the large cities, especially the capital. Often a whole family had to live in one rented room. The economic crisis affected in particular the recent rural migrants who had been attracted to the cities by the urban oil boom, which had now given way to recession. The regime's symbolic manoeuvres had left no impact on the life of the lower classes. The economic crisis was in no small measure due to the decline in agricultural production. The agricultural sector could not support consumption nationally. The land reforms, which had stimulated the disintegration of the countryside against a background of increasing urbanisation, had created small-holdings without increasing agricultural production. The public warehouses had stocks from the past, but corruption and hoarding were commonplace in the bureaucracy. The public thus had good reason for strong indignation and discontent.

The upper class was also discontented because of the economic recession and symbolic changes in government policy. The redistributive policies and the economic stabilisation programme had caused dissatisfaction among powerful economic interests which was manifested in flights of capital and capitalists. There were complaints about increasing state intervention in the economy. Within the single party, businessmen had already expressed their opposition to the domination of business interests by bureaucratic interests. Also, the increasing disunity in parliament led to the emergence of several 'fractions' (including the Pan-Iranist, the Freedom, the National Unity, the National Path and the National Ideal fractions). In particular, the Freedom Fraction was supported by business interests which had entered the Majles in 1975. There was also some direct support among the upper bourgeoisie for the revolution. For instance, T. Barkhordar, a major industrialist, paid 20 million rials 'in order to help the movement'.[1] Likewise some industrialists continued to pay striking workers. Merchants and traders in the bazaars set up funds to provide financial help for strikers and to distribute provisions during the revolution.[2]

Against this background of public discontent, in the beginning public protest was expressed by spontaneous crowds with little mobilisation and organisation. The economically motivated crowds reacted to rising prices, lower wages and food shortage. The expression of grievances was particularly encouraged by the liberalisation programme and was given some space in the official press. In August 1977, several crowds composed of high-school students and 'passers-by' spontaneously gathered in the vicinity of the Artillery Square near the bazaar in Tehran. They complained of high prices and food shortages.[3] Confrontation between the municipal police and rural immigrants who were building houses outside city limits led to several clashes between crowds and the police. A crowd of people whose houses had been demolished by the police set out from the south of Tehran to the Shah's Niavaran palace, but were prevented from approaching the palace by the police. Their representatives explained their action in terms of the liberalisation policy and the right to free expression, but they were arrested and accused of sedition, and in the end no answer to their complaints came from the Shah's special bureau.[4] During 1977, crowds of workers gathering in the south of Tehran clashed with the municipal police who continued to demolish the houses built outside city limits. In November and December sporadic and spontaneous strikes occurred in several factories as well as government departments. In December, coinciding with the religious month of Moharram, shopkeepers in the Tehran bazaar attending religious sermons held demonstrations against government economic policy.[5] From December there was a gradual transition from spontaneous and economically motivated crowds to more organised rallies and demonstrations. One special event acted as the precipitant of the revolution. In December, Mostafa Khomeini, son of the exiled religious leader Ayatollah Khomeini, died in suspicious circumstances. Mournings were held in several towns and demonstrations were held in the Tehran bazaar in which the name of Ayatollah Khomeini was often proclaimed. This was followed by the publication of an article in *Ettelaat*, probably at the instigation of the court, in which the regime slandered and ridiculed Khomeini. From this time on, public protest became more organised and Islam as the ideology of the revolution became increasingly more apparent as religious mythology and rituals determined the shape of the unfolding revolutionary events. On 9 January 1978 the city of Qum, the headquarters of the Ulama, witnessed the first major incident of organised popular opposition. The bazaar and the religious schools closed down in protest at the above-mentioned article. A protest meeting organised by the Ulama called for the return of Khomeini from exile, the release of political prisoners, economic independence from foreign countries, dissolution of the single party and respect for religion and the Ulama.[6] A peaceful demonstration staged by religious students came under attack by the police, killing between forty and two hundred people; martial law was declared in the city. In a statement, the senior Ulama of Qum declared the regime to be anti-Islamic and illegitimate and called for public mournings. In response, the bazaars closed down in several cities and in Tehran the Society of Traders and Artisans of the bazaar called for a public strike in sympathy with the Ulama.

In the beginning, the emerging mass opposition had very few organisations of its own, but increasingly the traditional channels of communication such as the bazaar guilds, *heyat*s (religious sessions), mosques and coffee-houses provided the necessary means of communication. The mosques and the bazaars played the most significant role in the mobilisation and organisation of popular opposition.[7] After the Qum incident the bazaars began to organise massive memorial demonstrations at forty-day intervals, in accordance with the traditional pattern of mourning. On the fortieth day of the Qum incident the Ulama mobilised large demonstrations, especially in Tabriz where the bazaars closed down and severe clashes occurred between the crowds and the army.[8] After the Tabriz confrontation several more fortieth-day mournings were held in commemoration of preceding violent events. By the beginning of Ramadan, public demonstrations, rallies and surging crowds had become part of daily life. The Ulama and the bazaars undertook a massive mobilisation effort, promulgated the ideology of the revolution and articulated the grievances and hopes of the public. In this the most effective tool was the elaborate rituals of the Shiite religious processions, with all their emotional trappings. In September, large demonstrations were held throughout the country calling for 'Independence, Freedom, and Islamic government'. The bazaar-Ulama movement thus emerged as the leading force overtaking the constitutionalist parties. As the mobilisation was stepped up, the crowds became increasingly more ideological and less economically motivated, and the ideal of an Islamic state became widespread. On the whole, the revolution began with the moderate protests of the professional middle class and the intelligentsia with their open letters and petitions, but the bazaar and the Ulama soon took the initiative and organised massive demonstrations.

The Regime of 'National Reconciliation'

As the popular opposition became an increasingly formidable force to be reckoned with, the regime sought to redirect the movement by making attempts at reconciliation with the opposition. On the whole two opposition forces with distinct political tendencies emerged: the liberal constitutionalist opposition and the popular revolutionary opposition. The moderate opposition called for the implementation of the Constitution and included the National Front, the Freedom Movement, the Radical Movement (recently formed by a group of professional men), the Lawyers' Association, the Social Democrat Party (formed by the constitutionalist minority group in parliament) and Jonbesh (formed by the leading intellectual Dr Haj Seyed Javadi). Also, senior Ulama, especially Ayatollah Shariatmadari and Ayatollah Shirazi, called for the implementation of the Constitution. By contrast, the popular revolutionary opposition which had become associated with the name of Ayatollah Khomeini called for the establishment of a new, Islamic regime. Khomeini approved of no compromise and repeated his call for the destruction of the monarchy from exile.

Faced with the constitutionalist and popular oppositions the regime sought to make an alliance with the moderates and redirect the Islamic movement. Thus the court dismissed the cabinet of economic crisis only to institute one of political crisis, the cabinet of 'national reconciliation'. The new cabinet promised free elections; freedom of the press was granted, and moderate opposition leaders were called upon for negotiations. It also granted large sums towards wage settlement; members of the royal family were forbidden from any financial dealing with public companies, and records concerning profiteering by bazaar guilds which had accumulated for some years were written off. Also, the powers of the chamber of guilds were reduced and taxes were to be cut. The moderate opposition sought to seize the opportunity afforded for political reform. The National Front announced its willingness to negotiate with the regime and moderate religious leaders called for the implementation of the Constitution and especially the convention of the parliamentary committee of Mujtaheds to supervise legislation.[9]

While the regime's attempts at reconciliation with the moderate opposition had not yet borne fruit, mounting popular opposition led to events which made any compromise with the regime impossible. This was the bloody massacre of Black Friday on 8 September. Behind the scene of 'national reconciliation' the army generals, as well as some US advisers, urged the Shah to adopt a hard-line stance against the opposition.[10] Despite the moderates' attempt to dissuade popular street opposition, massive rallies and demonstrations were held. The moderate opposition refused to join public rallies and called on the people to give the government more opportunity to liberalise.[11] Then the regime, in a sudden reversal to repression, declared martial law in Tehran and other major cities. On Black Friday, between 700 and 3,000 people (according to different accounts) were massacred at the Zhaleh Square near Parliament. After Black Friday the moderate camp became increasingly radicalised. Even the parliamentary opposition minority considered the reconciliation attempts as being insincere. Increasingly the regime had to give more concessions to the moderates while they were increasingly less willing to accept them. From September the popular opposition overtook the constitutionalist opposition. Calls for strikes by Ayatollah Khomeini met with a positive response all over the country. In October, strikes occurred in government ministries, the post office, law courts, railroads, hospitals, radio and television stations, schools, the Central Bank, bus companies, banks, hotels, the bazaars, the oil industry and so on. The strike of 37,000 oil workers brought the whole economy to a standstill.[12] There were 1 million civil servants on strike.[13] In the beginning of the revolution the regime had been able to recruit some peasants and send them to the cities to attack the demonstrators. In December, the inhabitants of some of the villages involved 'repented' as the revolution spread to the countryside. On the whole, against this background of increasing popular opposition, the regime's attempt at reconciliation with the constitutionalist opposition did not fall on fertile ground. In fact, the regime was too slow with concessions to the moderate opposition so that it always remained one step behind developments.[14] In the beginning, the Shah thought that minimal changes would be sufficient, changes which did not satisfy the moderates; when eventually the Shah agreed to accept everything according to the Constitution, it was too late. In the end, the regime did not succeed in making an alliance with the moderates.

The Alliance of the Moderates and the Radicals

As the moderate opposition was radicalised, ground was prepared for the emergence of a revolutionary alliance between the liberal parties and the radical Ulama against the Shah's regime. In November, the leaders of the moderate opposition, Dr Sanjabi and M. Bazargan, flew to Paris to negotiate with Ayatollah Khomeini who approved of a policy of no compromise with the Shah. The moderates finally accepted Khomeini's leadership of the revolution and announced that no compromise was possible with the Shah. In a declaration issued in Paris on 5 November and signed by Khomeini and Sanjabi, it was agreed that the form of the government after the Shah would be determined by a referendum. The National Front declared that the monarchy lacked legitimacy.[15] At the same time, Ayatollah Beheshti, Khomeini's representative in Tehran, called on 'the Marxists, materialists and liberals to cooperate for some time and with one voice to continue the valuable struggle against the regime'.[16] As the possibility of an alliance with the moderates disappeared and the opposition became united against the regime, the Shah resorted to a hard-line policy of naked force.

The Praetorian Regime

The army was the last resort of the Shah. On 6 November, soon after the stance of the moderate opposition was made clear, the Shah dismissed the cabinet of 'reconciliation' and installed a new cabinet of seven generals headed by General Azhari, the chief of staff. This signified the impossibility of any alliance with the opposition. The military government was an *ad hoc* regime with no political or economic programmes. Its aim was to prevent the regime from further disintegration. The establishment of the military regime had the backing of the US administration, which encouraged the Shah to adopt an 'iron-fist' policy.[17] Under the generals' regime, the freedoms previously granted were withdrawn. Troops occupied press premises in Tehran and imposed censorship. The National Front leaders were arrested and the army occupied the oilfields. Yet the Shah was as half-hearted in his hard-line policy as he had been in his liberalisation programme.[18] Azhari was rather an old man, whereas the Shah could have chosen a younger and more ambitious officer such as General Khosrowdad, who had asked the Shah to give him permission 'to level Tehran'. After the establishment of military government, the Shah's conciliatory speech in which he said that he had 'heard the voice of the revolution' himself, caused confusion within the army elite. There were rumours that some army officers were seeking to come to power in a *coup* because of the Shah's weakness. There were also rumours that the Shah was fatally ill.[19]

Shortly after the army's assumption of power, however, popular opposition was heightened and the bazaars closed down indefinitely. The high point of popular opposition came in the holy month of Moharram when crowds appeared in white shrouds prepared for death. On the first day of the month alone, between 400 and 3,000 people (according to different accounts) were killed.[20] On *Ashura*, the tenth of the month and the peak of the mournings, between 1 and 3 million people demonstrated against the regime in Tehran alone.

At the same time, the military regime weakened from within as the army began to disintegrate. There were rumours of mutiny in the garrisons. Earlier, Khomeini had called upon soldiers to desert. As the majority of the rank and file of the army were conscripts, Khomeini's call found an increasingly positive response among them. In Tehran, soldiers and especially air force cadets deserted in large numbers. There were rumours of the arrest and execution of the cadets stationed on the ports of the Persian Gulf for supporting the revolution. There was news of the assassination of top army commanders by soldiers in the Lavizan garrison.[21]

Under the military regime the Shah still attempted a compromise with the moderate opposition which now proposed the formation of a regency council to replace the Shah. Dr Sanjabi was taken to the court by soldiers for negotiation but he only repeated that there could be no solution under the Shah. By now there was unanimous agreement among the opposition forces that he could not be part of any political deal. The military regime only intensified the crisis.

The Constitutional Regime: A Tenuous Alliance

The US administration had throughout declared its support for the regime, urging the Shah to arrive at a compromise with the moderate opposition.[22] This policy also worked the other way as the moderate opposition had made contacts with the US Embassy to present its case against the Shah's dictatorship. Internally the court's position had been totally undermined; the final 'push' came with the disintegration of its foreign support.[23] From December the US administration's support for the Shah wavered.[24] In general, the interests of the administration revolved around three issues: a peaceful solution to the political crisis, the preservation of the unity of the army and the prevention of the leftward radicalisation of the revolution and of the assumption of power by 'radical elements'.[25] Faced with the possibility of the Shah's imminent downfall, the administration attempted to mediate directly between the regime and the moderate opposition in order to find common ground between the two. Thus it sent the George Ball mission to Iran to negotiate with the moderate opposition. The mission's report recommended the Shah's resignation and the establishment of a regency council, reflecting the views of the moderate opposition.[26] This became the basis of the administration's new policy and its withdrawal of support from the Shah. The new policy was to persuade the Shah to choose a government and to leave Iran. The task of the General Huyser mission which was sent to Iran in early January 1979 was to implement the new policy, i.e. to obtain the army's acquiescence for the Shah's departure and to ensure its support for the new regime. It met and advised the Shah to take this course of action.[27] The Shah continued to seek, among the constitutionalists, someone willing to form a government, now on the basis of his departure and the formation of a regency council provided for by the Constitution. Due to the opposition's rejection of any government appointed by the Shah this development took the form of a personal adventure. Dr Shapour Bakhtiar, a leading member of the National Front, met the Shah and agreed to form a government on the conditions of the Shah's departure from Iran and his own assumption of real power. The issue of the Shah's departure caused some unease within the military elite. Diehard army generals disapproved of the Shah's departure and the 8,000-strong Imperial Guards declared their full support for the Shah. But it was the Huyser mission's task to prevent dissension within the army. At the same time, to ensure the loyalty of the army the Shah appointed three of his close military advisers to command the armed forces. Once Bakhtiar obtained parliament's vote of confidence the Shah prepared to leave. At the same time, according to Article 42 of the Constitution providing for the temporary absence of the monarch, a nine-man regency council was formed.[28] On 16 January the Shah left Tehran officially for a period of rest, which jubilant crowds saw as signalling the end of the monarchy.

As a full-blooded constitutional government, the Bakhtiar regime promised everything short of a revolution. Its programme included the dissolution of SAVAK, freedom of political prisoners, freedom of the press, the recognition of the Ulama's role in legislation and an end to government intervention in commerce and industry. But the new regime was from its inception rejected by moderate and popular opposition alike. The National Front dismissed Bakhtiar as a traitor to its cause. Everywhere the constitutional regime was denounced as being the agent of imperialism.[29] Government employees in the ministries rejected the new ministers appointed by Bakhtiar. Although his constitutional re- forms had the tacit support of the liberal opposition and the moderate Ulama, no major group was willing to run the risk of supporting a regime appointed by the Shah. When Bakhtiar sought to make political capital out of the silence of the moderate Ulama, they issued declarations and called his regime illegal. Some large demonstrations did take place in Tehran in support of the Constitution and Bakhtiar. 'Some 100,000 people mainly from the army and the rich, calling themselves the "sup- porters of the Constitution and social democracy" gathered in the Parliament Square to declare their support for the Bakhtiar regime.'[30] But the constitutional regime was confronted with the surging crowds of the revolution who were organising themselves into revolutionary committees and taking over the administration of the cities. Under Bakhtiar, while the Huyser mission ensured a measure of unity in the military elite, the rank and file of the army were in a process of further disintegration and passing to the side of the revolution.[31] There was a visible decline in discipline. Air force soldiers went on hunger strike in support of the revolution. In the provinces officers met local religious leaders on their own initiative. Everywhere demonstrations were held in the air force garrisons to demand the return of Khomeini.[32] On the whole, the constitutional regime was confronted with internal disinte- gration and the surging waves of the revolution. Members of parliament and of the regency council resigned one after another and strikes con- tinued in the bureaucracy. There were thus no good prospects for the political consolidation of the regime.

Dual Sovereignty

Ayatollah Khomeini had already formed an Islamic Revolutionary Council mainly composed of his clerical associates in order to form a provisional revolutionary government. Upon his return from exile, soon after the departure of the Shah, he appointed Mehdi Bazargan, the leader of the Freedom Movement, as the Prime Minister of the Pro- visional Revolutionary Government which was set up to take over from the constitutional regime. The PRG called upon the Bakhtiar regime to relinquish the reins of power and the constitutional regime threatened

to use force against the PRG. Between the constitutional regime and
the regime of the revolution stood the army, which initially supported
Bakhtiar. In order to pave the way for a smooth transition of power
the moderate opposition and the US Ambassador arranged meetings
between the two governments to discuss the possibility of a change
from constitutional monarchy to a republic. Bakhtiar proposed the
holding of a constituent assembly and urged that any political change
should take place on the basis of the Constitution. At the same time,
with the mediation of the US Embassy and the Huyser mission, the
PRG met with the military commanders in order to gain their support.
On 5 February a meeting was held between Bazargan, General Qarabaqi,
the Chief of Staff, and General Huyser, with the aim of convincing the
army that the Bakhtiar regime would not last long and that any attempt
at a military *coup d'état* would prove futile. These negotiations finally
led to an alliance between the army and the PRG.[33] General Qarabaqi
announced that the army would not interfere in politics and would
remain united to back any legal government. This meant the army's
withdrawal of support from the Bakhtiar regime and its neutrality in
the conflict between the two governments. The PRG in turn conceded
that the unity of the army must be preserved. With more defections by
air force cadets in support of Khomeini, General Rabii, the commander
of the air force, also declared the neutrality of his own forces. The army
in fact was more concerned about its own unity than the defence of the
Bakhtiar regime. The Huyser mission left Tehran on 7 February assuring
'the unity and neutrality' of the army. The disintegration of the army
and the declaration of its neutrality made the task of the final victory
of the revolution easier.

The Civil War

The increasing disintegration of the army led to open conflict between
forces which had sided with the revolution and those which had remained loyal to the old regime, a possibility which the army generals
had sought to avert by declaring their forces neutral. Yet on the same
day that the neutrality of the army was declared, air force cadets
marched before Ayatollah Khomeini and in support of the revolution.
On 9 February, a demonstration in the Doshan Tappeh air force garrison
in Tehran in support of the revolution led to a mutiny. The royalist
Imperial Guards arrived at the garrison in order to suppress the demonstration. Fierce fighting broke out between the two, drawing the crowds

to the side of the air force cadets. At this point the Fedaiyan and Mojahedin armed guerrillas and other armed groups arrived to fight the
Guards. No doubt the release of political prisoners throughout the
revolutionary period had enlarged the ranks of militant political groups.
Some 2,450 such prisoners had been released between October and
January alone. Barricades were set up all over east Tehran and the fighting continued for two days and nights. Some 200 to 300 people were
killed in Tehran alone.[34] Air force officers opened the armouries to the
crowds and guerrillas and finally the Imperial Guards retreated from
the garrison. Throughout 11 February thousands of armed civilians,
guerrillas and cadets fought for the control of several military garrisons
and police stations. At the Eshratabad garrison a fierce battle was fought
before it fell to the revolutionaries and was set ablaze. During the fighting a US military mission was attacked because it was rumoured that
the Americans were fighting on the side of the Imperial Guards. Similar
events took place in the provinces. In Tabriz heavy fighting continued
for three days. By 11 February the army was in great disarray and the
crowds had captured all military garrisons and police stations in Tehran.
On that day the High Defence Council ordered the retreat of all forces
into the barracks. In the evening General Qarabaqi assured Bazargan
that the army was on the side of the PRG. With the army surrendering
to the revolution, Bakhtiar and members of government, parliament
and regency council all resigned. During the fighting General Badrei,
Commander of Ground Forces, General Beglari, Deputy Commander of
Imperial Guards, and a few more senior officers were killed. Later the
top leadership of the Imperial army was decimated by executions. On
12 February the Shah's Niavaran Palace and the Imperial Guards' garrison fell and thus power was effectively transferred to the revolution.

The revolution succeeded because of the coincidence of several factors. The economic crisis and massive migration provided the necessary
background for mass mobilisation. The network of 80,000 mosques and
other religious institutions provided the organisational basis. Ayatollah
Khomeini's leadership and emphasis on demands appealing to all classes
and parties proved effective. The bazaars provided the necessary funds.
The general strike debilitated the regime. And in particular US policy
towards the regime proved instrumental. The liberalisation policy,
which was a pre-revolutionary policy, was juxtaposed by one of total
support for the Shah's authoritarian regime. Thus on the one hand the
US supported the Shah until just before the end; on the other hand it
pressed the Shah for liberalisation at the same time. Although this two-
tier policy might have worked in normal times, it proved contradictory

in the revolutionary situation. Thus the Shah's attempt at liberalisation and repression at the same time reduced the effectiveness of his repressive apparatus and encouraged increasing popular opposition.

Notes

1. *Kar*, 17 Khordad 1358.
2. Cf. 'The bourgeoisie invest in revolution as they would in anything else, spreading risk and covering all options by backing all promising movements': F.G. Hutchins, 'On Winning and Losing by Revolution', *Public Policy*, vol. 18 (1969), p. 27.
3. Sazeman-e Enghelabi, *Shuresh dar Tabriz (Rebellion in Tabriz)* (Tehran, 1357), pp. 1-5.
4. Fedaiyan-e Khalq, *Reports on Struggles Outside City Limits* (Tehran, Mordad 1357), pp. 97-9.
5. Sazeman-e Enghelabi, *Shuresh dar Tabriz*, pp. 1-5.
6. These were the first formulated demands put forward by the religious opposition; the list of demands in ibid.
7. In addition the communities of ethnic and rural groups, such as the Kurdish, Azarbayjani and Ardabili communities, resident in Tehran played a major role in linking rural and urban populations. They were usually organised on a religious basis and had their *hosseiniyeh*s, which during religious months organised trips to the native city of the community. Also in the holy city of Mashhad residents from other provinces had their own religious and charity centres.
8. An account of the Tabriz riots is given in Mojahedin-e Khalq, *Jonbesh-e Khalq-e Tabriz (Uprising in Tabriz)* (Tehran, 1358).
9. *Kayhan*, 5 Shahrivar 1357. The new government also set up a new Ministry for Religious Endowments in order to appease the Ulama. Its purpose was to 'finance theology schools, renovate shrines and mosques and provide scholarship grants for theology students'.
10. Within the US administration, there was some conflict over the extent of support for the Shah, and his adoption of a hard-line policy. The National Security Council urged the Shah to adopt an 'iron-fist' policy, whereas the State Department called for compromise with the moderate opposition. In November the Department drafted a cable to the US Embassy in Tehran to advise the Shah to transfer real power to a coalition government. The NSC, however, managed to cancel the cable and instead sent the Shah a message of full support for the installation of a military regime. See M. Ledeen and W. Lewis, 'Carter and the Fall of the Shah: The Inside Story', *Washington Quarterly*, vol. 3 (1980), pp. 3-40.
11. *Le Monde*, 17 September 1978.
12. The oil workers' demands included the lifting of martial law; release of all political prisoners; expulsion of foreigners from the oil industry and putting on trial the head of SAVAK, General Nasiri. As a result of the strike, oil exports were halted at the end of 1978; previously Iran had exported 6 million b.p.d., accounting for 80% of the government's foreign earnings.
13. By now political opposition to the regime had become rather autonomous from the economic grievances. Thus 400,000 striking teachers dropped their demand for pay increases and called for political reforms. Strikes continued despite government offers to meet the strikers' pay demands in full.
14. For instance in October 1978 the National Front had demanded the dissolution of SAVAK, release of all political prisoners, abolition of military courts

and legalisation of all parties. In October the regime was not prepared to accept these minimal demands; in December, due to the moderates' radicalisation, the National Front was not prepared even to form a coalition cabinet.

15. *The Times*, 3 November 1978. In Paris Sanjabi declared that the National Front was 'in complete accord with the religious movement of Iran'. This was the first time since the early 1950s that leading secular and religious leaders of opposition to the Shah had formed a coalition.

16. Khomeini, Beheshti *et al.*, *Hokumat-e Jomhuri-ye Islami* (*Essays on Islamic Government*) (Tehran, 1358), p. 69.

17. *New York Times*, 1 November 1978.

18. Thus on the same day as he installed the military government, he called on the people 'not to tolerate the past mistakes, oppression and corruption'. Clearly he had lost the sense of self-righteousness.

19. The army's attempt to appease the opposition further divided the ruling group. Already in October 34 senior SAVAK officials had been dismissed. In November the military regime ordered the arrest of 54 senior officials and businessmen, such as Hoveida, the former Premier, General Nasiri, the former head of SAVAK, and other former ministers (*New York Times*, 8 November 1978).

20. BBC and Radio Moscow broadcasts. According to one estimate, during the two months of military rule some 3,100 people were killed and many more wounded: Anonymous, *Veqaye-e Enghelab* (*A Chronology of the Revolution*) (Tehran, 1357).

21. On 14 December, three Imperial Guards killed 12 senior officers at the Lavizan barracks; on 18 December an armed unit in Tabriz refused to shoot and was recalled to the barracks; and on several occasions soldiers and demonstrators fraternised with one another.

22. Even after the Black Friday massacre President Carter had phoned the Shah expressing his support for the regime and calling for liberalisation (*Washington Post*, 10 September 1978).

23. During the year, as the crisis intensified, the Shah became increasingly uncertain about the US attitude to his regime. On the one hand he received total support from the embassy in Tehran, while on the other hand there were public calls for liberalisation from the US: M.R. Pahlavi, *The Shah's Story* (London, 1980), pp. 186ff.

24. On 7 December Carter declared that the Shah had the 'support and confidence' of the US, but his administration had 'no intention of interfering in the internal affairs of Iran'; it was up to the Iranian people to choose the kind of regime they wanted (*New York Times*, 13 December 1978).

25. State Department Statement, 20 January 1979.

26. Ball recommended that the army did not have any chance of reimposing order. His recommendation was opposed by the National Security Advisor, Z. Brzezinski, and other Shah supporters in the administration, but Carter decided to follow Ball's recommendation: M. Ledeen and W. Lewis, 'Carter and the Fall of the Shah', *Washington Quarterly*, vol. 3 (1980), pp. 3-40.

27. The US administration advised the Shah to leave; *New York Times*, 8 January 1979. Later Henry Kissinger wrote: 'Our government had concluded, I was informed, that the Shah must leave Iran,' if the moderate opposition were to have any chance of preventing Khomeini from obtaining total power: *For the Record: Selected Statements, 1977-1980* (London, 1981), p. 252.

28. The members of the council were: Bakhtiar, Ali Ardalan, the Court Minister, A. Entezam, the chairman of NIOC, Qarabaqi, Chief of Staff, A. Aliabadi, former Prosecutor-General, M. Varasteh, a former Finance Minister, the Speaker of the Majles, the President of the Senate and Jalal Tehrani, a loyal associate of the Shah.

29. The US support for Bakhtiar (*New York Times*, 4 and 12 January 1979) intensified anti-US feelings; from late December anti-American demonstrations outside the US Embassy increased.

30. *Kayhan*, 2 Bahman 1357; *International Herald Tribune*, 7 January 1979, described the Bakhtiar government as 'thoroughly middle class'.

31. The army leadership remained united behind the Bakhtiar government until early February (*New York Times*, 22 January 1979); the disintegration of the military began from the bottom due to family and religious influences among the rank and file: Sreedhar, 'The Role of the Armed Forces in the Iranian Revolution', *IDSA Journal*, vol. 12 (1979), pp. 121-42.

32. Cf. 'Armies never fail to join revolutions when all other causes of revolution are present and they never fail to oppose them when this is not the case': G. Pettee, *The Process of Revolution* (New York, 1938), p. 105.

33. Thus the Huyser mission played an important role in neutralising the army command and paving the way for negotiations. It also arranged a meeting between the army commanders and Ayatollah Beheshti. At the time these negotiations were kept secret; later Mehdi Bazargan disclosed some of them in a number of interviews, e.g. *Ettelaat*, 3 Azar 1358, and *Kayhan*, 20 Bahman 1358.

34. *New York Times*, 10 February 1979.

6 TOWARDS THE RECONSTITUTION OF THE STATE

In the last three chapters we tried to explain the causes of the revolution. We now go on to study the course of the revolution after the fall of the old regime, in terms of the proliferation of power centres and attempts by various classes and parties at achieving hegemony in the post-revolutionary state. We will discuss the rule of 'the moderates' and the ascendancy of 'the extremists'. The class struggles after the revolution, we will argue, are important in understanding the evolution of the revolution. The revolution has led to a change in the social location of political power, by transferring power to another class. It has also created new power arrangements and has led to the emergence of an ideology imbued with populist overtones.

Political Parties

For a decade and a half the royal dictatorship had sought to suppress open conflicts among social classes by a combination of sheer force and economic control. With the dictatorship out of the way, social class conflicts gradually resumed. The revolution brought into the political arena new social classes as well as ethnic groups with novel demands, seeking to influence the process of the reconstitution of the state. As the incompatibility of opposed socio-economic interests became increasingly evident, the existing political parties came to represent specific interests and specific interests tended to organise their own political parties. The political parties discussed in this chapter are classified according to the same class-ideological basis specified in Chapter 1. The political ideologies discussed there (the secular democracy of the middle class, non-liberal fundamentalism of the clergy allied to the petty bourgeoisie, and popular working-class ideology of the radical intelligentsia) had persisted, but in addition there was the emergence of the new ideological trend of revolutionary Islam, which had spread rapidly among the intelligentsia immediately prior to the revolution. A new category of parties was thus built on this ideology.

The Liberal-Bourgeois Parties of the Middle Class

This category included the better known of the old opposition parties
and wanted to maintain the social structure existing under the old regime, whilst changing the political structure. In general they advocated
the establishment of a liberal regime. In fact at one stage they had been
willing to accept the constitutional monarchy according to the old Constitution (of 1906), but later they insisted that the same Constitution
should provide the framework for the new political arrangements. As
parties of professionals and high officials they had put their emphasis on
a political change from authoritarianism to parliamentary democracy.
However, compared to the other parties, they were little known to the
mass of the people and their support came mainly from the judiciary,
the government bureaucracy and business circles.

The National Front was the major liberal-moderate party. It consisted of the Iran Party, led first by the lawyer, A. Saleh, and later by
Dr K. Sanjabi, and the Iranian Nationalist Party, led by D. Foruhar. The
Lawyers' Association and the Socialist Society also had close contacts
with the Front. After the revolution, the Front called for the ratification of a new constitution 'similar to the constitutions of the democratic countries of Western Europe'.[1] It also called on the government to
promote and encourage private enterprise. The goal of the revolution,
according to the National Front, 'was to destroy the dictatorship. The
revolution was a popular movement and not a class struggle, the struggle
of toilers against capitalists or of peasants against landlords.'[2]

The National Front was in a process of disintegration during the
revolution. The expulsion of Dr Bakhtiar prior to the revolution and
the defection of the Nationalist Party after it were followed by the departure of Dr Matine Daftari, a grandson of Dr Mosaddeq, who left to
form the National Democratic Party. This was a reaction to the National
Front submitting to the clerical line of the revolution, from the time of
the Paris Declaration. The National Democratic Front demanded the
dissolution of the Revolutionary Council set up by Ayatollah Khomeini
and the election of a new council from among government employees,
guilds and workers, and it opposed the intervention of the clergy in
politics.[3]

More Islamically inclined than the National Front was the Freedom
Movement which assumed power after the revolution. The leaders of
the party, engineers M. Bazargan, Y. Sahabi, E. Sahabi, A. Haj Seyed
Javadi and Amir Entezam, all obtained government positions in the
PRG. The party advocated national parliamentary democracy and was

opposed to clerical rule.[4] On socio-economic matters, it emphasised that

> what we need today is the private sector, for we have never had a private sector in our economy. In the past, the private sector was composed of a number of families associated with the court, therefore there was no free trade and no competition.[5]

The Freedom Movement had also been involved in contacts with the US Embassy in order to undermine the foreign support of the old regime. The party did not take 'imperialism' to be a real threat and in fact it believed that the 'Imperial powers' had been helpful in the success of the revolution.[6]

One of the new liberal parties formed after the revolution was the Moslem Peoples' Republican Party (MPRP). Initially the party originated among the associates of Ayatollah Shariatmadari, the moderate religious leader who, along with Ayatollahs Shirazi and Qumi, sided with the liberal parties. However, the MPRP went beyond the circle of clerics and included middle-class professionals and, as the ensuing conflicts unfolded, differences in the party led to the defection of clerics to the Islamic parties. The clerical founders of the party (Hojjatolislams H. Khosrowshahi, Sadr Bolaqi, R. Golsorkhi and G. Saidi) accused the more secular faction of the party of being 'capitalists', 'nationalists' and 'Westernised'. The moderate faction included businessmen, professionals and lawyers and after the defection of the clerical faction it continued party activities. Party leaders and members such as Dr A. Alizadeh, engineer R. Maraqii, Dr M. Enayat, a prominent journalist, Farrokh Daftari, a lawyer, H. Besharat, a landowner, and others of the same socio-economic status advocated a secular constitution to be passed by a national constituent assembly.[7] The party was most active in the province of Azarbayjan, where Ayatollah Shariatmadari had great following and found substantial support among businessmen and traders in Tabriz.

Associated with the MPRP and Ayatollah Shariatmadari was the Radical Party, organised after the revolution. The founders of the party were lawyers, engineers, university professors and high officials such as engineer R. Maraqii, Dr J. Momtaz, a Tehran University professor, Dr F. Nasseri, a lawyer, engineer T. Makkinezhad, Dr R. Abedi, Dr H. Emami and others. The Radical Party was a secular and liberal party and called for the 'restoration of private enterprise'.[8]

More democratic than liberal was the Jonbesh (Movement) created by a leading intellectual, Dr Haj Seyed Javadi, during the revolution.

Like the National Democratic Front, the Jonbesh was mainly composed of intellectuals, lawyers and professors, such as Dr N. Katuzian of Tehran University, Dr K. Lahiji, a prominent lawyer, and Dr M. Katbi. The party was supported by the Jurists' Association, the Association of Writers and the National Organisation of Academics.

On the whole, the bourgeois-liberal parties were small and elite-dominated parties with few links to the urban and rural masses. Lacking organisational resources and a broad social base, they relied heavily on the bureaucracy and the judiciary left from the old regime, at a time when real power was exercised elsewhere in the newly emerging popular organisations.

Non-liberal Fundamentalist Parties

The Islamic parties were mostly created after the revolution. In contrast to the liberal parties, the fundamentalists had a more drastic concept of revolution and were more hostile to the old regime. They were not content with a change in the political system from the monarchy to a republic; their main objective was the unification of religion and the state. In line with Ayatollah Khomeini's interpretation of Shiite political theory, the Islamic parties put forward the idea of 'the rule of the theologian' and considered the old Constitution based on Western liberalism as being alien to the spirit of their nationalist Shiism. The fundamentalist parties were made up mainly of the lower clergy and drew their active support from the bazaar guilds which were revived and reorganised after the revolution. The upper clergy, in the main, were aligned with the moderates.[9] The formal clerical organisations, in particular the theological colleges situated in shrine cities, were controlled by the upper clergy, namely the *ayatollah*s and *mujtahed*s, who are the source of all interpretation of Islamic law and the recipients of taxes and donations. The lower clergy, the *hojjatolislam*s and *modarresin*, were financially dependent on the ayatollahs, and since the clerical occupation had long lost its appeal among the urban classes, these people came mostly from a village background. Thus if the liberal parties were parties of professionals and high officials, the extremist parties were created by lowly clerics. Leonard Binder had described them in 1965 thus:

> Younger *ulama* and *tullab* realize that they are no longer on a par with the Westernized intelligentsia. Their learning is belittled, their behaviour is ridiculed, their clothing is mocked, and all the best government jobs are closed to them. Their incomes are bound to be

small unless they are related to the landed aristocracy. The *ulama*, both old and young are on the defensive. The government and Westernized intellectuals in the ministries are ashamed of the *ulama*.[10]

It was from among this lower clergy that the fundamentalists came. The core consisted of Ayatollah Khomeini's disciples and students. The main fundamentalist clerical party was the Islamic Republican Party formed in February 1979. The founders of the party were Ayatollahs Beheshti, Mosavi Ardabili, Mahdavi Kani and Hojjatolislams A. Khamenei, M. Bahonar, Hashemi Rafsanjani, H. Ghaffari, Golzadeh Ghafuri, Nategh Nuri and non-clerical associates such as Dr H. Habibi and Dr H. Ayat. The party held that sovereignty originates in God and that all laws must be based on the Islamic law, with the head of state a theologian or Imam.[11]

The lower clergy, especially in Tehran and in the shrine cities, organised several small groups including the Society of the Teachers of the Qum Theological Schools, the Society of the Militant Clergy of Tehran, the Islamic Organisation of Fajr, the Party of Towhid (Monotheists), the Islamic Organisation of Ashtar, the Society of the Committed Clergy of Tehran, the Defenders of Towhid, the Organisation of the Crusaders of Truth and the Mojahedin of the Islamic Revolution. Most of these were organised in the poorer districts of south Tehran. Associated with the Islamic Republican Party were the Party of Towhid and the Party of God (Hezbollah), both Tehran bazaar groups. The Party of God was the continuation of the fundamentalist coalition groups of the early 1960s which itself was part of the Fedaiyan-e Islam Party of the 1940s. After the revolution the Fedaiyan-e Islam was reorganised by Hojjatolislam Shojuni. The Society of the Committed Clergy established links with similar groups in the provinces in order to facilitate the coordinated nomination of electoral candidates. In addition, there were numerous local groups taking their names after the Shiite saints.

Compared to the liberal parties, the fundamentalist groups were in a better position to keep the population politically mobilised. The network of communication provided by the mosques and bazaars enabled the clergy to appeal to large numbers and to organise Islamic societies and guilds in the bazaars. Most importantly, the clergy were closely intertwined with the popular organisations created by the masses during and after the revolution.

The Radical Islamic Parties

This category of parties was built on the ideological trend of the spread of Islam among the modern intelligentsia before the revolution. The Islam of the radical intellectuals was highly nationalistic, putting emphasis on the struggle against imperialism and the influence of Western capitalism in Iran. The main parties in this category were the Movement of the Militant Moslems, the Revolutionary Movement of the Moslem People (Jama), the Islamic Movement of Councils and the Mojahedin-e Khalq. In contrast to the fundamentalist parties, these radical Islamic parties were mainly composed of intellectuals and students and had their own clientele among the urban educated youth. Their catch-word was 'council democracy' or the establishment of councils in all institutions, which according to their understanding was the basic concept of government in Islam.

The Movement of the Militant Moslems, led by Dr H. Payman, Dr Eftekhar and other intellectuals, had started as an underground party in 1965. After the revolution, the party called for the nationalisation of industries, the confiscation of large properties, the establishment of workers' councils and land reforms. The party believed that in true Islam ownership is communal and that property belongs to God. According to Dr Payman, the Prophet of Islam had changed the old relations based on private property and in his city-state, Madina, private property did not exist.[12]

Similarly the Mojahedin put forward demands for the nationalisation of industries, the formation of a people's army and the establishment of councils.[13] After the revolution, the Mojahedin expanded their organisation and established the Young Mojahedin Organisation with a large following among high-school and university students. The Revolutionary Movement of the Moslem People led by Dr K. Sami and other intellectuals also advocated radical socio-economic measures. Of the radical Islamic parties only the Mojahedin had a large following and organisational resources and emerged as a major contender for power. Combining Marxism and Islam in their ideology, the Mojahedin attracted support both from radical intellectuals and students as well as militant bazaaris. The party's political demands were not however much different from those of the secular left. In a letter they sent to Ayatollah Khomeini after the revolution the Mojahedin emphasised that in an Islamic state 'monopolistic classes should be abolished; the basis of ownership is labour; workers and peasants should be exempt from taxes and the national rights of ethnic minorities should be recognised'.[14] Elsewhere, however, the Mojahedin declared that 'at this stage we are not opposed to national capitalism and the bazaar'.[15] In addition to the Young Mojahedin Organisation, which was their overt, front organisation, the

Mojahedin also kept their prerevolutionary underground network. From the beginning the Mojahedin opposed the establishment of a theocratic state and advocated political decentralisation and the formation of a coalition government of Islamic and radical groups.

The Leftist Parties

The left included numerous factions and groupings and was mainly composed of intellectual and student movements and groups. They called for the nationalisation of industries and banks, ending the dependent relationship with US imperialism, creating a new popular military structure, and autonomy rights for ethnic groups. As the most active segment of opposition, the left was to have considerable influence on the ideological direction of the revolution. However, despite their principal common stance, the leftists were far from united on tactical grounds. Some wavered towards the liberals, some cooperated with the Islamic parties and some acted independently. Apart from internal differences, the left also found it difficult to broaden its social base and infiltrate into the rural and urban lower classes because of the effective mass mobilisation and politicisation already undertaken by the Islamic movement. A notable exception was the strike committees and workers' councils in the oil industry, with strong leftist influence within them. However, the working-class movement which emerged after the revolution was to a large extent unrelated to the leftist parties. Despite these obstacles, the left made a strong bid for power.

The main leftist parties and factions were: the Fedaiyan-e Khalq, the Paykar Organisation, the Tufan Organisation (Maoist), the Organisation for Communist Unity, the Communist Party of Iranian Workers and Peasants, the Revolutionary Organisation (which had splintered from the Tudeh in 1969), the Party of Socialist Workers (Trotskyist), the Organisation of the Militant Workers, the Communers Organisation, the Marxist-Leninist Committee, the Organisation of Revolutionary Youth, the Democratic Union (another Tudeh splinter group), the Tudeh Party and other smaller factions.

The Fedaiyan Organisation called for the formation of workers' and peasants' councils, the dissolution of the Imperial army and the nationalisation of all industrial and banking capital.[16] The organisation was uncertain about its programme of action immediately after the revolution and soon split into two main factions. The majority faction vacillated between supporting the moderates and the Islamic parties and was itself split into pro- and anti-Tudeh (-Soviet) factions. The minority faction (the Dehghani and Chupanzadeh groups) accused the majority of opportunism and called for arming the masses. In the minority's view the Islamic state was the regime of the dependent bourgeoisie rather than the national bourgeoisie.[17] Similarly the Paykar Organisation, which as a Marxist faction had defected from the Mojahedin before the revolution, rejected any compromise with the liberals and the Islamic parties who, in the party's view, all sanctioned the capitalist order.[18] From the start the Paykar and the Fedaiyan declared their opposition to the establishment of an Islamic state, and after a few months of political activity went underground. By contrast, the position of the pro-Soviet Tudeh Party was more equivocal in that the party was opposed to the 'infantile leftists' and from the start sided with the Islamic fundamentalists.[19] The Tudeh of the 1970s was very different from the Tudeh of the 1940s; due to suppression and exile as well as opportunism and attachment to the Soviet Union, it had lost much of its support and members. The Tudeh supported the Islamic Revolution for ideological and tactical reasons. It viewed the conflicts between the liberals and the Islamic extremists as a class conflict between the bourgeoisie and the masses, and believed that the Islamic parties were eventually heralding the working-class movement.[20] Rather than oppose it, the Tudeh sought to influence the course of the revolution so as to radicalise it, and thus to obtain a new power base in Iran. Thus it supported Ayatollah Khomeini's anti-imperialism and radical policies and sought to intensify further the anti-US hostility. In addition, the party called for agrarian reforms, nationalisation of industries and foreign trade, and expansion of state economic control. On the other hand, as in the early 1950s, the Tudeh opposed the National Front liberal parties.

On the whole, the leftist groups had important differences among themselves, in spite of the unsuccessful 'Conference of Unity' which some of the factions held after the revolution, in order to resolve the most controversial issues.

Political Conflicts

After the revolution, the power bloc was occupied by the liberal-secular parties of the new petty bourgeoisie and the non-liberal fundamentalist clerical parties, which drew their active support from the bazaar petty bourgeoisie. The two segments thus had distinct supporters and sympathisers. Entrepreneurs, civil servants, lawyers, judges, professionals, professors, engineers and high officials supported the modernist moderate parties while merchants, traders, mullahs and the petty bourgeoisie of the bazaars filled the ranks of the revolutionary committees, the 'action groups' of the extremists and the nation-wide network of the Islamic societies of bazaar guilds which formed the bedrock of support for the clerical parties.

The initial alliance between the two had been maintained during the early stage of the revolution in their common struggle against the old regime. Their alliance ultimately broke over their differing views of the nature of political authority in the new state. The clerical parties were anti-Western and extremely anti-imperialist and drew their intellectual strength from the traditional literati. The liberal parties were secularist and drew inspiration from diverse Western intellectual traditions.

Eventually, the moderates were ousted from the power bloc and the Islamic fundamentalists undertook a massive mobilisation effort to consolidate their power. In this process, one important factor was the 'social question', i.e. the economic class struggles going on in the society at a time of economic crisis. While the liberals proved incapable of dealing with this, the Islamic parties broke their alliance with the liberals, stepped up mass mobilisation and asserted their hegemony. Hence the regime they built was an authoritarian-populist regime.

The Rule of the Moderates

Dual sovereignty and the rule of the moderates had in fact started with the constitutional regime of Bakhtiar. Those who came to power after his fall were cut from the same constitutional and moderate cloth. After the revolution, the Provisional Revolutionary Government of the Freedom Movement, appointed by Ayatollah Khomeini, controlled the 'legal' apparatus of the state left from the old regime while the popular revolutionary institutions constituted the rival extra-legal government. If the PRG was appointed from above and comprised the 'revolutionary elite', the popular institutions emerged from below and were made up of the revolutionary masses. Revolutionary committees, guards and councils were organised in government departments, factories, bazaars and universities and gradually assumed the bulk of actual political power. Thus, as a result of dual sovereignty, the power bloc was divided into two main segments.

The 'legal' PRG took over the state apparatus, the army, the police and the judiciary left from the old regime. As the government of the moderate opposition, it had negotiated with the old regime for a smooth transition of power. Broad agreements had been reached between the moderates, the army and its American advisers on the necessity of a peaceful transfer of power in order to prevent the radicalisation of the revolution. In fact the civil war, which the PRG considered as being a 'grave disaster',[21] had interrupted the process of negotiations between the army and the PRG. The revolutionary committees arrested the army commanders who had been negotiating with the PRG. Thus, from the start, the government of the moderate parties was confronted with the power of popular organisations. Monarchist at heart, these parties represented the more highly placed of the old opposition. The PRG was the coalition of the liberal parties including the National Front (Iran Party), the Nationalist Party, the Freedom Movement and the Radical Party. Of the radical Islamic parties only the Jama participated in the PRG but it later resigned from the government on the grounds that the ruling parties were not radical and revolutionary enough. The PRG included industrialists, capitalists, large landowners and high officials of the old regime. Of the high officials of the old regime there were A. Moinfar (Oil Minister), an ex-Minister and chairman of the Plan Organisation under the old regime, A. Ardalan (Minister of Economy), a large landowner, holder of royal insignia and a close economic adviser of the old regime, Dr Mowlavi (chairman of the Central Bank) and M. Khalatbari (Finance Minister), high bureaucrats under the previous regime. Others were A. Izadi (Minister of Agriculture), a large landowner, A. Amir Entezam (Deputy Premier), a large industrialist, and R. Maraqii (Governor of Azarbayjan), a large construction industrialist. Bazargan himself was a share-holder in a company in Tehran, a fact which his opponents were to use to discredit him as a 'bourgeois capitalist'. Thus high officials of the old regime, appointed ministers under the PRG, allowed their colleagues in the bureaucracy to continue in office. Of the National Front, Dr Sanjabi and Dr Mobasheri (prominent lawyers) were given cabinet positions. On the whole, the PRG was the government of the bourgeoisie both in terms of the social background of its incumbents and the socio-economic policies which it was to adopt.

On the other hand, the popular revolutionary institutions were the creation of the masses and the result of their involvement in the revolution. Revolutionary committees, Guards and courts emerged and exercised real power. There were a number of local revolutionary committees in every town. In Tehran there were 14 committees under the authority of the Central Revolutionary Committee, operating in the building of the old parliament. There were 34 rival revolutionary committees in Tabriz and 17 in Esfahan. In smaller towns there were usually two or three committees acting as the police and sometimes as the law court. There were also revolutionary courts in opposition to the civil courts, dealing especially with counterrevolutionary activities. The

Revolutionary Guards, providing an alternative security force to the army and the gendarmerie and numbering 10,000, were formed by order of Ayatollah Khomeini to protect the revolution and spread it abroad. At the head of this extra-legal government stood the Revolutionary Council, which had authority over the committees, the Guards and the revolutionary courts. The popular revolutionary institutions were mainly made up of urban lower strata rather than rural masses (but in several places the peasants formed their own councils or unions) and of the petty bourgeoisie rather than the industrial working class (but the latter also formed their own organisations). The revolutionary committees sprang up mainly in the bazaars and were made up of mullahs, merchants, bazaar apprentices, shopkeepers and the unemployed. For instance, in the city of Hamadan there were two revolutionary committees headed by two rival mullahs. One was located in the bazaar and was made up of shopkeepers and apprentices from less affluent trades such as blacksmiths and shoemakers and mullahs. The other was located in another old district of the town and was made up of soldiers who had deserted from the army, high-school students, apprentices in the bazaar and a few unemployed. In the rural areas, especially in Kurdestan, Azarbayjan and Gonbad, the committees were dominated by local landlords and clerics, and in the provincial centres on the whole, revolutionary committees were dominated by the local clergy and bazaar merchants. Everywhere the committees were led by *hojjatolislams* or the lower clergy. The revolutionary courts were also formed by mullahs despatched from the city of Qum. A revolutionary court usually consisted of a cleric, a civilian judge and a local trustee, but the cleric had the dominant position and usually carried with him a religious code recently issued by Ayatollah Montazeri containing instructions on how to deal with counterrevolutionaries. The courts were under the authority of the revolutionary general prosecutor appointed by Khomeini. The Revolutionary Council had supreme authority over this extra-legal government and it was composed of Ayatollahs Beheshti, Montazeri, Mosavi Ardabili, Kani, Khamenei, Bahonar, Rafsanjani, Taleqani and Khomeini's non-clerical associates, A. Bani-Sadr and S. Qotbzadeh.

The struggle for power between the PRG and the extra-legal government began immediately after the revolution. The PRG from the beginning sought to control the revolutionary committees and courts, transfer their power to the 'legal' government or tried to dissolve them. Much to the chagrin of the PRG, revolutionary committees obtained full power, especially in the provinces where the PRG did not command much authority, and the revolutionary courts continued to execute the associates of the old regime. By the beginning of March, the interim government had become impatient with the activities of popular organisations. Bazargan complained that 'the committees hinder the course of affairs and interfere in the administration and this is in contrast to the functions of the legal government'.[22] The PRG also called for the incorporation of the Revolutionary Guards into the armed forces. In response to the PRG's threats of resignation, the Revolutionary Council urged the committees to cooperate with the government. The PRG proposed regulations in order to eliminate the independent power of the popular institutions. According to these, the committees were to pave the way for the transfer of their powers to the government and prepare for their dissolution.[23] In the face of Bazargan's criticism of Khomeini on the grounds of his interfering in specific government affairs, Khomeini in effect withdrew from everyday politics and left Tehran for Qum at the beginning of March. By this time the PRG had managed to exert some control over the popular institutions.

In spite of the differences between the PRG and the revolutionary organisations, the alliance of forces which occupied the power bloc was dominated by the PRG and its policies. From the start the PRG declared that it was not a revolutionary government and did not believe in radical actions. Instead, it professed to be following a 'step-by-step' policy. Bazargan was opposed to 'those who have extreme revolutionary ideas and say that weapons must remain in the hands of the people and since the army is an imperialist army it must be smashed, and that factories must be run by the workers'.[24] He appointed deputies of the military commanders of the Shah's army, many of whom had been arrested during the revolution, to high military positions in the new government. The PRG's policy towards the army brought about protests from the military rank and file, especially amongst the air force, who demanded democratic appointment of commanders through soldiers' councils. The policy of the PRG was to strengthen the state apparatus and to preserve the army and its hierarchy.

On economic grounds, the overall policy of the PRG was to promote the private sector. Soon the government invited the fugitive industrialists who had fled the country during the revolution to return to their businesses, for 'the government is now considering amnesty for capitalists. Islamic government in fact supports honest capitalists. Those who have money should have no fear.'[25] The government also offered loans for the reopening of factories; up to July 1979 it had recommended payment for 260 applications for loans out of 950 such requests.[26] The Central Bank promised every facility for those industrialists who wished to return. The PRG banned all strikes and abolished the workers' profit-sharing scheme, under the excuse of seeking to nationalise industries. The police, the Revolutionary Guards and committees suppressed strikes and attacked workers' demonstrations.

The PRG policy concerning agricultural land and peasants sought to preserve the *status quo* in the rural areas established after the land reforms. According to a government bill, private landed property was legal irrespective of the size of the holding, hence lands belonging to landlords exempted from the land reforms were legally protected and any occupation of such lands by peasants was illegal. Such large holdings still existed in several areas: for instance in Gorgan and Gonbad on the Caspian, only 20 per cent of land was peasant property, the remaining 80 per cent belonging to 800 large landowners, including the Pahlavi family.[27] Large landlord properties also existed in Azarbayjan and Kurdestan. The Revolutionary Council passed a resolution forbidding any expropriation of lands by peasants and made such action punishable by death.[28] The PRG formed a five-man commission and a special force of the Revolutionary Guards for the securing of lands occupied by peasants in the course of the revolution. This exacerbated the ongoing conflicts between peasants and landowners, especially in Kurdestan, West Azarbayjan and Sistan (see below). In these areas the government distributed arms among the landlords 'in order to restore order'.[29] In West Azarbayjan the revolutionary committees were in close cooperation with armed local landlords who had taken back their lands formerly distributed among peasants in the land reforms.[30] According to the Land Ownership Law passed by the Revolutionary Council, exploitation of land on the basis of *mozarei* (the five-element formula practised mainly before the land reforms) was legal. The law, however, recognised as legal all land transactions carried out under the land reforms of 1963.

While the PRG was trying to demobilise the already politicised strata, Ayatollah Khomeini and some of his clerical associates sought to keep the population mobilised. Thus he urged the PRG to take steps to the benefit of the *mostazafin* (the downtrodden). He made water and electricity free for these people, ordered the establishment of the Mostazafin Housing Foundation and instructed the government to compensate the losses of those hardest hit during the revolution. The PRG was opposed to such 'hasty' actions. The question of housing the poor led to sharp disagreements between the PRG and the revolutionary organisations. People from south Tehran occupied empty houses in the north with the approval of Ayatollah Karrubi, the guardian of the Housing Foundation. The PRG disagreed with such measures and stopped the grant of government credits to the Foundation. Increasingly the poor occupied houses in the north while revolutionary committee men despatched by the government to evacuate the squatters instead transferred more houses to the homeless. The conflict between the PRG and the revolutionary institutions mounted as Ayatollah Karrubi acted swiftly in housing the homeless. In this process, Karrubi seemed to have acted in an extreme manner, as he soon had to go into hiding, and shortly his Revolutionary Guards were disarmed. Subsequently many of the squatters were forced out.[31]

The PRG had announced from the beginning that it did not intend to nationalise banks and large industries, partly in order to encourage the fugitive industrialists to return. But since the government imposed no restrictions on the flight of capital and capitalists, private banks and industries came close to the verge of bankruptcy.[32] Because of the dominance of financial capital private companies were indebted to the banks and the banks themselves were nearly bankrupt. Thus the government was forced to take some action. By nationalising private banks and large industries the government sought to save them from total collapse. The industries nationalised included those belonging to 51 major industrialists who had fled the country and industries whose total debt to the banks was more than their capital. The latter were also compensated. The PRG, however, announced that the industries would be returned to private control once they were rehabilitated.[33]

In foreign policy, the PRG attempted to improve relations with the United States. The government of the liberals had from the start had the support of the US. During the revolution, the moderate opposition leaders had frequently visited the US Embassy in order to present their case against the regime. By the time the US administration had finally withdrawn its full support from the Shah it had established good relations with the moderates.[34] After the revolution, members of the PRG frequently visited the US Embassy to pave the way for better relations. In February, Bazargan himself had several meetings with the US Ambassador.[35] The Iran-America Commerce Bureau resumed its activities and the PRG paid the private banks' debts to American banks in order to attract foreign investment. It also endorsed the existing military agreements between Iran and the US and the army was to receive necessary spare parts supplies from America.[36] In February a group of the Fedaiyan-e Khalq attacked and occupied the US Embassy, but the government forced them out and assured the Embassy of full protection. The PRG was, however, careful not to attract public attention to its attempts at improving relations with the United States.[37]

On the whole, under the PRG an uneasy alliance obtained between the moderates and the fundamentalists. The government sought to curb as much as possible the power of the revolutionary committees and courts and in this it had the support of the bourgeoisie. On several occasions, industrialists petitioned the PRG to control the revolutionary committees and workers' syndicates. For instance the management boards of the Lime Company and of the Industrial Group of Varzidikar in Tehran sent a petition to the PRG to dissolve all revolutionary committees, courts and Guards.[38] The government had already managed to exclude the affairs of commercial companies from the jurisdiction of revolutionary courts. As to the workers' syndicates, which were made up of the workers alone, the PRG sought to replace them with consultative councils representing workers and the management. The moderates, however, were confronted with a wholesale class conflict between workers and capitalists, peasants and landowners, with communal conflicts superimposed by class conflicts and with the masses who, in the words of an exasperated moderate, 'for years had suffered under the oppression of the kings and could not even complain and now they think they can get everything they want'.[39] In short, the PRG was confronted with a quest for more social revolution. Bazargan himself frequently said, 'we were only expecting a fall of rain. Now there is coming a storm.'

The Social Question and the Quest for More Revolution

In explaining the political evolution of revolution, Hanna Arendt has referred to the 'social question' or the 'existence of poverty', which, she argues, has been a major factor in all revolutions since 1789. Arendt argues that a liberal revolution or the liberal phase of a revolution will not succeed because liberals, as individualists, underestimate the importance of the social and public spheres of life in general. Instead they overvalue the individual and his private rights. They ignore the fact that revolutions pose more than mere political problems, that they involve social and economic problems as well. Arendt argues that faced with an acute 'social question', a revolution will fail to create the political order advocated by the liberals, and as the social question becomes more dominant and tends to direct the course of the revolution, the liberals are increasingly left behind. While the liberals ignore the social question of raising the masses above poverty, the radicals claim to have the ability to solve it politically, and hence tend to ignore the individual and his private concerns. Arendt's conclusion is that political action by the radicals cannot solve the social question and the quest for such a solution destroys freedom and sends revolutions to their doom.[40]

The social question will inevitably affect the political course of revolution, however, by contributing to the discredit and fall of the liberals and by providing a justification for the ascendancy of the extremists. In Iran, the moderates viewed the revolution only as a political affair, concerning the form of government. With the monarchy overthrown, they considered that the revolution had gone far enough, if not too far already. Yet the revolution itself was 'degenerating' into a social conflict. Class struggle began in the countryside where peasants and landlords became involved over the appropriation of large areas of disputed land; in the cities, where industrial workers and capitalists fought over industrial management, decision making and profit; in the areas of minority settlement, where peasant-landlord conflicts became intertwined with communal conflicts; and between the urban masses and the propertied classes.

In the rural zones, the peculiar nature of the land issue (in particular due to the agrarian reforms of 1963) had made the peasantry a very diverse social stratum. While the better-off peasants who had obtained land under the land reform feared expropriation at the hands of the remnants of the landlords, the poorer peasants and agricultural labourers pushed for the immediate redistribution of large lands. The landlords sought to reoccupy lands previously redistributed among peasants, giving grounds to the widespread fears about the revolution expressed among the peasants. As already mentioned, the old regime had managed to mobilise peasant groups to attack urban demonstrations. After the revolution, peasant support for the old regime and the Shah was detectable wherever landlords reappeared as a major force on the scene.[41] While landlords formed their own unions in several places, small-holders and poor peasants throughout the country established peasant councils and unions to fight the landlords who were often supported by the PRG and the army. The land issue became a cause of sharp class conflict everywhere.

Due to the provisions of the 1963 Land Reform Law, landlords retained parts of their estate such as land under mechanised farming and tea-farms, as well as up to 500 hectares, usually including the best lands of the estate. Under false pretences, they usually retained more than the Law had allowed. In addition, in several areas such as Turkoman Sahra on the Caspian, West Azarbayjan and Kurdestan, the land reforms had not been thoroughly implemented. In the area of Turkoman Sahra (Gorgan and Gonbad) the Pahlavi family itself owned large tracts of the best land (amounting to more than 10,000 hectares), the Yazdani family of the upper bourgeoisie owned 30,000 hectares and army generals also owned extensive holdings in the area.[42] In the areas of minority settlement such as Urumieh (in Azarbayjan), despite the redistribution of some land among the peasants, landlords still retained their special status as the head of peasant communities. In Kurdestan the old regime had preferred to cooperate with the landlords in order to ensure the security of the borders and landlords had had links with the army and the gendarmerie. As a result, the majority of the Kurdish peasantry (up to 72 per cent)[43] were landless agricultural labourers. After the revolution, landlords in several areas seized peasant holdings or demanded a share of the crop. In March 1979, landlords in Char Mahal in Urumieh demanded their share of the crop for the previous twelve years, and claimed that all the laws of the old regime, including the Land Reform Law, were now null and void. Char Mahal includes four areas, each containing between 50 and 100 villages. In several of these, the pressure of the landlords for the 'ownership-share' led to armed conflict between the peasants and the landlords' bands, and hundreds of peasant families were driven off the land. Peasant refugee camps were set up in the area while threats of violent attacks by landlords forced peasants in other villages to pay the 'ownership-share'. The revolutionary committees in the area were themselves under landlord influence and in order to ensure security in the border areas the army distributed arms amongst the landlords. In response to landlord attacks, Char Mahal peasants formed peasant councils and established a Central Union in order to enable them to present their case to the government, and to establish peasant cooperatives. During the revolution, peasants of the same area had frequently attacked revolutionary demonstrators in the town of Urumieh and had been known for their support of the Shah.[44] Landlord attacks also occurred in other areas of the province. On one occasion, armed landlords with influence on the local revolutionary committee attacked peasants in the village of Qara-Agja, and in order to create widespread fear they castrated two peasants with the animal-castrating machine and went on to occupy peasant lands.[45] In Astara on the Caspian, ex-landlords and their gunmen formed a revolutionary committee and attacked peasants and took back the previously redistributed lands. In Tavalesh, Gilan, peasant demonstrations were held against ex-landlords who were returning to the area from the cities to reclaim 'their' land. In several villages peasants were driven off their land. In Fars, the army distributed arms amongst landlords and Khosrow Qashqai, a prominent tribal leader, was sent to the province as the representative of the PRG to ensure the obedience of the tribes. Wherever the landlord class was strong, as was the case in West Azarbayjan and Kurdestan, landlords

established their own unions. The Voshmgir Union of landlords in Gonbad was especially formed to confront the emerging peasant unions in
the area.

The peasants also sought to seize large holdings, and demanded swift
and meaningful land reforms. Peasant councils were organised both
among the better-off peasants who sought to fight off landlords and
among agricultural labourers and poorer peasants who sought to appropriate land. Among the first councils to be formed were Kurdish peasant
councils in Marivan and other areas, composed of armed peasants and
established under the guidance of the Kurdish Communist Kumala
Party. To ward off the landlords supported by the government forces,
peasants attacked gendarmerie stations and obtained arms. The Central
Peasant Union, which was composed of 32 village councils, became involved in a conflict with the landlords which formed a major dimension
of the Kurdish question (see below). Peasant councils and unions were
also organised in Turkoman Sahra. Amongst the more important of
these was the Central Peasant Council of Tatar Olya, composed of nine
councils. All Turkoman peasant councils were united in Setad, the
central headquarters of the peasant councils, in Gonbad which closely
cooperated with the local branch of the Fedaiyan-e Khalq. The councils
proposed that large holdings belonging to the favourites of the old
regime and landlords be cultivated by the peasant councils. The PRG
responded that the peasants had no right to such lands and finally agreed
that the peasants could take 20 per cent of the crops. The peasant councils, however, occupied the lands despite the attempts of the revolutionary committees and Guards to prevent them, while the landlords
appealed to the PRG for help. A PRG mission sent to the area failed
to solve the question and was accused by the councils of ignoring the
demands of the peasants. The land issue was also one of the major issues
in the conflict between the PRG and the Turkoman minority. Peasant
councils were also organised in Gilan, Yazd, Baluchestan and Urumieh.
The demands of the councils included the appropriation of large estates,
the cancellation of peasants' debts to the banks and cooperatives, the
abolition of all remaining landlord rents and dues and real land reforms.
The popular slogan was 'land to those who work it'. In several places
peasants occupied large estates. In Lurestan, the lands of General Paliz-
ban, a royalist rebel stationed in Kurdestan, were occupied by the peasants. In Hamadan, peasants occupied the Bani-Sadr estate belonging to
F. Bani-Sadr, the public prosecutor. Everywhere agricultural labourers
demanded the dissolution of agricultural companies and agri-business
complexes which had been formed on the lands of local peasants. In

the Qum area, peasants confiscated some land, but landlords had the support of religious ranks in Qum. In other areas mullahs were often reported to have told peasants that confiscated lands were like stolen property and on these lands prayers could not be said according to religious law.

The policies of the PRG and the Revolutionary Council regarding the agrarian question in effect worked to the benefit of large landowners, especially in areas like Kurdestan and Gonbad. The Land Ownership Law passed by the Revolutionary Council recognised the *status quo* and the existing rights on land obtained through purchase and transfer under the 1963 Law. The government thus regarded as illegal any confiscation of land by peasants. The Revolutionary Council passed a bill according to which those confiscating land would be prosecuted in the revolutionary courts and could be sentenced to death. The Law also prohibited ex-landlords from occupying peasant lands. The government policy thus meant that, for the time being at least, there could be no more land reforms. Responding to the left's accusation that the government was supporting 'feudalism', Dr Izadi, the Minister of Agriculture (who was himself a large landowner) commented that in Iran, feudalism had never existed. What had existed was landed property, because landlords could sell their land independent of the peasants working it.[46] Landlords, especially in West Azarbayjan, interpreted the Law to their own benefit, claiming that since confiscation of land was illegal the land reforms had also been confiscation of property, and hence they sought to take back the lands distributed in 1963. In practice, however, the PRG took the side of the landlords, especially in areas of minority settlement, in the name of ensuring security in the border areas.[47]

As the PRG failed to implement agrarian reform, increasing complaints came from peasants, to the effect that the revolution had changed nothing in their lives. A letter from the governor of Garmsar to the PRG read:

> The local landless peasants had hoped to obtain land after the revolution. In spite of the just expectations of these exploited people I am ashamed to declare that I could not take any appropriate measures because in the event of any action in this regard the revolutionary courts and the five-man commission, on the basis of the Land Law and in response to the complaints of the landlords, would rule against any confiscation and occupation of land.[48]

In the urban areas, especially in Tehran, Tabriz and Esfahan, the revolution had made the proletariat and sub-proletariat highly politicised and assertive. Promises for a better life given by the revolutionary leaders, as well as political publicity by radical parties, created widespread expectations for an immediate improvement in social conditions. In Tehran, workers and the unemployed would gather on Revolution Street by the University to listen to the heated debates on the great political questions of the day. Workers would listen to the Mojahedin, who would accuse the PRG of adopting anti-revolutionary policies, and to the Fedaiyan, who would tell them of the plots of the imperialists. Some activist workers were themselves members of leftist groups and workers' councils. These factory councils or committees had sprung up all over the country during and after the revolution. Originally they were strike committees, but later they sought to take over the management of the factories. Workers reopened some factories, closed because of the flight of owners and managers, and took over the management themselves. On other occasions, they expelled the managers. In the Tabriz tractor factory the workers chased out all the managers and set up a factory council to manage the works. The Council of Railway Workers, with 57 representatives from 35,000 workers throughout the country, was established in the early days of the revolution and declared that since the railway workers had contributed a great deal to the victory of the revolution, they would expect that the government would swiftly respond to their just demands.[49] The demands of the workers' councils included a forty-hour week, higher wages, the payment of a share of the profits, the recognition of workers' councils, the legalisation of strikes, setting up an unemployment fund in the Ministry of Labour and a daily meal. Most important of all were demands for higher wages to catch up with rising prices. During the first six months of the revolution, the rate of inflation was put at 47 per cent, while the number of unemployed was more than 3 million (out of an economically active population of 11 million).[50] Unemployed workers held marches in several places and often clashed with revolutionary committees. In Esfahan, 10,000 unemployed workers from 24 factories marched to the governor's office asking for 'work, bread and housing', but they were confronted by armed Revolutionary Guards who dispersed them with violence.[51] On many occasions factory owners stopped the delivery of supplies or closed their factories in the face of workers' attempts to take over the management.

Workers' councils organised numerous strikes to press their demands on the management and the government. On a single day thousands of workers in 34 large factories in Gilan went on strike and demanded the

payment of their shares in the company profits. As the working-class
movement gained momentum, the PRG sought to control workers'
councils. It passed a law concerning the formation of employers' councils in place of workers' councils. They were to be composed of the
representatives of the management, employees and workers. Workers
in many factories refused to deliver the products. In October, fishermen
working for the Fishing Company in Anzali on the Caspian occupied the
company on the grounds that the company, which had the monopoly
of fishing, had breached its recent agreement with fishermen on free
fishing. They staged large demonstrations and clashed with the Revolutionary Guards. Finally the PRG sent in the army and several fishermen
were killed. The demands of the workers' councils were far from being
met. The oil workers demanded, in vain, to have a representative in the
Revolutionary Council but this remained a secret organisation.[52] Even
after the Revolutionary Council approved the forty-hour week, the
PRG insisted on 48 hours and the council revoked its earlier decision.
A worker, writing to the PRG, complained: 'the dispute settlement
board represents the employer, the Minister of Labour represents the
employer, and the representative of workers represents the employer'.[53]
Another worker wrote: 'Mr Bazargan, whenever he talks about workers,
his words are like those of the factory owner. All his words and actions
are in the interest of the greedy managers. Neither did the Imam go to
a factory to see what is happening to workers.'[54] Amid this increasing
economic class struggle, the moderate policies of the PRG could only
alienate the urban and rural masses.

Like the industrial workers, the rank and file of the army also organised committees and councils and demanded fundamental changes in
the structure of the army. In particular, the air force rank and file were
opposed to the reconstitution of the armed forces in the Imperial style,
and were also opposed to the restoration of the authority of the former
military high command. Young air force officers and the rank and file
organised the 'Military Wing of the Revolution', which called for the
dissolution of the Imperial army and the creation of a people's Islamic
army, with the democratic appointment of commanders by councils.
From the beginning, such councils established in the naval bases and
garrisons met with the opposition of officers, who demanded from their
soldiers the same kind of discipline as had existed in the Shah's military.
But the soldiers were clamouring for the democratisation of the armed
forces. After all, it was the air force and military rank and file who had
fought the army officers in the last days of the old regime and so had
contributed to the victory of the revolution. In June, 18,000 air force

cadets staged sit-ins demanding the dismissal of army commanders and the recognition of soldiers' councils. They called for the abolition of rank and the creation of a 'classless' army and accused the PRG of recalling old officers to high military command while revolutionary courts ordered the execution of mostly low-ranking soldiers for shooting the people during the revolution.[55]

The moderates had hardly expected that the revolution would reach such a pass. Every day deputations arrived in Qum from the provinces and tribal areas to complain about their local economic conditions. There were expectations of a swift change in social conditions. The economic crisis continuing from before the revolution hit the urban lower classes the hardest. Alongside workers and peasants' councils there emerged numerous other societies and councils such as the Society of the Indebted, the Association of the Injured (during the revolution), the Society of the Families of the Martyrs of the Revolution, the councils of the unemployed, the society of pit-dwellers, and so on. In July, in Tabriz, complaints about profiteering led to a food riot. Several processions of the poor converged on the main square and smashed any shop they could reach in the city, looting the food. Several capitalists were assassinated in Tehran, Esfahan and Gilan. In Amol, the 'supporters of Islam', a local popular group, identified the moneylenders of the town and called for their execution. Everywhere social inequality was considered to be a political evil which had been created by the old regime.

Closely intertwined with the social question was the communal question. Communal opposition to the PRG began as it became clear that the government was to ensure the continuity of the state structures that had existed under the old regime. The revolution not only brought new social forces into the conflict arena but also ethnic and religious minority groups. Iran is a country of ethnic and religious minorities. Ethnically, the majority of the population is divided into six sections: Persians (50 per cent), Azaris (23 per cent), Kurds (11 per cent), Arabs (5 per cent), Turkomans (3 per cent) and Baluchis (3 per cent). After the revolution, the new (Shiite Persian) regime was confronted with demands from Kurds, Turkomans and Arabs for land reforms and limited political autonomy from the central government.

The Kurdish question was intimately tied up with the land issue. Among the areas which had been little affected by the 1963 land reforms were Kurdestan and West Azarbayjan, the homeland of the Kurds. This was due to the sensitivity of the region, the traditional rebelliousness of the Kurds and their historical demands for a measure of autonomy. The old regime had thus maintained links with local landlords and notables and, as a result, the remnants of the landed class were considerably more powerful in Kurdestan than in any other province. The Kurds expected that the fall of the monarchy, which had crushed the Kurdish republic of Mahabad after the Second World War and had suppressed their 1967-8 armed movements, would provide an opportunity for the redress of their ethnic and economic grievances. Yet after the revolution the landed class, which already had a strong power basis in the area, emerged forcefully on to the political scene, formed unions and employed armed men, seeking to re-establish their traditional authority over the peasants. They were also either members of local revolutionary committees or had a powerful influence on them. On the other hand peasants, with the particular encouragement of the Kumala Communist Party (whose history went back to the time of the Kurdish republic) organised their own councils and unions. In the conflicts between the peasants and the landlords the latter received the support of the local committees and the army, which distributed arms among them in order to ensure security. There were a number of parties and groups active in Kurdestan, including the Kurdish religious leaders (*mamosta*s), the Kurdish Democratic Party and the Kurdish radical left. Sheikh Ezzedin Hosseini, the religious leader of Mahabad, emerged as the national leader of the Kurds and stood for the autonomy of Kurdestan from Tehran. The Kurdish Democratic Party, led by Dr A. Qassemlu, had been a branch of the Tudeh Party at the time of the post-war Kurdish movement. The party demanded autonomy for Kurdestan, including the establishment of a local parliament, government and judicial system. It organised its own fighting force, *pishmargeh*, and had a large following, especially in the Kurdish cities. More radical than the KDP was the Kumala Party, mainly composed of Kurdish and Persian intellectuals. As an originally Maoist party, Kumala sought to mobilise landless peasants and organised its own *pishmargeh* from among them. The organisation of peasant councils and unions in Kurdestan was in the main the work of Kumala. Party activists travelled through the Kurdish country propagating their cause and with the help of the peasants attacked and disarmed gendarmerie posts. Armed peasants marched on the cities and clashed with landlords. This enabled the landlords to obtain arms from the government on the grounds that peasant unions and movements were part of 'Communist subversion'. Kumala called for 'land to the tiller', confiscated large lands and redistributed them among the peasants. Thus while KDP support came mainly from the cities, Kumala was supported mostly in the villages. The government in Tehran did not recognise peasant unions and the leftist parties, hence government forces supported landlords and local notables against the left and the peasants. Confronted with demands for Kurdish autonomy soon after the revolution, the PRG sent a delegation to Mahabad to negotiate with Kurdish leaders. The delegation failed to reach any agreement and in March fighting broke out between the KDP *pishmargeh* and the Revolutionary Guards. Later an agreement was reached on limited autonomy, including the establishment of Kurdish councils to administer local affairs and the recognition of cultural rights. However, more disputes arose and the Revolutionary Guards and the army moved into Kurdestan. The conflict continued until August when a full-scale war broke out.[56] The Kumala Party was wiped out and Kurdish cities fell to the army. The war and the presence of the army strengthened the landlords who cooperated with the army. On one occasion, which became known as the massacre of Garna, some fifty people of the village of Garna were massacred by the revolutionary committee of Urumieh, composed of local landlords, in order to 'create fear among the peasants'.[57] The Kurdish war was to continue for three months.

The situation in Turkoman Sahra was similar to the Kurdish situation. Turkoman Sahra had been the personal estate of Reza Shah and after the land reforms the royal family retained the best of the Turkoman lands. Senior bureaucrats and army officers also had large holdings in the area. After the revolution, Turkoman peasants and labourers in more than four hundred villages confiscated lands belonging to absentee landlords, established peasant unions and cultivated the land communally. The peasant councils organised the Central Organisation of Peasant Councils in Gonbad which was supported by the local Fedaiyan Organisation. On the other hand, the landlords of the region, along with local mullahs, dominated the revolutionary committee in Gonbad. Conflicts began between the committee, Guards and the army on the one hand, and the Central Peasant Council and the Turkomans of Gonbad on the other. The Turkomans demanded representation on the committees dominated by the Persians, and limited autonomy. Landlords began to return to the region after the revolution to reclaim their lands. They sent petitions to the PRG and cooperated with the army, but the peasant movement in the area had already gained momentum and become organised, and the government could not do much in that regard.[58]

Unlike the Turkomans who worked on the land, the Shiite Arabs of Khuzestan were mostly employed in the industrial sector, especially in the oil industry. While the Arabs formed the bulk of the labouring class, the industrial, commercial and shipping companies were owned by Persian merchants and industrialists. After the revolution, the Arabs formed their own political organisations to express their economic and ethnic demands, including the formation of a local parliament, direct representation in the national parliament and the allocation of a share of oil revenues for local development. Open conflict began between the Arab political organisations and the revolutionary committees in Khuzestan, leading to the intervention of the army. The Arab separatist movement was thus suppressed.

The communal and class conflicts which occurred soon after the fall of the old regime signified that large sections of the rural, urban and tribal masses had become disenchanted with the performance of the revolution. The liberals in the power bloc could not realise that it was impossible to demobilise a population which was going through a revolution. Neither did they have the organisational capability to undertake a massive mobilisation of the lower classes. The liberal regime was dominated by professionals and businessmen and relied on the largely defunct state machine left from the old regime. On the other hand, the military lacked the necessary leadership and discipline to emerge as a viable contender for power against the debilitated liberal regime.[59] On the whole, the PRG increasingly lost touch with the masses and was left behind by the revolutionary upsurge. The social question was at least in part to justify the ascendancy of the extremists. While the PRG failed to demobilise the population, the fundamentalist clergy in power stepped up mass mobilisation.

The Demise of the Moderates and the Ascendancy of the Extremists

The conflict between the liberals and the Islamic fundamentalists began not long after the overthrow of the monarchy. Immediately after the revolution there was little dispute that the new regime would be an 'Islamic Republic'; but different parties had different implicit interpretations of such a system of government. In the first referendum to decide on the form of government (held in March 1979) almost all parties voted for an Islamic republic. For a short while it looked as if the PRG dominated the state, but as soon as the Islamic Republican Party was formed by the clerical members of the Revolutionary Council — who were also in control of the revolutionary committees, Guards and courts — the dual nature of state power became more pronounced. Dr Sanjabi, the leader of the National Front and the Minister of Foreign Affairs, resigned on the grounds that there existed a state within the state. Dr Mobasheri, a member of the National Front and Minister of Justice, continued to demand the abolition of the 'other government'. The lawyer, H. Nazih, chairman of the oil industry and a member of the

National Front, urged that Islam must be kept away from the affairs of the state and the economy and that freedom had been the only aim of the revolution.[60] The PRG's complaints of its inability to govern and the strengthening of the extremists' power structure led to an agreement in July to merge the two 'governments'. The PRG and the Revolutionary Council were to govern jointly. Five members of the council were to hold deputy ministerial posts in the PRG and in return five members of the PRG were admitted to the Revolutionary Council.

The main difference between the moderates and the extremists emerged over the nature of the constitution of the new state. The PRG published a draft constitution to be debated in a proposed constituent assembly.[61] Like the 1906 Constitution, the draft constitution was secular and liberal and provided for a council of guardians made up of five religious leaders and six jurists, in order to ensure the conformity of legislation with Islamic laws. The draft caused much controversy between the liberals and the extremists. The Islamic parties rejected both the draft constitution and the convening of a constituent assembly. Ayatollah Khomeini and the clerics of the Revolutionary Council on several occasions told Bazargan not to mention the word 'democratic' in relation to the Constitution. After the publication of the draft, a congress of its critics was held by the Revolutionary Council and the Islamic Republican Party in the University of Tehran. At the Congress, the principle of *velayat-e faghih* (rule of the theologian), in line with the theories of Ayatollah Khomeini, was put forward and the Congress concluded that in the Constitution, sovereignty must be said to originate in God, all laws must be based on Islam and that executive powers must be wielded by the ruling theologian.[62] This brought a sharp reaction from the moderates. Dr Sahabi, a PRG Minister and a member of the Freedom Movement, declared that *velayat* would destroy national sovereignty. Ayatollah Shariatmadari announced that according to Shiite jurisprudence *velayat* was applicable only in a very limited number of cases and anyway could not legally negate national sovereignty.[63]

The size of the constituent assembly which was to approve the draft constitution was a matter of further dispute. The moderates proposed a national constituent assembly, whereas the Revolutionary Council and Ayatollah Khomeini preferred a smaller body of experts on Islamic law. Finally, it was agreed between the PRG and the Revolutionary Council that a Constituent Council of Experts composed of 73 members would be elected to approve the Constitution. The elections to the council clearly divided the moderates from the extremists. In Tehran two major coalitions of parties were formed for the elections: the coalition of Islamic parties, including the Islamic Republican Party, the Mojahedin of the Islamic Revolution, the Revolutionary Guards, the Revolutionary Council, Fedaiyan-e Islam, the Clerical Society of Tehran and other smaller Islamic factions presented a ten-member slate, mostly comprising members of the Islamic Republican Party; a coalition of the moderate parties, including the National Front, the MPRP, the Radical Party and some high officials of the PRG, boycotted the elections. The Freedom Movement, however, stood for the elections but its candidates had only one person in common with those of the Islamic coalition's slate (Ayatollah Taleqani) and while of the latter seven out of ten were religious leaders, eight out of ten candidates of the Freedom Movement were doctors. Two other coalitions were formed: the coalition of the radical Islamic parties, including the Mojahedin-e Khalq, the Islamic Organisation of Counsel, Jama and the Movement of Militant Moslems. The slate of the coalition had four out of ten in common with that of the Freedom Movement and two in common with the Islamic coalition. The leftist coalition, including the Fedaiyan, Paykar and four smaller factions, had two in common with the Islamic Radicals' coalition and one with the extremists' coalition. These coalitions were formed only in Tehran; in the whole of the country 80 per cent of the candidates were members of the clergy.[64]

In the elections to the Constitutional Council (held on 3 August) the Islamic coalition of parties used their influence in the media, revolutionary committees and mosques to ensure victory and oust their opponents. Ayatollah Khomeini urged the electorate to vote for the Islamic candidates. Thus the Islamic parties managed to get their candidates elected both in Tehran and in the provinces. Out of the 73 elected, 60 were clerics and members of the IRP, the Clerical Society of Tehran and the Society of the Teachers of Qum Seminaries. The remainder were members and associates of the Freedom Movement. Thus the Constitutional Council was dominated by the extremists.

The division between the moderates and the extremists intensified with the disintegration of the Moslem People's Republican Party. As mentioned earlier, the party was composed of clerics as well as secular moderates and was associated with Ayatollah Shariatmadari. In the elections, while the moderate group which was associated with the Jurist Association sided with the liberal parties, the clerical group broke away from the party and joined the IRP. The party, however, stood for elections and won twelve seats, mostly in Azarbayjan. Yet the IRP, in cooperation with the clerical faction of the MPRP, declared the party dissolved; the names of the successful candidates of the MPRP were not announced and instead IRP supporters were sent to the council. Already the liberals were charging the Islamic extremists with seeking to obtain a monopoly of power by foul means. Thus the Constitutional Council was filled by the members of the extremist parties. Chaired by Ayatollah Beheshti, the leader of the IRP, the council put aside the draft Constitution and prepared its own draft drawn from the conclusions of the clerical Congress of Critics of the draft Constitution. The domination of the Constitutional Council was a major step towards the future hegemony of the extremists. From then on, they were to oust the moderates from power in three stages which finally led to the fall of the PRG, the suppression of the MPRP and the ousting of the first President of the Republic.

Before all this happened, further events led to the strengthening of the extremists. In response to mounting criticism of their actions during the Constitutional Council elections, the extremists introduced a press law which made any criticism of the clerical leaders punishable by imprisonment. The first open conflict between the moderate parties and the bazaar-based clerical parties occurred after a liberal daily paper, *Ayandegan*, which had been critical of the extremists' rise to power, was closed down by the Revolutionary Guards according to the new press law. The moderate parties called for a protest rally during which the Mojahedin of the Islamic Revolution, the Towhid Party and the Hezbollah, all south Tehran organisations associated with the IRP, clashed with the supporters of the National Democratic Front, the Radical Movement and the Lawyers' Association. On the one side there were employees of the Plan Organisation, members of the Engineers' and Jurists' Associations and students of Tehran University; and on the other was a crowd of bazaaris and apprentices mobilised by the revolutionary committees. The latter arrived from the south of the city with a truck-load of bricks to fight the supporters of *Ayandegan*. The same crowd, with the aid of the Revolutionary Guards, attacked and occupied the offices of the Mojahedin and the Fedaiyan-e Khalq. The incident further intensified the war of words between the moderates and the extremists. Ayatollah Khomeini, addressing the members of the Radical Movement, said: 'lawyers and intellectuals say that Islam is no good and want to cause trouble whereas it was Islam that freed them all. All our problems stem from these Westernised intellectuals; they will not be allowed to stand against Islam.'[65] Several of the Ulama issued statements and warned about the 'danger' of the liberal intellectuals for the Islamic Revolution.[66] Another defeat for the moderates came with the ousting of Hasan Nazih, chairman of the oil industry and of the Jurists' Association, who was a vocal opponent of the interference of the clergy in political affairs. He was accused of maintaining the 'Westernised experts' within the industry. By August, the PRG was on the defensive. The Constitutional Council continued to pass more articles of a full-blooded theocratic constitution and approved the principle of the rule of the theologian. As it became known later, some PRG ministers planned to have the Council dissolved in a *'coup d'état'*, but nothing came of the 'plot'. From Qum, Ayatollah Khomeini, unlike his earlier pronouncements, prescribed that the clergy should increasingly engage in politics. In exasperation Bazargan continued to ask Ayatollah Khomeini to move to Tehran so that he would be closer to the centre of decision making.

The PRG had to deal with both conflicts in the power bloc and the ever pressing social question. Strikes and work stoppages were everyday occurrences and there were clear indications that large segments of the population had become disenchanted with the work of the revolution. So far the liberals had sought to demobilise the population. Having failed in this, they now attempted to undertake a mobilisation effort by raising minimum wages and passing legislation for the exemption of the lower classes from taxes and for the redistribution of land among the peasants.[67] But with increasing loss of power, the government was not able to carry out many more reforms. Furthermore, the PRG was ideologically cut off from the mass of the population and lacked the necessary organisational resources to undertake a successful mobilisation effort. On the other hand, the extremists had so far been concerned with the consolidation of their own power position, without attempting mass mobilisation. One indication of the growing discredit of those in power was the turn-out of voters for elections to provincial and city councils. Barely 10 per cent of the electorate turned out to vote and there were outcries by the extremists that the revolution was in danger.

It seemed that only the extremists had the ideological and organisational resources to break through this immobilism. In particular, the personal leadership of Ayatollah Khomeini and the power structure at the extremists' disposal provided the necessary means for mass mobilisation. Thus with a crisis in the power bloc, the Islamic parties began to step up mass mobilisation, in order to break from the liberals in power and assert their power by aligning themselves with the masses. Ayatollah Khomeini's appeal was strongly nationalistic. He stepped up his attacks on US imperialism and attributed all the problems of the revolution to the machinations of America. The Islamic parties mobilised large processions at the same time that the Shah, for the first time after his departure from Iran, was admitted to the United States for medical treatment.[68] The extremists stepped up their criticisms of the moderates for their 'cooperation' with the imperialists, and on 4 November militant students in Tehran attacked and occupied the US Embassy.[69] This marked a decisive stage in the struggles between the moderates and the extremists, for the PRG had maintained normal relations with the US and Bazargan had only recently met an American political delegation. Coming under fierce attack, Bazargan soon resigned, stating his opposition to the capture of the Embassy. The Revolutionary Council took over from the PRG and although some of the liberals remained in office, and Bazargan himself became a member of the Revolutionary Council, there was no doubt that some of the internal conflicts of the power bloc had been resolved in the interest of the extremists. The liberal regime had evidently remained behind the upsurge of the revolution and it was duly thrust aside by the new wave of nationalistic radicalism.

In the struggle between the extremists and the moderates the files of the occupied American Embassy served as the marker. The students occupying the Embassy translated documents revealing the connections between US officials and the moderates. The documents were related to the contacts between the constitutional opposition and the Embassy before the revolution as well as contacts made by the PRG and the liberal parties. The Freedom Movement, the Radical Movement and the MPRP were accused of cooperation with imperialism and some members and officials of the PRG were either arrested and imprisoned or went into hiding. Of course some of the clerical leaders such as Ayatollah Beheshti had also participated in negotiations with US officials before the revolution, but for them only cheering could be heard.

The occupation of the Embassy led to the emergence of the students as a major power group. In fact, they emerged as a rival of the increasingly powerful IRP and made direct contact with Ayatollah Khomeini through his son, Ahmad. Yet the continuing 'revelations' of the students remained confined to the Freedom and Radical movements. This situation was due to the IRP's success in gradually subduing the Embassy power centre. The seizure of the Embassy had been a spontaneous move by a number of students with different political persuasions. By declaring support for the students, the IRP managed to infiltrate into the Embassy and as a result some of the more radical students were gradually expelled and replaced by the Revolutionary Guards of the IRP. Thus the 'revelations' of the Embassy remained selective and confined to the moderates.

With the newly emerged hegemony of the extremists, a wave of populism and radicalism set in. The new regime sought to mobilise the lower classes and promised to redress their economic grievances. The Revolutionary Council which had taken over now began to blame the PRG for hindering the advance of the revolution and proposed to take more radical measures, such as solving the agrarian question, the struggle against 'feudalism', preventing the flight of capital and welfare measures for the lower classes. Those criticisms of the liberal policies of the PRG which had appeared only in the leftist press, such as the PRG's support for the bourgeoisie, now found expression in government papers. Of course, the Revolutionary Council and its main component, the IRP, had been partners of the PRG, but now the IRP was jumping on the bandwagon of the new radicalism. The extremists' declaration of 'war on imperialism' also attracted the support of the left. The Fedaiyan declared their approval of Ayatollah Khomeini's anti-imperialist drive and they even proscribed demonstrations by unemployed workers as harmful to the anti-imperialist cause.[70]

Concerning the question of peasants and landlords, it was now admitted that a major cause of the provincial revolts had been the land issue, and the silence or indifference of the PRG in that regard — or frequently its active support for the landlords. More immediately, a major turn-around occurred on the Kurdish question. The government ordered a halt to all fighting and Ayatollah Khomeini sent a message to the Kurds in which he said that within the Islamic Republic, all ethnic minorities would be granted the right of self-rule in internal affairs. Celebrations were held all over Kurdestan in support of Ayatollah Khomeini. Clerical leaders of the IRP were now at pains to explain that Islam did not support large land ownership or 'feudalism', that the Islamic principle of *mozarei* was applicable only in exceptional cases and that in principle, land belonged to the tiller. Members and supporters of the IRP, taking over the Ministry of Agriculture, now put forward plans for Islamic land reforms. Ayatollah Dastgheib, complaining to the Revolutionary Council, wrote from Shiraz: 'Landlords and feudals have infiltrated high places in the government. The silence of the Revolutionary Council is by no means acceptable. Peasants should not wait for the government to give them land; they should themselves confiscate the large estates.'[71] IRP newspapers now approvingly reported confiscation of land by peasants. In Gonbad, the government reportedly confiscated large estates of local landlords to redistribute among peasants.[72] Revolutionary Guards and committees which had previously prevented the confiscation of land by peasants now encouraged them to take the land of the 'feudals'. In Gilan, Revolutionary Guards joined the local peasants in asking the government to dissolve the five-man commission (formed under the PRG) which, they claimed, was composed of local landlords.[73]

Regarding the industrial working class, the extremists also sought to adopt a more radical platform than that of the PRG. The PRG had decided to abolish the profit-sharing of workers in the recently nationalised industries, on the grounds that the industries now belonged not to the employers but to the public. The workers, however, continued to demand a share in the profit. One of the early acts of the Revolutionary Council after the fall of the PRG was to reintroduce the 1963 profit-sharing law with little change. As to the workers' syndicates which had emerged during the revolution, the IRP introduced Islamic councils (*shoura*) in their place. The imposition of such councils, which were only to be consultative, met with some opposition from independent workers' syndicates. In response, the regime, while declaring strikes counterrevolutionary, continued to incorporate workers' syndicates within the ruling party.

The first round of the ousting of the moderates enabled the extremists to go ahead with the making of their Islamic Constitution. The principle of *velayat-e faghih* inserted in the new Constitution alarmed the moderates with a spectre of impending 'dictatorship'. Even after the fall of the PRG, 17 out of 22 cabinet ministers sent a petition to Ayatollah Khomeini to drop the principle from the Constitution. According to the Constitution, the Islamic Republic was a theocratic state in which sovereignty originated in God, and in the absence of the Hidden Imam, leadership of the community was vested in a just and pious theologian whose powers ranged from the appointment of the Council of Guardians to supervise legislation and the command of the army, to the power to dismiss the President. However, the new atmosphere of populism and mobilisation, and the fact that the extremists were more directly in charge of the government, paved the way for an easy passing of the Constitution through a referendum. The clerical leaders had to give some assurances. Ayatollah Khomeini reassured the nation that 'the *Faghih* will not interfere inappropriately. He will only control the three powers so that they may not deviate. *Velayat* is not dictatorship but anti-dictatorship.' Whereas in mid-October barely 10 per cent of the electorate had turned out in the elections to city councils, by the beginning of December, after stepping up mass mobilisation, the turn-out was 79 per cent. The moderate parties, however, did not participate in the referendum.

The passing of the Constitution unleashed the second phase of struggle between the extremists in power and the active moderate opposition. While the National Front and the Freedom Movement had been cowed by the rise of the IRP, the MPRP and its spiritual leader Ayatollah Shariatmadari put up more resistance to the centralisation of power by the extremists. Before the constitutional referendum was held, Shariatmadari declared his opposition to Article 110 of the Constitution referring to *velayat-e faghih*. In Tabriz, Shariatmadari's home town and religious constituency, clashes occurred between rival revolutionary committees supporting Shariatmadari and Khomeini. The MPRP had armed revolutionary committees of its own and mobilised large demonstrations in Tabriz in support of Shariatmadari. Crowds took over the whole city with the support of the local police, Revolutionary Guards and the army and the MPRP demanded autonomy for Azarbayjan. Finally, Revolutionary Guards despatched from Tehran seized MPRP offices and committees and arrested party leaders. Under pressure from religious leaders Shariatmadari withdrew his support from the party which was declared counterrevolutionary. Eleven party leaders and members were executed and a number of large Tabrizi businessmen were arrested and imprisoned for supporting and financing the MPRP. As to Shariatmadari, he became confined to his house and was put virtually under house arrest.

So far in the struggle between the moderates and the extremists, it was the IRP which had emerged victorious. The leaders of the party, including Ayatollahs Beheshti, Ardabili, Kani, Khamenei, Bahonar and Rafsanjani, controlled the Revolutionary Council, important government ministries, high judicial offices and the Revolutionary Guards and committees. The IRP also had control over the Embassy students who provided a major centre of power and propaganda. Yet there were more positions of power to be won. Prior to the presidential elections which were to be held following the passing of the Islamic Constitution, it was widely expected that the first President of the Republic would be one of the leaders of the IRP and most probably Ayatollah Beheshti. However, the successive victories of the IRP had already brought the party the reputation of monopolism. In an unexpected move Ayatollah Khomeini prohibited clerics from standing in the presidential elections. This seemed to be a response to the mounting criticism by the moderate parties, as the IRP's rise to power had already become too blatant. Although the prohibition disappointed the IRP leaders, the party did what it could to prevent those moderates still around from standing in the elections. It was shortly before election day that the Embassy students issued their documents relating to the political record of the Freedom Movement and the Radical Movement; Bazargan, Entezam and Maraqii, who had declared their candidacy, soon withdrew from the elections. Several candidates stood for election, including D. Foruhar, the leader of the Nationalist Party, General Madani, a member of the National Front, and Dr Sami, the leader of Jama. Among the candidates, the one who stood the best chance of being elected was A. Bani-Sadr, a close associate of Ayatollah Khomeini. Despite being a member of the Revolutionary Council and the government, he had managed to remain 'untainted' by the liberalism of the PRG and the monopolism of the IRP. Although politically a liberal, Bani-Sadr was more radical than Bazargan and put forward his ideas about a 'godly classless society' and 'Islamic economics' which he had formulated before the revolution. Yet like other moderates, Bani-Sadr was critical of the 'monopoly of power' held by the IRP. From the beginning he declared 'decentralisation of power' as one of his major objectives which clearly ran counter to the tendency of the IRP and the trend of the revolution. The IRP gathered petitions from merchants and shopkeepers in the bazaar, its main constituency, against Bani-Sadr's electoral platform of abolishing banking interest and introducing an 'Islamic banking system'. In this heated struggle for power the IRP had to withdraw its own nominee unexpectedly, because it became known that the party's candidate was not a native of Iran. This was a setback for the party which had to nominate a new candidate hastily. In any case, Bani-Sadr obtained the majority of the votes and became the first President of the Republic. Upon Bani-Sadr's election, however, Beheshti warned of the 'danger of the liberals' and made it clear that he would oppose Bani-Sadr unless he 'went along with the revolution'. From the beginning Bani-Sadr became involved in a conflict for power with the extremists. The Revolutionary Council, dominated by the latter, still continued to rule. He sought in vain to curb the power of the revolutionary courts, committees and Guards. In terms of ideology, Bani-Sadr remained in a limbo between the moderates and the extremists. He was shrewd enough to change position on such matters as *velayat-e faghih* which earlier he had found unacceptable,[74] yet his ideological pronouncements drove him closer to the Islamic radicals, especially the Mojahedin-e Khalq.

Bani-Sadr's election was a victory for the moderates and a setback for the extremists in that some of the moderate parties which had already lost ground reappeared on the political scene and the IRP's rapid concentration of power was interrupted. With the elections for the first parliament of the Republic ahead, the IRP sought to reorganise its forces and use its electoral skills in order to regain some of the ground lost. Apart from controlling the media, the party had also already appointed its supporters to provincial and city governorships. These were to prove important assets for the party during the elections. The IRP formed an 'Islamic coalition' with eight other Islamic groups including the Tehran Clerical Society, the Islamic Mojahedin and the Islamic Teachers' Society. The candidates of the coalition were all IRP members. For the elections, Bani-Sadr formed a temporary bureau for the nomination of candidates which closely cooperated with the Freedom Movement and the National Front. During the elections the IRP used all the means available to it to obtain the majority of the seats. The Revolutionary Council and the IRP had already endorsed the simple majority double ballot system, in order to put the smaller parties of the left and the Islamic radicals at a disadvantage. During the elections, the IRP made exclusive use of the media and put its own supporters on supervisory boards. In cities where the leftist parties had influence and following such as Marivan and Sanandaj in Kurdestan, elections were not allowed to be held. Thus the Islamic coalition, using the Revolutionary Guards and committees and wielding its influence among the local clergy, managed to obtain the majority of the seats. Out of 245 deputies elected, 85 were members of the IRP alone (mostly clerics). The IRP deputies once again formed an 'Islamic coalition' with 45 deputies of the other Islamic parties such as the Tehran Clerical Society and the Fedaiyan-e Islam and thus initially held a majority of 130 deputies. Seventy-five of the deputies initially emerged as the liberal faction, including members of the Freedom Movement, the National Front and supporters of Bani-Sadr. Within the liberal faction there were also a number of clerics. The left and the Mojahedin-e Khalq did not obtain any seats. Soon the Islamic majority faction set up a committee to investigate the credentials of the moderate deputies, initially leading to the expulsion of three prominent members of the National Front charged with cooperation with the old regime.

Although the presidential and parliamentary elections strengthened the liberal tendency within the power bloc, the liberal opposition on the whole had been cowed. Parties such as the MPRP and the National Front retreated into silence. Yet with Bani-Sadr's election, the moderate opposition had found a strong voice within the power bloc. Bani-Sadr emerged as the spearhead of liberal and secular opposition to the growing power of the IRP. The issues over which he found himself in conflict with the extremists were the same as those which the other liberal parties had raised, with the difference that Bani-Sadr was the incumbent of the highest political office which he owed to popular vote. From the beginning the President's appointments of ministers and high officials were disputed by the extremist-dominated parliament. While Bani-Sadr in his appointments put emphasis on modern education, for the extremists the main requirement for political office was faith in the doctrine of the Islamic Revolution, i.e. the line of the Imam. Bani-Sadr's isolation began with the parliament's appointment of M.A. Rejai to premiership (who was a doctrinaire supporter of the extremists) despite Bani-Sadr's objection. Thus the IRP added the executive power to its domination of parliament, the judicial institutions and the revolutionary organisations. Bani-Sadr's support came from the moderate parties and groups which had gathered in the 'Presidential bureau'. Members of the Nationalist Party, the National Front and the Freedom Movement were active in the bureau which, according to one of its members, '[was] composed of literate and intellectual people and those who thought of themselves as experts. They ridiculed Islam and the Islamic doctrinaires.'[75] Faced with the increasing loss of power, Bani-Sadr intensified his criticism of the IRP in his daily paper, *Islamic Revolution.*[76] His opposition to the regime, from a position as high as the presidency, was not only effective in itself, it also had behind it the opposition of the liberals and the Islamic radical parties. Among the political allies of the President were the Mojahedin Organisation and its young followers. For some time Ayatollah Khomeini had urged the IRP and the President to cooperate, but Mojahedin support for Bani-Sadr helped Ayatollah Khomeini in turning against him. Following the closure of his newspaper by the revolutionary public prosecutor, Bani-Sadr called for public 'resistance against the dictatorship' as his Mojahedin supporters took to the streets and clashed with the Revolutionary Guards. Ayatollah Khomeini interpreted this as revolt against Islam and dismissed him as Commander-in-Chief of the army. Soon after, the extremist-dominated parliament, surrounded by crowds from the bazaar mobilised by the IRP, proclaimed Bani-Sadr incompetent to stay in office. Only twenty moderate deputies risked supporting the President and not attending the session. Some demonstrations occurred in provincial centres in support of Bani-Sadr and the Mojahedin and Paykar organisations clashed with IRP supporters. Bani-Sadr wrote his will as he became a hunted counterrevolutionary. Later, with the help of the Mojahedin, he fled to France. The Bani-Sadr affair further intensified the hostility of the fundamentalists to the 'line of the liberals'. Ayatollah Khomeini condemned the National Front and the Freedom Movement as enemies of Islam and 'parties of pagans'. It was vigorously declared that the aim of the revolution was to create an anti-liberal and anti-democratic and purely Islamic state. After the fall of Bani-Sadr, the presidential office was taken over by Ayatollah Beheshti, the leader of the IRP, Rafsanjani, the Speaker of parliament, and Rejai, the Prime Minister. In a rapid chain of events which followed amidst mounting terror and conflict between the extremists and their opponents, Beheshti, Rejai, several members of parliament and cabinet ministers were assassinated in bomb explosions which were believed to have been the work of the Mojahedin and Bani-Sadr's supporters. This made the fundamentalists even more determined to dispose of all their opponents, especially the Mojahedin, who set out to 'unleash a war' against the IRP. A small leftist-Islamic guerrilla group before the revolution, the Mojahedin Organisation had gathered a large following afterwards, with a membership of 150,000, mostly students and urban youth.[77] It had appropriated a large number of arms during the revolution and refused to give them up to the PRG. The organisation had some support among the air force rank and file and it was with their help that it arranged the flight of Bani-Sadr to France shortly after his fall. The ideological differences between the Revolutionary Council/IRP and the Mojahedin had become most pronounced in the constitutional referendum. The Mojahedin did not approve of the Islamic Constitution and the principle of *velayat-e faghih*, but their opposition to the government had remained vocal until the fall of Bani-Sadr in June 1981. For two weeks the spectre of civil war emerged as the Mojahedin and the Revolutionary Guards fought behind barricades. The Mojahedin declared war on the Republic and Ayatollah Khomeini, and during two weeks in June some 150 of their members were executed by the revolutionary courts on charges of rebellion against the state.[78] The Mojahedin and Bani-Sadr signed a 'covenant' for the overthrow of the government and the establishment of a 'democratic Islamic republic'. Later in exile they formed a 'provisional government-in-exile' calling for 'social democracy based on the system of councils'.[79] Allied to the Mojahedin, the radical left, including the Paykar Organisation, the Fedaiyan-e Khalq (minority) and the Communist Union, also engaged in armed struggle against the government. In January 1981, the Communist Union in league with the Mojahedin embarked on an 'armed uprising' and made a major offensive against revolutionary committees and Guards in the northern city of Amol. Fierce fighting caused heavy casualties, but the guerrillas were arrested.

Before and after the fall of Bani-Sadr, a number of attempts were also made by the armed forces to seize power. In July 1980 a number of air force officers in the Nuzheh air base attempted a *coup d'état*.

They had planned to bombard the residence of Ayatollah Khomeini, and to establish a 'social-democratic government' under Shapour Bakhtiar, the last Prime Minister appointed by the former Shah, who had since his fall formed 'The Iranian National Movement of Resistance' in France. Another attempted military *coup d'état* planned by a number of colonels was aborted in June 1982. In August 1982, twenty army officers were arrested and some executed in connection with a *coup d'état* planned by Sadeq Qotbzadeh, one of the early leaders of the revolution and a former associate of Ayatollah Khomeini. He was executed in September. The Qotbzadeh plot had had the support of Ayatollah Shariatmadari, who was then condemned as a counterrevolutionary and had to apologise to the government publicly. In Tehran the Zolfegar armed division was made responsible for detecting and aborting any attempt at a military *coup d'état*.

The Bani-Sadr affair unleashed a new wave of opposition by the liberal parties and intelligentsia. In February 1981, 133 university professors, lawyers and writers criticised purges in the bureaucracy, the closing of the universities and the 'monopolisation of power' by the regime. At the same time some opposition was expressed by bazaar merchants. Traditionally being the ideological and social base of support for the clergy, the higher echelons of the bazaar now found themselves squeezed by a revolutionary regime which seemed most concerned with *raison d'état*. Some leading bazaar merchants thus supported the liberal National Front parties, and after Bani-Sadr's fall two major merchants of the Tehran bazaar and a few more provincial merchants were executed for their support of Bani-Sadr and the liberal groups. The political disputes obviously split the ranks of the bazaar. Usually the more educated members of religious bazaari families supported the Mojahedin, whereas the less educated or those who worked in the bazaar supported the Hezbollah.

Together Bani-Sadr and the Mojahedin had posed the most serious threat to the clerical Islamic state; their suppression was a major step forward in the hegemony of the Islamic extremists. If the fall of Bani-Sadr signified the end of the rule of the liberals, the assassination of Ayatollah Beheshti marked the beginning of the IRP's complete ascendancy.

Notes

1. Interview with Dr Sanjabi, *Kayhan*, 3 Teer 1358.

2. *Ayandegan*, 10 Khordad 1358.

3. Party statement in *Kayhan*, 8 Esfand 1358.

4. Party statement in *Ettelaat*, 28 Shahrivar 1358.

5. E. Sahabi quoted in ibid.

6. Bazargan's speech on Tehran Radio, 15 Khordad 1358.

7. *Kayhan*, 20 and 21 Mordad 1358.

8. *Ettelaat*, 2 Mordad 1358.

9. Some high clerics had not even wholeheartedly supported the revolutionary movement. For instance it is reported that Ayatollah Qumi of Mashhad, on the eve of the revolution, had accepted some money from a businessman in Mashhad in return for prohibiting the strike in his factory and hotel: Seyyed Mahdi, *Ruhaniyat (The Clergy)* (Tehran, 1358).

10. L. Binder, 'The Proofs of Islam: Religion and Politics in Iran' in G. Maqdisi (ed.), *Arabic and Islamic Studies in Honor of H.A.R. Gibb* (Cambridge, Massachusetts, 1965), p. 138.

11. *Jomhuri-ye Islami*, 25 Teer 1358.

12. *Ommat*, the organ of the Movement of the Militant Moslems, 24 Mordad 1358.

13. Mojahedin statement in *Ettelaat*, 6 Esfand 1357.

14. A letter sent by the Mojahedin, Jonbesh, Jama and Sash reprinted in *Didgah-haye Mojahedin-e Khalq dar bareye Qanun-e Asasi (Mojahedin Views on the Constitution)* (Tehran, 1358).

15. Ibid., p. 28.

16. Fedaiyan statement in *Ettelaat*, 5 Esfand 1357.

17. *Mosahebe ba Rafiq Ashraf Dehqani (An Interview with Comrade Ashraf Dehqani)* (Tehran, Khordad 1358).

18. Paykar Organisation, *Sazeman-e Mojahedin dar Dame Liberalizm (Mojahedin in the Trap of Liberalism)* (Tehran, 1359), pp. 1-15.

19. The party's opposition to the radical left was specified in N. Kianuri, *Ma va Chapgarayan (We and the Infantile Left)* (Tehran, 1358).

20. N. Kianuri, *Hezb-e Tudeh-ye Iran Che Miguyad (What does the Tudeh Say?)* (Tehran, 1358).

21. Bazargan quoted in *Ettelaat*, 3 Azar 1358.

22. *Kayhan*, 10 Esfand 1357.

23. The text of the regulations in *Kayhan*, 14 Esfand 1357.

24. *Kayhan*, 17 Mordad 1358.

25. Ibid., 20 Khordad 1358.

26. Ibid., 11 Teer 1358.

27. *Jomhuri-ye Islami*, 4 Day 1358.

28. Ayatollah Khomeini was also reported to have said that in Islam there is no limit on private property; *Enghelab-e Islami*, 19 Mehr 1359.

29. Ibid., 24 Khordad 1358.

30. *Kar*, 29 Mordad 1358.

31. *Kayhan*, 21 Mordad and 11 Shahrivar 1358.

32. The Central Bank estimated that within six months after the revolution foreign exchange worth $2 billion had been smuggled out of the country. The number of foreigners was reduced from 250,000 before the revolution to 10,000 in April 1979. According to *Tehran Times*, 15 September 1979, 100,000 businessmen and professionals had left Iran since the revolution. This included some 18,000 Jews.

33. *Ayandegan*, 19 Khordad 1358. The nationalisation of the industries and banks under the PRG was mostly due to the efforts of A. Bani-Sadr, who was superintendent of the Ministry of Economy.

34. Bazargan referred to this on several occasions, e.g. in an interview in *Kayhan*, 20 Bahman 1358.

35. *New York Times*, 21 February 1979. Bazargan said that the PRG would not disrupt economic relations with the US: ibid., 17 February 1979.

36. *Kayhan*, 30 Mordad 1358.

37. However, in May the PRG abrogated the 1964 Iran-US Status-of-Forces Agreement which had granted US military personnel in Iran diplomatic immunity. At the same time Iran rescinded its arms contracts with the US worth $9 billion (except for spare parts supply).

38. *Ettelaat*, 14 Khordad 1358.

39. General Ahmad Madani quoted in *Ayandegan*, 6 Mordad 1358.

40. H. Arendt, *On Revolution* (Harmondsworth, 1965), pp. 59-114. For Arendt, the social question is a major but unsolvable question. For Marx, on the contrary, without solving the social question there could be no revolution and no liberty. The social question for Marx revolved around class exploitation and this was also considered to be a political question capable of resolution by political action (ibid., pp. 61-2). Arendt's concept is based on the Aristotelian view that revolutions tend to give rise to anarchy in their wake; and anarchy usually produces dictatorship. For a comparison of Arendt's and Hegel's views see P. Stillman, 'Freedom as Participation: The Revolutionary Theories of Hegel and Arendt', *American Behavioral Scientist* (1977), pp. 477-92.

41. F. Soltani, *Ettehadiyeh-haye Dehqani* (*Peasant Unions*) (a report from Kurdestan, Pishgam Press, 1358), pp. 17-19.

42. *Jomhuri-ye Islami*, 4 Day 1358.

43. *Rahai*, 27 Azar 1358, p. 10.

44. A report on Char Mahal in *Rahai*, 27 Azar 1358. The events in the area were also reported in *Kayhan*.

45. *Kar*, 29 Mordad 1358.

46. *Paygham-e Emruz*, 18 Farvardin 1358.

47. In this connection M. Chamran, the Defence Minister, held several meetings with some of the chiefs and landlords of the tribal areas.

48. *Enghelab-e Islami*, 20 Day 1358.

49. *Kar*, 28 Teer 1358.

50. *Kayhan*, 18 Mordad 1358

51. *Kar*, 23 Farvardin 1358.

52. In September 1979 the Oil Minister was badly beaten up by angry oil workers in the Abadan refinery.

53. *Kar*, 3 Khordad 1358.

54. Ibid., 19 Khordad 1358.

55. *Ayandegan*, 10 Khordad 1358.

56. An eight-point plan for Kurdish autonomy signed by the KDP, Kumala and the Fedaiyan was presented to the government in November 1979, specifying Kurdish demands in detail. These were: recognition of Kurdish autonomy in the Constitution; unifying the four Kurdish provinces into one autonomous unit; establishment of a Kurdish national assembly and local government; recognition of the Kurdish language as the primary language in Kurdestan; allocation of part of national budget to Kurdestan; Kurdish representation in the central government; exclusive responsibility of the central government in foreign policy and national defence; and the establishment of democratic freedoms in Iran: *The Times*, 3 December 1979.

57. Pishgam Organisation, *Qarna* (Tabriz, 1358), p. 15.

58. This description is based on Peasant Unions, 'Turkoman Sahra News Sheet', nos. 9 to 15 (1358).

59. Apart from those army officers executed immediately after the revolution, some 7,000 officers were sacked in the first year of the revolution. In February 1979 alone 200 generals were retired.

60. *Ettelaat*, 15 Mordad 1358.

61. Published in *Kayhan*, 1 Esfand 1357.

62. *Jomhuri-ye Islami*, 25 Teer 1358.

63. *Bamdad*, 29 Shahrivar 1358.

64. *Kayhan*, 8-12 Mordad 1358.

65. *Ettelaat*, 2 Mordad 1358.

66. Ayatollahs Khonsari and Ruhani quoted in *Ettelaat*, 15 Mordad 1358.

67. *Ettelaat*, 4 Day 1358. At the same time the PRG allocated a special month-ly fund for loans to the Tehran unemployed.

68. Earlier the US administration had assured the PRG that it would not allow the former Shah into the US. However, due to pressure from the Shah's friends, especially the Rockefeller family, he was admitted.

69. Their immediate demand was the extradition of the former Shah from the US. The hostages were held until January 1981. In the meantime the US imposed a trade embargo on Iran and froze Iranian official deposits in the US; Iran abro-gated the 1959 defence treaty with the US, and cancelled licences of US banks operating in Iran; in April 1980 the US broke off diplomatic relations with Iran and the trade embargo was supported by the European Economic Community. Finally, through Algerian mediation an agreement was signed to resolve political and financial differences between the two countries, leading to the release of the hostages. According to the agreement, the US undertook not to interfere in Iran's affairs in any way; to freeze the assets of the Shah in the US pending the resolu-tion of Iran's claim to them; to bar any lawsuit against Iran arising from the host-age issue; to end all trade sanctions against Iran; and to return Iran's frozen assets. Subsequently some $7 billion were transferred to Iran.

70. *Kar*, 28 Aban 1358.

71. *Kayhan*, 6 Day 1358.

72. *Jomhuri-ye Islami*, 15 Esfand 1358.

73. *Mardom*, 23 Day 1358.

74. *Ettelaat*, 28 Shahrivar 1358.

75. Quoted in *Jomhuri-ye Islami*, 16 Teer 1360.

76. In March the Majles passed a bill authorising the Prime Minister to appoint acting ministers, thus bypassing the need for the President's approval. Bani-Sadr refused to sign this and other bills. Thereupon Ayatollah Khomeini warned 'those who defy the Majles'. In May the three-man commission which had been set up earlier to arbitrate between the President and his rivals accused Bani-Sadr of 'incit-ing people to rebellion and obstructing the course of legislation'.

77. Estimated by *The Economist* (London), 5 September 1981.

78. Ibid. According to the government, the Mojahedin killed 124 people be-tween June and September 1982, among them members of Revolutionary Guards, clerics, Hezbollahi shopkeepers and members of revolutionary committees. Accord-ing to *The Economist*, 13-19 February 1982, the government said some 2,000 members of the organisation were killed between September 1981 and February 1982.

79. *Nashriye-ye Anjoman-heye Daneshjuyan-e Mosalman* (*Journal of the Mos-lem Students' Societies*) (London), no. 7, 2 September 1981.

7 THE RULE OF THE FUNDAMENTALIST CLERGY

Having described the political conflicts which ended with the ascendancy of the Islamic Republican Party and the non-liberal populist clergy, we now arrive at an analysis of the regime they built. Taking full advantage of their mass base of support, the revolutionary clergy broke their alliance with the liberals in the power bloc and tried to assert their hegemony by undertaking mass mobilisation and attempting to solve the 'social question'. Hence within the capacity of the men of property who directed the revolution, the new regime took a radical direction.

The revolution produced a new power structure dominated by a new ruling group. The extremists in power were few in number and it was from among the lower clergy that they were drawn. The clergy numbered around 80,000 but were themselves split. In addition to the fundamentalists there were the liberal-moderates, the apathetic and the cautious who did not have enough confidence in the stability of the political situation and thus stayed out of politics. The members of the new ruling bodies were mainly drawn from the fundamentalist parties of the Fedaiyan-e Islam, Mojahedin-e Islam, the coalition groups, the Party of Islamic Nations and the IRP. Like the 'Twelve Who Ruled' in Revolutionary France,[1] a handful of clerics, mostly previous students of Ayatollah Khomeini in Qum, emerged as pillars of the revolutionary regime. These were Ayatollahs Beheshti, Ardabili, Rafsanjani, Khamenei, Montazeri, Kani, Bahonar, Amlashi, Nateq-Nuri, Ghuddusi and Mosavi-Tehrani. These and others supported the establishment of a theocratic state according to the original Shiite political theory propounded by Ayatollah Khomeini, who thence emerged as Imam and *Vali-ye Faghih* (Ruling Theologian). Other major clerics continued to adhere to the 'constitutionalist tradition' advocating an institutional separation of religion and politics. Thus Ayatollahs Shariatmadari, Qumi, Shirazi, Mahallati and Zanjani maintained that in line with the Shiite tradition practised ever since the time of the Imams, the role of the clergy should be confined to moral guidance of the state and society. Shariatmadari in particular believed that the Ulama should not go any further than supervising parliamentary legislation.[2] The moderate Ulama thus found the notion of *velayat-e faghih*, in the sense of supreme political and religious authority embodied in one *mujtahed* or a council of *mujtaheds*, to be a complete break from tradition. On religious grounds they

166

maintained that in Iran there have always existed a number of *mujtaheds*, from among whom the believers have been free to choose their *Marjaa Taqlid*. Politically, they believed that *velayat-e faghih* is a very narrowly defined legal institution referring to the Ulama's duty to care for orphans and the poor.[3]

Other religious leaders who were influenced by radical thought, such as Ayatollah Taleqani, who was sympathetic to the Mojahedin-e Khalq until his death in September 1979, and Sheikh Ali Tehrani, the former teacher of Ali Shariati, called for the implementation of the principle of *shoura* (consultation) which they interpreted as the basis of government in Islam.[4]

However, Imam Khomeini and his disciples succeeded in fusing religious and political authority in the principle of *velayat-e faghih* embodied in Article 110 of the new Constitution. Accordingly, Imam Khomeini as *Faghih* is the representative of the Hidden Imam, and as *Rahbar* is the supreme head of state. As discussed in Chapter 3, Shiism was itself a political opposition movement in Islam and although it later became the official religion of the monarchical state in Iran, its original political ideals remained theoretic. According to this, legitimate authority belonged to the Imams, and in the absence of the last Hidden Imam the Ulama were considered as His general agency, in religious as well as in political affairs. Now, the Islamic Revolution institutionalised this concept of authority in the principle of the 'rule of the theologian' as the agency of the Imam. Thus authority originates in God, and in the absence of the Imam is vested in a just and pious jurist. According to the Constitution, 'the Islamic Republic is a system based upon: faith in God as the source of sovereignty and legitimacy; divine revelations and their basic role in legislation; . . . and continuous Imamate' (Article 2). And 'in the absence of the Hidden Imam, the administration of affairs and the leadership of the nation is vested in a just, pious, brave and thoughtful theologian' (Article 5). In case the eligible theologian who 'emerges and is accepted by the majority of the people' does not emerge, then 'the experts elected by the people shall confer about all those eligible for leadership and shall introduce one whom they find outstanding, or they may introduce three to five theologians as members of the council of leadership' (Article 107). The *Faghih* is accorded extensive powers by the Constitution, similar to the powers that a ruling Shiite Imam would have. They include: the appointment of the Council of Guardians, which is held in parliament in order to ensure the conformity of legislation with the Constitution and Islamic law (composed of six theologians appointed by the *Faghih* and six lawyers approved by the Majles);[5] the appointment of the members of the High Judicial Council; the command of the armed forces; the endorsement of the President after his election. The eligibility of presidential candidates must be endorsed by the Council of Guardians; the dismissal of the President on the recommendation of the Supreme Court or parliament; clemency and commutation of punishment (Article 110). The three legislative, executive and judicial powers operate under the *Faghih*'s supervision (Article 57). Parliament does not legally exist in the absence of the Council of Guardians, half of whose members are appointed by the *Faghih*. The *Faghih* also appoints the Chief Justice of the Supreme Court. Clearly the new Constitution is not a 'republicanised' version of the 1906 Constitution, as the bases of authority and legitimacy differ in the two texts. In the new Constitution, authority originates in God rather than in the nation, and the centrality of parliament is reduced.[6]

Of particular interest to the clerics was the judiciary, which – given that Islam is an elaborate body of laws – would be the most important branch of government in an Islamic state. The judicial system had in fact been a major domain of clerical power before the secularisation of the state. According to the Constitution, the highest judicial authority, the Supreme Judicial Council, consists of five *mujtahed*s, two of whom are appointed by the *Faghih*. In August 1982, all prerevolutionary codes (adopted since 1907) were declared by Imam Khomeini to be null and void, and the Supreme Judicial Council ordered the magistrates to judge on the basis of the *Shariat*. At the same time some 5,000 religious students of the Qum seminaries (*Tullab*) were urged to concentrate on law in order to replace the civilian judges.

As we have seen, it was the clergy's effective control of political institutions arising from the revolution that enabled them to consolidate their power. In the provinces the new power structure was consolidated by Ayatollah Khomeini's representatives rivalling the PRG-appointed governors. These representatives, the nation-wide Revolutionary Guards, the courts and the local committees constituted a vast apparatus of administrative and political control. In addition, the clergy in power also created a number of populist organisations, such as the Crusade for Reconstruction responsible for rural development programmes and for achieving agricultural self-sufficiency, the Housing Foundation, the Mostazafin Foundation responsible for the administration of confiscated property, the Martyrs' Foundation, the Relief Committee and the Mobilisation Organisation responsible for keeping up popular political mobilisation and for government distribution of goods. This centralisation of power enabled the fundamentalist clerics to undertake a mass mobilisation programme. With the fall of the liberal PRG, the IRP stepped up mass mobilisation, marked by the initiation of some land reforms, the incorporation of workers' unions into the ruling party as well as by attempts to reorganise the bazaar guilds. Certainly the economic crisis continuing from before the revolution swelled the ranks of the urban lower classes, who demanded radical socio-economic policies. While the economic crisis provided the necessary background for mobilisation, it was also the important role of party organisation which facilitated mass mobilisation.

The economic crisis, which had been aggravated by flight of capital and the decline of the private sector immediately after the revolution, was further intensified as a result of disruption in economic relations between Iran and the West and the outbreak of a full-scale war between Iran and Iraq. All this resulted in the emergence of a dictated economy and a large apparatus of state economic control. Following the seizure of the US Embassy in Tehran in November 1979, the US administration imposed a trade embargo on Iran and blocked Iranian assets in US banks worth about $10 billion. In May 1980 the trade boycott of Iran was also supported by the Western European countries, affecting the export of goods to Iran contracted after November 1979. The adverse impact of this trade embargo was obvious, as the Iranian economy had grown highly dependent on the West during the previous decades. In particular it led to increases in the price of manufactured goods. The embargo, which lasted until January 1981, coincided with the outbreak of the war with Iraq.

The war broke out in mid-September 1980 after Iraq had unilaterally abrogated the Reconciliation Treaty of 1975 recognising the common border in the previously disputed Arvand Rud (Shatt al-Arab) waterway as running along the Thalweg line. Obviously the revolution in Iran and the Arab separatist movement in Khuzestan had encouraged the regime in Iraq to harbour hopes of expanding its regional influence. Already in October 1979 it had demanded full sovereignty over the waterway, the evacuation by Iran of three Persian Gulf islands occupied in 1971 after the departure of the British from the area, and granting of autonomy by Iran to its Kurd, Baluch and Arab minorities. Iraq's concern about the probable impact of the Islamic Revolution on its Shiites, who constitute the majority of the population, was shown when in April 1980 the regime executed Ayatollah Sadr, the Shiite leader. On the other hand Iran announced the formation of a Revolutionary Islamic Army for the liberation of Iraq. In September 1980 the Iraqi army occupied large areas of border land inside Iran, including the port of

Khorramshahr, and encircled the oil city of Abadan. The war reached a
stalemate, however, until the latter half of 1981 when the Iranian army
and Revolutionary Guards made a number of successful offensives and
liberated almost all the territory under Iraqi occupation. However, this
apparent border conflict showed the persistence of the conflict between
Pan-Arabism represented by Iraq, and Pan-Islamism represented by the
revolution in Iran.[7]

The combined impact of the trade embargo and the war on the economic situation further aggravated the economic crisis and necessitated
increasing state intervention in the economy. The volume of paper
money was expanded. Between September 1980 and March 1981 the
Central Bank issued the equivalent of $5.4 billion in new notes to cover
the budget deficit of $10.6 billion. Some 16 per cent of the annual
budget of $44 billion was allocated for the war effort. As a result of
the war, oil output fell from 1,700,000 to 500,000 barrels per day.
During the war the Central Bank put the rate of inflation at 35 per cent,
but it was well above 50 per cent, especially for essential goods. Industry, which had employed 33 per cent of the labour force, declined in
production by a third.[8]

The revolutionary regime did not have a consistent body of doctrine
for regulating the economy; in fact economic regulation had had no
basis in the regime's ideology. Instead it found itself increasingly regulating and conducting the economy due to the persistent pressures of the
lower classes, the increasing dissatisfaction of the bourgeoisie with the
revolution and other circumstances. The array of measures adopted for
extending state economic control included nationalisation of industries
and trade, the economic mobilisation programme, the anti-profiteering
campaign, price fixing and land redistribution. In November 1980 the
Majles approved a bill for the nationalisation of foreign trade, but it was
opposed by the Council of Guardians which found it contrary to Islamic
law. The bill was however passed by the Majles in May 1982 providing
for direct state control of all imports and exports. The government also
created a vast apparatus for the control of production and distribution
in the form of the Economic Mobilisation Organisation. As a consumer
service, the organisation brought the distribution of consumer goods
under government control. Through this a relative measure of equality
in consumption was imposed, although the black market thrived. The
local revolutionary committees and economic mobilisation bureaux
distributed goods and raw materials to producers and then bought up
the finished products for distribution. For instance confectioners received their supply of sugar from the committees at the official price

and sold their products back to them for a profit of some 20 per cent. According to the Constitution there are three economic sectors: private, cooperative and state sectors, but the regime sought to restrict the role of the private sector and expand the cooperative sector in order to avoid 'the concentration of wealth in a few hands and the emergence of the state as a large employer' (Article 43). In the cooperative sector a number of production, distribution and other cooperatives were established. In Tehran all the private transport companies were amalgamated into cooperatives. Distribution cooperatives were set up in most neighbourhoods by the revolutionary committees and the people were urged to join them. In the (nationalised) banking sector the government amalgamated all the banks into four groups: industrial, commercial, construction and agricultural. In sum, the revolutionary situation increased still further the political and economic powers of the state machine.

After the fall of the liberals, the fundamentalist clergy articulated a state ideology imbued with populism. It advocated redistributive policies, and sought to antagonise the lower classes against the *mostakbarin* (predators). It thus quickly picked up the language of class struggle. Imam Khomeini declared that 'we will not leave alone all these large properties'.[9] The IRP newspaper wrote that 'the bourgeoisie think that the ownership of capital has no limit, oppose executions and confiscation of property and any step taken in the benefit of the *mostazafin* [the downtrodden]. They pose a danger to Islam and their elimination is a revolutionary task.'[10] The policy of the regime was declared to be based on the 'line of the Imam', or the 'line of the *mostazafin*'. The IRP started a campaign against the 'liberal bourgeoisie', and undertook a purge of factory managers, replacing them by party members. Everywhere confiscation of property was acclaimed to show that the regime was opposed to the wealthy class. The radicalism of the extremists was the necessary rhetoric of the phase of the revolution following the fall of the liberals. After the revolution, the liberals had sought to restore liberalism after two decades of corporatist and populist ideology under the old regime. They effectively demonstrated the inability of their ideology to deal with socio-economic questions. The extremists at least did not miss the point that any attempt to establish a stable domination would require the articulation of the pressures of the lower classes.

The *mostazafin* line involved some considerable challenge to the interests of the bazaar, the regime's main active source of support. Increasing state intervention in the economy caused some opposition among the bazaaris. In the summer of 1982, some 20,000 shops in the bazaars were closed because of profiteering. In the provincial cities, the

Hezbollahis occasionally attacked the bazaar and smashed the shops which had refused to close on a religious or revolutionary occasion, despite a call for a public gathering. The differences within the clergy over the economic policy of the state finally resulted in internal dissension and factionalism. The supporters of the line of the Imam advocated state economic intervention. On the other hand the traditionalist clergy who organised the Hojjatiyeh Association expressed the opposition of the bazaar sector to the nationalisation of foreign trade, land redistribution, confiscation of property and other forms of centralised economic intervention.

The populist ideology of the supporters of the line of the Imam put emphasis on the mobilisation of the working class, the peasantry and the small producers. Although it took the IRP some time to learn how to penetrate the workers' syndicates and how to modify its ideology to absorb their demands, the incoherence of the working-class movement after the revolution facilitated the reimposition of corporatist control of that class. Islamic workers' councils were encouraged to replace the independent syndicates. The IRP established a workers' section to encourage the establishment of such councils, and the Revolutionary Guards also created a special bureau for factories. All factory councils in every town were organised into a central council. The articulation of the workers' councils to the Islamic ideology was justified on the grounds that in Islam the affairs of the community must be conducted on the basis of the principle of counsel (*shoura*). Similar councils were organised in all government offices and private institutions, which in fact constituted IRP cells throughout the country. The Islamic councils of workers and employees enjoyed a good deal of power, especially in government departments regarding the choice of managers, dismissals, the administration of offices and the allocation of resources. For instance in September 1982, the Islamic Council of the clerical employees of the Tehran judiciary identified a number of senior judges as counter-revolutionary and expelled them from office. Only after the government intervened on the side of the judges and strongly criticised the council did the employees reluctantly lift their siege of the judicial headquarters. Similarly in schools, the councils of Islamic teachers laid down the code of conduct and had a dominant position.[11]

The regime also encouraged land redistribution among peasants. Seven-man land redistribution committees were set up and despatched to the provinces in order to establish peasant councils and investigate the land issue. According to the government, up to December 1981 1 million hectares of land had been temporarily transferred to landless peasants before the establishment of their legal basis. The clerical Council of Guardians in the Majles opposed the land redistribution programme as being contrary to Islamic law. However, Imam Khomeini, accusing the clerics (who had been appointed by himself to ensure the conformity of legislation with Islamic law) of preventing the progress of the revolution, ordered the Majles to ignore their views and proceed with radical legislation. He declared that large landed property had been originally obtained through confiscation and had no legal basis. The regime also established some 15,000 Islamic peasant councils throughout the country.[12]

The establishment and mobilisation of guilds and Islamic societies in the bazaars, which constituted the regime's bedrock of support, formed the centrepiece of the mobilisation programme. In Tehran, the epicentre of the revolution, all the bazaar guilds were organised in the Society of Guilds. The guilds were mostly affiliated with the IRP which had established a guilds section. The party mobilised its most active supporters, the Hezbollah, from among the guilds to confront opposition rallies. The Hezbollahis were mostly recruited from small shopkeepers, had two hundred stations in Tehran and were always on the alert to gather and fight the opponents of the regime. They also had links with the Revolutionary Guards and committees. Under the old regime the influence of the guilds had declined, and they had lost their position as a corporate unit for the determination of taxes. After the revolution, however, the bazaar guilds began to regain this position and were represented in the Ministry of Economy's tax commission. According to a tax law passed in 1981 the guilds were to have a say in the determination of taxes.[13] Thus the traditional complex of the bazaars, mosques and religious schools constituted the social basis of the Islamic regime.

The mobilisation of guilds, workers' and peasants' councils formed the basis of the populism of the regime. However, the major dominant social class within the power bloc itself was the bazaar national and petty bourgeoisie allied to the lower clergy. Also, in terms of class ideology the Islamic regime was the regime of the traditional petty bourgeoisie. Of the 19 members of cabinet appointed after the fall of the PRG, 4 were *hojjatolislams*, 9 were professional men from bazaar-clerical families, 1 was a Tehran bazaar merchant and 5 were professionals from new middle-class homes.[14] The composition of the first Majles of the Islamic Republic also indicated the social basis of the class alliance in the power bloc. Out of 216 deputies elected by spring 1980, 98 were *hojjatolislams* and *modarresin* (lower clergy), 51 were from a bazaar background, 64 were doctors, lawyers, teachers and civil servants, 2 were women and daughters of clerics and 1 was a worker.[15] The extremist faction (the Grand Islamic Coalition), which continued to expand, was mainly composed of the clergy and bazaaris, but there were also professionals and civil servants in their ranks. By contrast the moderate faction, which continued to dwindle, was composed mainly of civil servants and professionals, who were all members of the liberal National Front and Freedom Movement parties. Within the liberal faction there were also a number of clerics. A dwindling 'independent' faction composed of clerics and civil servants also existed, but it increasingly took the side of the majority extremist faction.

In terms of class ideology, the ideology of the Islamic Revolution was basically the continuation of the Islamic nationalism of the late nineteenth century, based on the reaction of the Ulama and the bazaar to Western economic and political penetration. It was intensely anti-imperialist and its nationalism was expressed in terms of Islam. The ideology of the Islamic Revolution, especially in its populist phase, portrayed the images and aspirations of small producers, peasants and the petty bourgeoisie. According to Ayatollah Montazeri:

> In an Islamic economy exploitation will cease; the product of the worker's labour shall belong to himself; the situation of class exploitation will be ended; all the relations of capitalism and exploitation will be destroyed and Islamic regulations will govern over production, exchange and market. Economic production will be put back into the right order.[16]

The society that the fundamentalists portrayed was one in which everybody would be directly involved in production, which would take place on an individual basis, so that the product of labour would return directly to the individual producer. The slogan that the product of labour should belong to the labourer projects a society made up of small producers where everybody owns his own workshop and where production on a mass scale and the relations of wage-labour do not arise. In line with this ideology the regime put the emphasis on small production and national economic self-sufficiency and independence. It was extremely protectionist, at least theoretically, and associated the freedom of international trade with imperialist domination. In order to achieve agricultural self-sufficiency, it launched the Rural Reconstruction Crusade which despatched townspeople to help the farmers.[17]

However, the clergy are more than the mere representatives of the traditional bazaar sector and its socio-political order; they are real men with specific images of themselves and their role in history. Thus to complement our analysis of the revolutionary regime we shall conclude by looking at the world of the immediate consciousness of the men who directed the revolution. One revolutionary slogan has caught this consciousness by portraying the eschatology of the revolution: 'The Revolution shall continue until the return of the Mahdi, the Lord of the Age.' In the eyes of the extremists and their followers the revolution was heading towards a divine destination and to that end they have sought to eliminate evil and promote revolutionary/religious virtue. The aims of the Islamic Revolution included *Paksazi* (purgation), *Bazsazi* (restoration) and *Nawsazi* (renovation). The fundamentalists believed that the lingering immorality and corruption of the old regime had to be eradicated before righteousness could be established; the laws and bases of the faith which had been suppressed by the old *Taqut* (Idolater) regime must be restored; and new organisations had to be established to reorganise the community of believers. They viewed the foundation of 'nation-state' as a result of infidel influence and sought to revive the *Ommat* (community of believers) which had once encompassed all the followers of the faith. Hence they sought to export the revolution to other Islamic lands riven with parochial national divisions. Both revolutionary and Shiite asceticism required the eradication of all vices. Drinking, gambling and sexual misconduct evoked suppression. Music was banned as the 'opium of the youth'; the minimum age for marriage was lowered to 15 for boys and 13 for girls; and simple marriages were arranged by the revolutionary committees. Imam Khomeini ordered the deletion of all un-Islamic provisions from the family laws passed by the old regime. In the Islamic Republic, 'all civil, penal, fiscal, economic, administrative, cultural, military, political and other laws must be based upon Islamic law' (Article 4 of the Constitution). It may be said that this is not in line with the traditional Shiite faith which had recommended patience in the face of evil until the Second Coming. But the revolutionary interpretation of the religious doctrine had furnished the idea that the way must be paved for the advent of the Second Coming. When it was admitted that the deputy of the Imam could rule on His behalf (the idea embodied in the institution of *velayat-e faghih*), then his rule would naturally have to partake of the virtuousness of the promised Utopia. Thus for the fundamentalists, the revolution was not a lonely moment in history but a link in the nexus of the history to which Shiite consciousness gives meaning. Thus in bringing about the kingdom of God, the fundamentalists were deterministic; they believed that the revolution happening here below was heralding the Second Coming of the Mahdi. In the Tehran bazaar rumour was rife among the faithful that the Imam had been in contact with the Hidden Imam several times. This was natural to follow, given that the fundamentalists saw the will of God, rather than any socio-economic causes, behind the success of the revolution — as they publicly admitted. And if there was conflict, war and bloodshed, so much the better, for Shiite eschatology also has it that the Second Coming of the Mahdi will itself be a bloody revolution in which water-mills will be turned by currents of blood shed by the sword of the Imam. Thus the Islamic Revolution portended the millennium. And this was confirmed in the predictions left from the Shiite saints and doctors of divinity. For instance, a Qum clerical newspaper researched the Traditions of the Prophet and the Imams and presented the following account about the nature and the future of the revolution:

> According to the Traditions of the Prophet and the Imams concerning the Revolution before the coming of the Lord of the Age quoted in *Bahar ol-Anvar* (volume 60, chapter 36), 'The Awaited Mahdi' (chapter 24) and 'On Awaiting the Imam' (page 145), it is foreordained that: 'There will rise a great man from Qum. He will call on the people to turn towards Truth and he will be helped by a number of brave men solid like mountains, fearless of war and reliant on God, who will carry black flags. They will call on the tyrant of the day to obey Islamic laws but he will not accept. Then they will take arms, fight with the enemy and sacrifice martyrs until the tyrant is defeated. They then begin to implement God's laws. Qum will emerge as the centre of virtue and knowledge and the news will spread to people in east and west and to man and to genie and even to women in harems until the truth of Islam and Shiism is proved to everyone. The tyrants of earth will forget Qum as they will forget God but this is near the reappearance of the Hidden Imam and the men in Qum are the deputies of the Imam and will rule until the Imam will take charge of the state. Then the Imam will take revenge on all those who disobeyed the righteous men of Qum.'[18]

The men of Qum thus believed that the revolution was following a course which could not be altered by those who opposed it. Accordingly they considered their opponents not as political rivals but as apostates who hindered the onward march of the revolution and thus had to be dealt with according to the religious code of sin. And as the opponents grew in number, the extremists became even more convinced that the mere existence of so much opposition by the 'corrupt on earth' was proof enough of the righteousness of their Republic.

The fundamentalists thus put into practice the theocratic Shiite idea of the indivisibility of temporal and spiritual powers. The new source of legitimacy introduced by the new Constitution was not a diffuse religious legitimisation of power, but a total subordination of the political institution to the religious office. With this theocratic Constitution as its base of legitimacy, a party of true believers as its crusaders and new coercive institutions under its control, the regime of the Islamic Revolution has thus consolidated its power. In the new power structure, religion, apart from anything else, has been a power resource at the disposal of the regime. The power of the old regime had been partly based on economic stability. In turn the political stability of that regime had been disrupted by an economic crisis. The power resource of the Islamic regime has been of a different nature, relating to the consciousness of men, which has put mass mobilisation at its disposal and has so far made the omnipresence of the revolutionary regime complete.

Notes

1. R. Palmer, *The Twelve Who Ruled: The Year of the Terror in the French Revolution* (Princeton, 1971).

2. *Ettelaat*, 20 Khordad 1358.

3. Shariatmadari's views in *Bamdad*, 29 Shahrivar 1358.

4. *Nazarat-e Ostad Ali Tehrani* (interview with Tehrani by the Mojahedin) (Tehran, 5 Teer 1359). He accused those in power of mixing Islam with other ideologies. Tehrani was among the few who voted against Bani-Sadr's impeachment.

5. Decisions as to whether legislation is in accord with Islamic precepts are reached by the majority of the six Islamic jurisprudents, and those regarding the conformity of legislation with the Constitution by the majority of the council.

6. However, despite the renunciation of democracy as a Western import by the leaders of the revolution, the Constitution is in part democratic as the main democratic procedures, i.e. popular representation, majority vote, parliament, etc., have been adopted.

7. On this see B. Crowther, 'Iran and Iraq at War: The Effects on Development', *The Round Table*, no. 281 (1981), pp. 61-9.

8. *The Economist*, 13-19 February 1982, p. 58.

9. *Jomhuri-ye Islami*, 28 Shahrivar 1360.

10. Ibid., 4 Mehr 1360.

11. According to the 1349 Labour Law still in operation after the revolution (Article 32), the employer can dismiss a worker on any grounds approved by the Ministry of Labour. The government amended the article to the effect that the members of Islamic councils cannot be dismissed because they are considered as the representatives of the workers: *Kayhan*, 18 Mordad 1360.

12. The Rural Reconstruction Crusade (Jehad-e Sazandegi) carried out the task of the mobilisation of the countryside through the implementation of development projects in rural areas. According to official figures by June 1981 it had built 15,000 km. of rural roads and distributed 15 billion rls in loans to peasants.

M. Mohajeri, *Islamic Revolution – Future Path of the Nations* (Tehran, 1982), pp. 178-80.

13. *Ettelaat*, 23 Esfand 1361.

14. The background information was obtained from biographies of ministers published in various issues of *Jomhuri-ye Islami*.

15. The background information was gathered from various newspapers. According to Mohajeri, *Islamic Revolution*, p. 133, the occupations of the fathers of the deputies were as follows: 96 were born into rural families; 19 into bazaari traditional working-class families; 51 into bazaar merchant families; 69 into clerical families; 8 into new middle-class families (civil servants, professionals).

16. Quoted in *Ettelaat*, 29 Mehr 1358.

17. However, despite this nationalistic ideology, due to the circumstances mentioned above, Iran became more dependent on the import of foreign goods after the revolution, especially foodstuffs. Imports of food increased from $2.2 billion in 1977, to $3.6 billion in 1978, to $9 billion in 1979, to $12.2 billion in 1980 and to $10 billion in 1981: World Bank, *World Development Report: 1982* (Oxford, 1982), p. 125; G.T. Kurian, *Encyclopedia of the Third World* (London, 1982), vol. 2. British exports to Iran increased from £50.6 million in 1981 to £333.7 million in 1982: UK Department of Trade, *Overseas Trade Statistics* (London, December 1982), p. v25.

18. *Barresi* (weekly), Qum Publications, no. 6 (Khordad, 1358).

POSTSCRIPT: THE THERMIDOR

The Islamic Revolution now seems to be approaching that final stage of all revolutions which, in the classical literature, is called the Thermidor. On the ninth of Thermidor Year II of the French poetic revolutionary calendar (27 July 1794) Robespierre was overthrown in a conspiracy by a faction of the deputies to the Convention and was later guillotined. The end of the French Revolution has been dated from that event. Abstracted from this, the Thermidor has come to mean 'a convalescence from the fever of revolution'.[1] During the Thermidorian phase the politically proscribed is amnestied; mass rallies gradually disappear; the government adopts a policy of demobilisation; state economic intervention is gradually abandoned; and in sum the revolution which in the populist phase had gone 'from Right to Left, comes back from Left to Right'.[2]

In Iran a measure of the Thermidor seems to be setting in. During three years following the collapse of the old regime a new Leviathan has emerged from that Hobbesian 'state of nature' which characterises all revolutions, in which the mechanisms of social control disintegrate for some time and the base interests of individuals, groups and classes overwhelm and swamp the political arena. In general revolutions tend to politicise the society all over and obliterate the distinction between the political and the economic, the public and the private. Before the political system is rebuilt the economic question exerts itself and demands resolution. Mass participation in politics leads to extremism, and the extremists' main concern becomes to respond to the masses with revolutionary rhetoric. The extremism of the first three years of the Islamic Revolution alienated the upper bourgeoisie, and led to massive purges of the bureaucracy and the judiciary, confiscation of property, nationalisation of foreign trade, and government control of much of domestic trade. The main body of the Western and modern educated class which has staffed the liberal and radical parties became alienated from the Republic. It was not difficult to find rich bazaari *hajji*s who, disappointed with the failure of the revolution to produce liberalism, had in exasperation even stopped their daily prayers. Relations between government and business deteriorated as banking credit was short in coming. The result was increasing state intervention in the economy.

179

If the mobilisation of the masses in the populist phase of the revolution has been necessary for an attempt to establish a relatively stable political domination, now an economic mobilisation of the middle class is deemed essential for reconstructing the economy. The revolution began to take a new turn in December 1982 when Imam Khomeini called for respect for individual rights and freedoms and a relaxing of the existing political repression and urged entrepreneurs and industrialists in exile to return home. He called on the revolutionary prosecutors, judges, Guards and committees against abuses of people's rights, and declared that the people 'should be confident and engage in economic investment. We are not here to expropriate them.'[3] Following the Imam's orders a committee was set up to implement them and a number of commissions were formed to travel around the country and investigate public grievances. Imam Khomeini approved the appointment of a court to try revolutionary prosecutors and religious judges charged with the abuse of individual rights. In January 1983 a purge of Islamic tribunals and revolutionary committees began, some 400 political prisoners were pardoned, the purges of the bureaucracy were stopped, and a large number of extremist officials and judges, including the revolutionary prosecutors of Tehran, Qum, Bushahr and Birjand, were dismissed. The new move was declared to be a 'judicial revolution'. In a public survey carried out by the daily paper *Ettelaat*, one hundred people from different social classes and occupations were asked about the reasons for the new turn in the revolution. The reasons given were: public discontent with the authorities; the failure to implement divine laws; inflation and unemployment; the purges; and the domination of capitalists and landowners.[4]

The populist policies had not only alienated a segment of the propertied class; they had also caused friction within the ruling group as manifested in the differences between the 'line of the Imam' supporters and the Hojjatiyeh Association over state economic policy. An indication of the impending Thermidor was the growing influence of the Hojjatiyeh Association in the government. The association is led by a lower cleric, Sheikh Mahmud Halabi, and is associated with the Mashhad-based Ulama, especially Ayatollahs Qumi and Shirazi. It has been opposed to the radicalisation of the revolution and the populist Qum-based clergy. It supported the Council of Guardians in their opposition to the land redistribution bill, and with bazaar support, also opposed the nationalisation of foreign trade. Within the council, Ayatollah Kani has supported the Hojjatiyeh line. The association has viewed the radical policies of the regime as being a result of the Tudeh Party's influence within the government, and is strongly anti-Tudeh. The Hojjatiyeh clergy have strong influence in the Majles and have also obtained a powerful position in the recently elected Council of Experts, which is to decide on a successor to Imam Khomeini.

Reminiscent of the disputes of early Islam, the succession issue has caused friction within the clergy. The line of the Imam supporters within the IRP have supported Ayatollah Montazeri as the next *Faghih* since the ratification of the principle of *velayat-e faghih* in the Constitution. Montazeri, a radical lower cleric, comes from a peasant background. According to the Constitution if the *Faghih* does not emerge himself, as has been the case of Imam Khomeini, an elected body of experts will choose a single *Faghih* or a council of leadership composed of three or five theologians. In December 1982, the first Assembly of Experts of 84 jurists was elected to appoint the next ruling theologian. The Hojjatiyeh supporters in the assembly do not consider Ayatollah Montazeri as a man of equal stature to Imam Khomeini, and instead advocate a collective *velayat*. Some clerics even argue that the *Faghih* should 'emerge' himself in line with traditional practice, rather than being appointed by an elected assembly. The Hojjatiyeh group seems to have obtained a dominant position in the Assembly.

A major side-effect of the Thermidorian phase of the revolution is the recent dissolution and suppression of the pro-Soviet Tudeh Party, which had supported the Islamic Republic since its inception. According to the government, the Tudeh and the majority Fedaiyan had conspired to seize power and assassinate all the major figures of the Republic with Soviet support. In April and May 1983 the Tudeh leaders were arrested and some three hundred Soviet nationals were expelled. However the Tudeh had become more vocal recently and had opposed the recent policy changes as a 'right-wing swing', charging that even Imam Khomeini was 'abandoning the line of the Imam'. In any attempt to seize power, the party would apparently look to the extremist faction in power for support.

The Thermidorian turn has resulted in a number of policy reversals in the economic field. The policy of price control and anti-profiteering has been relaxed, and the government has sought to stabilise wages. All this has brought complaints from the Islamic societies of factories and of government employees. According to one account, 'since the government has lifted its control over the trade and distribution of rice, the prices have risen phenomenally and the hoarders have pocketed huge profits'.[5] As to the wage policy and the Islamic councils, the Ministry of Labour has announced that 'the government policy is to freeze the minimum wages . . . but we will not agree with the dismissal of committed Moslem elements from the Islamic societies'.[6] To relax the anti-profiteering, the Guilds Court of Tehran has been purged of extremist judges. There are outcries from the extremist clerics that 'the Revolution's main confrontation is with the capitalists; . . . who can support the millionaires in the name of Islam?'[7] The Thermidorians retort: 'we do not think in terms of classes; there may be worthless persons among workers, and humane individuals among the employers'.[8] Imam Khomeini has recently expressed his concern about the clergy's total preoccupation with politics, and their failure to pay sufficient attention to religious education.[9] The extremists still call on the religious students to 'devote themselves to the administration of the Islamic Revolution'.[10]

The Thermidorian turn and the attempt at liberalisation seem to be the necessary rhetoric of the present phase of the revolution, which is most concerned with economic reconstruction. Although it is declared that the liberalisation effort is not political, in the sense of compromising the fundamentals of the Republic, liberalisation efforts are never initially political and usually bring political changes in their wake, as happened in the case of the old regime. However, there is a major difference between the liberalisation efforts of the old and revolutionary regimes. The liberalisation and demobilisation efforts of the old regime in the 1976-8 period, which had likewise come after a period of populism, proved perilous to that regime, and not only because there was an economic crisis which was thus politicised. It was mainly because the regime itself could not mobilise the populace and instead there was a massive countermobilisation against the regime by the bazaar-Ulama movement. Under the Islamic Republic, although there has been a gesture of liberalisation, the economic crisis is at its height and there are a number of active opposition groups, but there is no effective countermobilisation against the state as the regime controls all the modern as well as traditional means of mass communication, mobilisation and organisation.

Notes

1. C. Brinton, *The Anatomy of Revolution* (New York, 1960), p. 206.
2. Ibid., p. 209.
3. *Payam-e Enghelab*, Third Year, no. 75, p. 8.
4. *Ettelaat*, 6 Bahman 1361, pp. 5, 10.
5. Ibid., 27 Ordibehesht 1362, p. 6.
6. *Sobh-e Azadegan*, 28 Ordibehesht 1362, p. 2.

7. *Jomhuri-ye Islami*, 22 Esfand 1361, p. 4 (Ayatollah Karrubi).
8. *Ettelaat*, 3 Ordibehesht 1362 (Hojjatolislam Rafsanjani).
9. *Imam* (March 1983) (monthly), p. 46.
10. *Imam* (April 1983), p. 26.

CONCLUSION

It has been the aim of the present study to explain the characteristics of the state and the dynamics of revolutionary change in Iran. In general, revolutions tend to create sharp and long-lasting divisions in society. Since the Constitutional Revolution, the continuous conflict for power has prevented the emergence of a stable and viable state structure. The liberal regime which was to be produced by that revolution did not become established, and instead modern Iranian politics has been one of authoritarian rule and mass mobilisation. The recurrent crises of the capitalist economy and the inability of liberalism to deal with the economic problems in particular have significantly contributed to the emergence of authoritarian rule. In fact authoritarianism emerged at the junctures of economic crises when one segment in the power bloc broke with the other segments and undertook mass mobilisation. The 1921-41 period did not produce a politics of mass mobilisation, but Reza Shah's authoritarian rule was greatly enhanced after the 1930 world economic depression, leading to the emergence of state capitalism. The economic crisis of the early 1960s prompted the emergence of the Shah's authoritarian-corporate regime. The deeper economic crisis of the mid-1970s led to an intensification of authoritarian rule towards populist-fascism under the Shah, and provided the necessary background for the revolutionary mass mobilisation of the 1978-9 period. The continuing economic crisis also jeopardised the prospects for political consolidation after the revolution, prompting the fall of the liberals and the rise of populism. On the whole, due to the recurring economic and political crises and the need for mobilisation, the state structure has remained fluid.

As to the revolution of 1979-82, its origins stretch back to the late nineteenth century when the process of the expansion of the world capitalist economy and the incorporation of Iran into the Western socio-economic system began. This process had two interrelated yet contradictory effects. On the one hand it resulted in a partial structural convergence between the Iranian socio-political structure and Western capitalism. On the other hand it resulted in a partial divergence, in the form of a reaction against this process leading to the emergence of indigenous Iranian nationalism. The social base of this early nationalism was the bazaar sector whose petty commodity mode of production was being undermined by the onset of Western penetration. As a protest movement, the early nationalism was expressed in terms of Islam. Thus the expansion of Western economic influence, while weakening the economic substructure of the society, curiously strengthened the cultural-religious superstructure. The Ulama and the bazaar asserted themselves against Western influence and emerged as the bastion of indigenous nationalism. These fundamental developments in the social structure and in national consciousness have since reverberated in twentieth-century Iran. The indigenous nationalist movement has been a force behind religio-political doctrinal developments. At the turn of the century, the Ulama's opposition to the state resulted in their withdrawal of legitimisation from absolutism and their acceptance of constitutionalism. But for various reasons, the Islamic-nationalist movement was further intensified under the Shah, leading to a new doctrinal development in the form of reviving the original Shiite political ideal. Thus the ideology of the Islamic Revolution is the continuation of the same early indigenous nationalism, expressed in terms of Islam. Its social base is the bazaar sector, and it has an anti-Western character which expresses the bitter hostility of the petty bourgeoisie towards the modern capitalist world and its social and cultural features. The ideology of political Islam portrays a society made up of small producers in which every individual is the owner of his own workshop and there is no need for wage-labour. If the constitutional movement of 1905-11 had been a major step forward in the secularisation and Westernisation of Iran, the Islamic Revolution seeks to undo the work of that movement. After the Constitutional Revolution the modern intelligentsia and their ideas had won out; after the Islamic Revolution the Ulama have emerged dominant. The theocratic Shiite idea of the indivisibility of political and religious powers which has been put into practice is the first indigenous political formula which has been offered for the reconstitution of the bases of state in modern Iran. The revolution is thus the expression of the local economy and the national consciousness; thus it is a petty bourgeois, Islamic-nationalist revolution.

SELECT BIBLIOGRAPHY

1. Theoretical Background

Abercrombie, N. and Turner, B. 'The Dominant Ideology Thesis', *British Journal of Sociology*, vol. 29, no. 2 (1978), pp. 149-70

Allardt, E. 'Revolutionary Ideologies', *International Journal of Comparative Sociology*, vol. 12 (1971), pp. 24-40

Almond, G. *et al.* (eds.) *Crisis, Choice and Change: Historical Studies of Political Development* (Little, Brown, Boston, 1973)

Althusser, L. 'Contradiction and Overdetermination' in his *For Marx* (Allen Lane, London, 1979)

Amann, P. 'Revolution: A Redefinition', *Political Science Quarterly*, vol. 77 (1962), pp. 36-56

Amin, S. *Unequal Development: An Essay on the Social Formations of Peripheral Capitalism* (Harvester Press, Hassocks, 1976)

Arendt, H. *On Revolution* (Penguin, Harmondsworth, 1965)

Aya, R. 'Theories of Revolution Reconsidered', *Theory and Society*, vol. 8, no. 1 (1979), pp. 39-99

Binder, L. *The Ideological Revolution in the Middle East* (John Wiley, New York, 1964)

Bloomfield, J. (ed.) *Class, Hegemony and Party* (Lawrence and Wishart, London, 1977)

Brinton, C. *The Anatomy of Revolution* (Vintage Books, New York, 1960)

Cameron, D. 'Towards a Theory of Political Mobilization', *Journal of Politics*, vol. 36 (1974), pp. 138-71

Cohn, N. *The Pursuit of Millennium* (Paladin, London, 1978)

Cole, G. 'The Conception of the Middle Classes', *British Journal of Sociology*, vol. 1 (1950), pp. 278-90

Cox, R. *Ideology, Politics and Political Theory* (California University Press, Berkeley and Los Angeles, 1969)

Dahrendorf, R. *Class and Class Conflict in Industrial Society* (Routledge and Kegan Paul, London, 1959)

Davies, J. 'Towards a Theory of Revolution', *American Sociological Review*, vol. 27 (1962), pp. 3-19

—— (ed.) *When Men Revolt and Why, A Reader in Political Violence and Revolution* (Free Press, New York, 1971)

Draper, H. *Karl Marx's Theory of Revolution* (3 vols., Monthly Review Press, New York, 1977, 1978)

Dunn, J. *Modern Revolutions. An Introduction to the Analysis of a Political Phenomenon* (Cambridge University Press, Cambridge, 1972)

Eckstein, H. 'On the Etiology of Internal Wars', *History and Theory*, vol. 4 (1965), pp. 133-63

Edwards, L. *The Natural History of Revolution* (Chicago University Press, Chicago, 1970)

Eisenstadt, S. 'Social Change, Differentiation and Evolution', *American Sociological Review*, vol. 29 (1964), pp. 375-86

—— *The Political Systems of Empires* (Free Press, New York, 1969)

Freeman, M. 'Theories of Revolution', *British Journal of Political Science*, vol. 2 (1972), pp. 339-58

Geschwender, J. 'Explorations in the Theory of Social Movements and Revolutions', *Social Forces*, vol. 42 (1968), pp. 127-35

Goiten, L. 'The Rise of Near Eastern Bourgeoisie', *Journal of World History*, vol. 3, no. 3 (1958-9)

Goldstone, J. 'Theories of Revolution: The Third Generation', *World Politics*, vol. 32 (1979-80), pp. 425-53

Gothschalk, L. 'Causes of Revolution', *American Journal of Sociology*, vol. 50 (1944), pp. 1-18

Gregor, J. *The Fascist Persuasion in Radical Politics* (Princeton University Press, Princeton, 1974)

Hagopian, M. *The Phenomenon of Revolution* (Harper and Row, New York, 1974)

Halpern, M. *The Politics of Social Change in the Middle East and North Africa* (Princeton University Press, Princeton, 1963)

Hayes, C. *The Historical Evolution of Modern Nationalism* (Macmillan, New York, 1931)

Hechter, M. *Internal Colonialism: The Celtic Fringe in British National Development* (University of California Press, Berkeley and Los Angeles, 1975)

Hopper, R. 'The Revolutionary Process', *Social Forces*, vol. 28 (1950), pp. 270-9

Hotinger, A. 'How the Arab Bourgeoisie Lost Power', *Journal of Contemporary History*, vol. 3 (1968), pp. 111-28

Huntington, S. *Political Order in Changing Societies* (Yale University Press, New Haven, 1970)

Hutchins, F. 'On Winning and Losing by Revolution', *Public Policy*, vol. 18 (1969), pp. 1-40

Johnson, C. *Revolutionary Change* (Little, Brown, Boston, 1966)

Kamenka, E. 'The Concept of a Political Revolution' in C.J. Friedrich (ed.), *Revolution* (Atherton Press, New York, 1966)

Kautsky, J. (ed.) *Political Change in Underdeveloped Countries* (John Wiley, New York, 1964)

Khadduri, M. *Political Trends in the Arab World: The Role of Ideas and Ideals in Politics* (Johns Hopkins University Press, Baltimore, 1970)

Kohn, H. *Nationalism: Its Meaning and History* (Von Nostrand, Princeton, 1955)

Kramnick, I. 'Reflections on Revolution', *History and Theory*, vol. 11 (1972), pp. 26-63

Laclau, E. *Politics and Ideology in Marxist Theory: Capitalism, Fascism, Populism* (New Left Books, London, 1979)

Leiden, C. and Schmitt, K. *The Politics of Violence: Revolution in the Modern World* (Prentice-Hall, Englewood Cliffs, NJ, 1968)

Lewy, G. *Religion and Revolution* (Oxford University Press, Oxford, 1974)

Lowi, T. 'American Business and Public Policy: Case Studies and Political Theory', *World Politics*, vol. 16 (1964), pp. 677-715

Lukács, G. *History and Class Consciousness* (Merlin Press, London, 1971)

Malloy, J. (ed.) *Authoritarianism and Corporatism in Latin America* (University of Pittsburgh Press, Pittsburgh, 1977)

Mandel, E. 'The Laws of Uneven Development', *New Left Review*, no. 59 (1969)

Maravall, J. 'Subjective Conditions and Revolutionary Conflict', *British Journal of Sociology*, vol. 27, no. 1 (1976), pp. 21-34

Marx, K. 'The Class Struggles in France, 1848-1850' and 'The Eighteenth Brumaire of Louis Bonaparte' in K. Marx and F. Engels, *Selected Works* (Foreign Languages Publishing House, Moscow, 1958)

Mazor, A. 'Conflict and Coalition', *Journal of Conflict Resolution*, vol. 12 (1968), pp. 169-83

Moore, B., Jr. *Social Origins of Dictatorship and Democracy: Lord and Peasant in the Making of the Modern World* (Beacon Press, Boston, 1966)

Nedelman, B. and Meier, K. 'Theories of Contemporary Corporatism: Static or Dynamic', *Comparative Political Studies*, vol. 10, no. 1 (1977)

Oppello, W. 'A Framework for the Analysis of Revolution', *International Journal of Group Tensions*, vol. 4 (1974), pp. 455-93

Orridge, A. 'Uneven Development and Nationalism', *Political Studies*, vol. 29 (1981), pp. 1-15 and 181-90

Orum, A. 'Mobilizing People for Collective Political Action', *Journal of Political and Military Sociology*, vol. 4 (1976), pp. 187-202

Panitch, L. 'Recent Theorizations of Corporatism: Reflections on a Growth Industry', *British Journal of Sociology*, vol. 31, no. 2 (1980), pp. 159-87

Payton, C. and Blackey, R. (eds.) *Why Revolution?* (Schenkman, Cambridge, Mass., 1971)

Perlmutter, A. 'Egypt and the Myth of the New Middle Class', *Contemporary Studies in Society and History*, vol. 10 (1967), pp. 46-65

Pettee, G. *The Process of Revolution* (Harper and Row, New York, 1938)

Poulántzas, N. *Political Power and Social Classes* (New Left Books, London, 1973)
––––– *Fascism and Dictatorship* (New Left Books, London, 1974)
––––– *Classes in Contemporary Capitalism* (New Left Books, London, 1975)
––––– *The Crisis of the Dictatorships: Portugal, Greece and Spain* (New Left Books, London, 1976)

Russell, D. *Rebellion, Revolution and Armed Force* (Academic Press, New York, 1974)

Schmitter, P. 'Still the Century of Corporatism?', *Review of Politics*, vol. 30, no. 1 (1974), pp. 85-131

Skocpol, T. *States and Social Revolutions: A Comparative Study of France, Russia and China* (Cambridge University Press, Cambridge, 1979)

Smelser, N. *Theory of Collective Behaviour* (Free Press of Glencoe, New York, 1963)

Smith, A. 'Nationalism and Social Change', *International Journal of Comparative Sociology*, vol. 13, no. 1 (1972), pp. 1-20

Snyder, L. *The New Nationalism* (Cornell University Press, Ithaca, 1968)

Stone, L. 'Theories of Revolution', *World Politics*, vol. 18 (1966), pp. 159-76
––––– *The Causes of the English Revolution: 1529-1642* (Routledge and Kegan Paul, London, 1972)

Tocqueville, A. de *The Old Regime and the French Revolution* (Anchor Books, New York, 1955)

Trimberger, K. *Revolution from Above: Military Bureaucrats and Development in Japan, Turkey, Egypt and Peru* (Transaction Books, New Brunswick, 1978)

Uldricks, T. 'The Crowd in the Russian Revolution', *Polity and Society*, vol. 4 (1974), pp. 357-412

Walzer, M. 'Revolutionary Ideology: The Case of the Marian Exiles', *American Political Science Review*, vol. 57 (1963), pp. 643-54
––––– 'Puritanism as a Revolutionary Ideology' in J.N. Shklar (ed.), *Political Theory and Ideology* (Macmillan, London, 1966), pp. 49-66

Wittfogel, K. *Oriental Despotism: A Comparative Study of Total Power* (Yale University Press, New Haven, 1957)

Yoder, D. 'Current Definitions of Revolution', *The American Journal of Sociology*, vol. 32 (1926-7), pp. 433-41

Zollschan, G.K. and Willer, D. 'Prolegomenon to a Theory of Revolutions' in G.K. Zollschan and W. Hirsch (eds.), *Explorations in Social Change* (Houghton, New York, 1968), pp. 125-51

2. Books, Unpublished Works and Articles in English on Iran

Abrahamian, E. 'The Crowd in Iranian Politics 1905-1953', *Past and Present*, no. 41 (1968), pp. 184-210
—— 'The Social Bases of Iranian Politics: The Tudeh Party, 1941-53', unpublished PhD thesis, Columbia University, New York, 1969
—— 'Oriental Despotism: The Case of Qajar Iran', *International Journal of Middle East Studies*, vol. 5 (1974), pp. 3-31
Akhavi, S. *Religion and Politics in Contemporary Iran: Clergy-State Relations in the Pahlavi Period* (State University of New York Press, New York, 1980)
Algar, H. *Religion and State in Iran: 1785-1906, The Role of the Ulama in the Qajar Period* (California University Press, Berkeley and Los Angeles, 1970)
Arjomand, S. 'The Shiite Hierocracy and the State in Pre-Modern Iran: 1785-1890', *European Journal of Sociology*, vol. 22 (1981), pp. 40-78
Ashraf, A. 'Historical Obstacles to the Development of a Bourgeoisie in Iran' in M.A. Cook (ed.), *Studies in the Economic History of the Middle East* (Oxford University Press, London, 1970)
Avery, P. *Modern Iran* (Ernest Benn, London, 1965)
Bashiriyeh, H. 'Political Power, Political Culture and Political Institutionalization: The Case of Iran', unpublished MA dissertation, University of Essex, 1979
Bayne, E. *Persian Kingship in Transition* (American Universities Field Staff, New York, 1968)
Bharier, J. *Economic Development in Iran: 1900-1970* (Oxford University Press, Oxford, 1971)
Bill, J. 'The Social and Economic Foundations of Power in Contemporary Iran', *The Middle East Journal*, vol. 17 (1963), pp. 400-18
Binder, L. *Iran: Political Development in a Changing Society* (University of California Press, Berkeley and Los Angeles, 1962)
—— 'The Proofs of Islam: Religion and Politics in Iran' in G. Maqdisi (ed.), *Arabic and Islamic Studies in Honor of H.A.R. Gibb* (Harvard University Press, Cambridge, Mass., 1965)
Browne, E. *The Persian Revolution, 1905-1909* (Cambridge University Press, 1910)
Calder, N. 'Accommodation and Revolution in Imami Shiite Jurisprudence: Khomeini and the Classical Tradition', *Middle East Studies*, vol. 18 (1982), pp. 3-20
Costello, V. 'The Industrial Structure of a Traditional Iranian City', *TESG*, vol. 64 (1973), pp. 108-20
Cottom, R. 'Political Party Development in Iran', *Iranian Studies* (Summer 1968), pp. 82-96
Djamalzadeh, M. 'Social and Economic Structure of Iran', *International Labour Review*, vol. 53 (1951), pp. 23-40
Effimemo, M. 'An Experiment with Civilian Dictatorship in Iran: The Case of Dr. Mossadegh', *Journal of Politics*, vol. 17 (1955), pp. 390-406
Elwell-Sutton, L. 'Political Parties in Iran: 1941-1948', *The Middle East Journal*, vol. 3 (1949), pp. 45-62
Enayat, H. *Modern Islamic Political Thought* (University of Texas Press, Austin, 1982)
Gallagher, C. *Contemporary Islam: The Plateau of Particularism, Problems of Religion and Nationalism in Iran* (American Universities Field Staff Reports, vol. 15, no. 2, 1966)
Hairi, A. *Shiism and Constitutionalism in Iran* (E.J. Brill, Leiden, 1977)
Halliday, F. *Iran: Dictatorship and Development* (Penguin Books, Harmondsworth, 1979)

Issawi, C. (ed.) *The Economic History of Iran: 1850-1914* (Chicago University Press, Chicago, 1971)

Jacobs, N. *The Sociology of Development: Iran as an Asian Case-Study* (Praeger, New York, 1966)

Jafri, H. *Origins and Early Development of Shia Islam* (Longman, London, 1979)

Kazemzadeh, F. *Britain and Russia in Iran: 1864-1914* (Yale University Press, New Haven, 1968)

Keddie, N. *Historical Obstacles to Agrarian Change in Iran* (California University Press, Claremont, 1960)

—— 'Religion and Irreligion in Early Iranian Nationalism', *Comparative Studies in Society and History*, vol. 4 (1962), pp. 265-95

—— 'The Origins of Religious-Radical Alliance in Iran', *Past and Present*, no. 34 (1966), pp. 70-86

—— 'The Iranian Power Structure and Social Change', *International Journal of Middle East Studies*, vol. 2 (1971), pp. 3-20

—— (ed.) *Scholars, Saints and Sufis: Muslem Institutions in the Middle East Since 1500* (University of California Press, Berkeley, 1972)

Lambton, A. *Landlord and Peasant in Persia* (Oxford University Press, London, 1953)

—— 'The Impact of the West on Persia', *International Affairs*, vol. 33 (1957), pp. 12-25

—— 'A Reconsideration of the Position of the Marja al Taqlid', *Studia Islamica*, vol. 20 (1964), pp. 114-35

—— 'The Evolution of Iqta in Medieval Iran', *The Journal of British Institute of Persian Studies*, vol. 5 (1967), pp. 41-50

—— *The Persian Land Reforms: 1962-66* (Clarendon Press, London, 1969)

—— 'Some New Trends in Islamic Political Thought in Late Eighteenth and Early Nineteenth Century Persia', *Studia Islamica*, vol. 11 (1974)

Ledeen, M. and Lewis, W. 'Carter and the Fall of the Shah: The Inside Story', *Washington Quarterly*, vol. 3 (1980), pp. 3-40

Miller, W. 'Political Organization in Iran: From Dowreh to Political Party', *The Middle East Journal*, vol. 23 (1969)

Minorsky, V. 'Iran: Opposition, Martyrdom and Revolt' in G.E. von Grunebaum (ed.), *Unity and Variety in Muslem Civilization* (Chicago University Press, Chicago, 1955), pp. 183-206

Morgan, J. *Feudalism in Persia: Its Origins, Development and Present Conditions* (Annual Reports of the Board of Regents, Smithsonian Institution, Washington, DC, 1914)

Philipp, M. 'The Concepts of Religion and Government in the Thought of Mirza Aqa Khan Kermani, A Nineteenth-Century Persian Revolutionary', *International Journal of Middle East Studies*, vol. 5 (1974), pp. 381-400

Rotblat, H. 'Social Organisation and Development in a Provincial Iranian Bazaar', *Economic Development and Cultural Change*, vol. 23 (1974-5), pp. 292-305

Rudulph, C. 'The Land Reform Programme in Iran and Its Political Implications', unpublished PhD thesis, The American University, Beirut, 1971

Savory, R. 'The Problem of Sovereignty in Ithna Ashari ("Twelver") Shii State', *Middle East Review*, vol. 11 (1979)

Sreedhar, M. 'The Role of the Armed Forces in the Iranian Revolution', *IDSA Journal*, vol. 12 (1979), pp. 121-42

Upton, J. *The History of Modern Iran, An Interpretation* (Harvard University Press, Cambridge, Mass, 1960)

Weinbaum, M. 'Iran Finds a Party System: The Institutionalization of the Iran-e Novin Party', *The Middle East Journal*, vol. 27 (1973), pp. 439-55

—— 'Agricultural Policy and Development Politics in Iran', *The Middle East*

Journal, vol. 31 (1977), pp. 434-50

Westwood, A. 'Elections and Politics in Iran', *The Middle East Journal*, vol. 15 (1960), pp. 397-415

Wilber, D. *Iran: Past and Present* (Princeton University Press, Princeton, 1958)

Young, T. 'The Problem of Westernization in Iran', *The Middle East Journal*, vol. 2 (1948), pp. 47-59

—— 'The Social Support of Current Iranian Policy', *The Middle East Journal*, vol. 6 (1952), pp. 125-43

Zabih, S. *The Communist Movement in Iran* (University of California Press, Berkeley, 1966)

3. Official Publications

Bank Markazi *The Annual Report and Balance Sheet* (Tehran, 1953-79)

—— *The National Income of Iran: 1335-1350* (Tehran, 1972)

—— *Majalleh-ye Bank-e Markazi* (*Journal of the Central Bank*) (Tehran, 1974-8)

Echo of Iran *Iran Almanac and Book of Facts* (The Echo of Iran Publications, Tehran, 1963-77)

Ministry of Economy *Iranian Industrial Statistics* (Bureau of Statistics, Tehran, 1969)

—— *Industrial Development of Iran* (Research Centre for Industrial and Trade Development, Tehran, 1971)

Ministry of Interior *The First Census of Iran: 1335* (2 vols., Tehran, 1961)

—— *National Census of Population and Housing: 1345* (Tehran, 1966)

Plan and Budget Organisation *Current Trends and Patterns of Urbanization in Iran: 1956-1976* (Population Studies Series, Report no. 1, Tehran, 1976)

—— *The Main Economic Indicators* (3rd Report, Tehran, 1976)

—— *The Statistical Yearbook* (Tehran, 1976)

—— *The Fifth Economic Plan: 1352-1356* (revised) (Tehran, 1975)

—— *The General Census of Population and Housing* (Tehran, 1978)

—— *Population Growth Survey of Iran* (Final Report: 1973-76, Tehran, 1978)

—— *The Social Indicators of Iran* (Tehran, 1978)

4. Books, Documents and Reports in Persian

Abidi, H. *Tabaqeh-ye Motavasset-e Jadid dar Iran* (*The New Middle Class in Iran*) (Jamei Publications, Tehran, 1358)

Akbari, A. *Elal-e Zaaf-e Tarikhi-ye Burzhuizi dar Iran* (*The Causes of the Historical Weakness of the Bourgeoisie in Iran*) (Sepehr Publications, Tehran, 1357)

—— *Naqdi bar Didgah-e Ejtemai-Eqtesadi-ye Bani-Sadr* (*A Critique of the Socioeconomic Views of Bani-Sadr*) (A Publications, Tehran, 1358)

Akhgar, K. *A Report on Unemployment* (no pub., n.p., Farvardin 1358)

Al-e Ahmad, J. *Gharbzedegi* (*The Western Affliction*) (no pub., Tehran, 1346)

—— *Khasi dar Miqat* (*Dust in the Desert*) (no pub., Tehran, 1348)

—— *Dar Khedmat va Khiyanat-e Roushanfekran* (*On the Services and Disservices of Intellectuals*) (Ravaq Publications, Tehran, 1357)

Anonymous *Asnadi az Jamiyat-haye Motalefe-ye Islami, Jama va Hezb-e Melal-e Islami* (*Documents about the Coalition Groups, the Jama, and the Party of the Islamic Nations*) (Panzdah Khordad Publications, Tehran, 1350)

—— *A Report on the Black Friday* (no pub., Tehran, 1357)

—— *A Report on the Workers in Irana Factory* (no pub., Tehran, 1358)

—— *What do the Unemployed Workers Say?* (no pub., Tehran, 1358)

Ashraf, A. *Nezam-e Feodali ya Nezam-e Asiai* (*Feudalism or Asiatic Despotism*) (Institute of Social Research, Tehran, 1347)

Atiqpur, M. *Bazar va Bazariha dar Enghelab-e Iran* (*The Bazaar and the Bazaaris in the Iranian Revolution*) (Kayhan Publications, Tehran, 1358)

Bahar, M. *Tarikh-e Mokhtasar-e Ahzab-e Siyasi-ye Iran* (*A Short History of Political Parties in Iran*) (2 vols., Amir Kabir Press, Tehran, 1322)

Bani-Sadr, A. *Osule Paye va Zabete-ye Hokumat-e Islami* (*The Basic Principles of Islamic Government*) (no pub., n.p., 1354)

—— *Kish-e Shakhsiyat* (*The Cult of Personality*) (no pub., n.p., 1355)

—— *Eqtesad-e Towhidi* (*Islamic Economics*) (Jonbesh Press, Tehran, 1357)

—— *Bayaniye-ye Jomhuri-ye Islami* (*The Manifesto of the Islamic Republic*) (Imam Publications, Tehran, 1358)

Barahani, R. *Dar Enghelab-e Iran Che Shodeh ast va Che Khahad Shud* (*What has happened and what will happen in the Iranian Revolution?*) (Zaman Publications, Tehran, 1357)

Bazargan, M. *et al. Bahsi dar Bareh-ye Marjaiyat va Ruhaniyat* (*A Discussion about the Highest Religious Authority and the Clergy*) (Sherkat-e Enteshar, Tehran, 1340)

Esfandiari, Y. *Maseleh-ye Bikari* (*The Question of Unemployment*) (Socialist Workers Party, n.p., 1358)

Ettehad-e Mobarazeh (a political group) *Marxist-Leninist-ha va Qiyam-e Bahman* (*The Marxist-Leninists and the Bahman Revolution*) (no pub., Tehran, 1358)

—— *Toghyan dar Tabriz va Towtei dar Qum* (*Revolt in Tabriz and Conspiracy in Qum*) (no pub., Tehran, 1358)

Fedaiyan-e Khalq *Grouh-e Jazani-Zarifi* (*The Jazani-Zarifi Group*) (Mehdi Publications, Tehran, 1352)

—— *A Report of the Struggles of People Living Outside of City Limits* (Fedai Publications, Tehran, 1357)

—— *Hokumat-e Enhesar Talaban* (*The Government of the Monopolists*) (Rah-e Fedai, no. 2, 1358)

—— *Strikes of Workers in the Pars Factory* (Fedaiyan Press, Tehran, 1358)

Grouh e Kar (a political group) *Jang, Solh va Siasat-e Hayat-e Hakemeh dar Kurdestan* (*War, Peace and Government Policy in Kurdestan*) (no pub., Tehran, 1358)

Haj Seyed Javadi, A. *Daftar-haye Siasi-ye Jonbesh* (*Political Notebooks of the Movement*) (Jonbesh Press, Tehran, 1357)

Ivanov, M. *Tarikh-e Novin-e Iran* (*Contemporary History of Iran*), trans. H. Tizabi and H. Qaempanah (Tudeh Publications, Tehran, n.d.)

'Jami' *Gozashteh Cherag-e Rah-e Ayandeh ast: Tarikh-e Iran dar Fasele-ye Do Kudeta* (*The Past is the Guide to the Future: The History of Iran between Two Coups d'Etat*) (Jami Publications, Tehran, n.d.)

Javanan-e Enghelabi (a political group) *Yek Sal-e Gozashteh, Taeed-e Khat-e Mashye Osuli-ye Ma* (*The Past Year Confirms Our Views*) (no pub., Tehran, 1358)

Javid, Dr *Demokrasi-ye Naghes: 1320-1332* (*Incomplete Democracy*) (Tudeh Publications, Tehran, n.d.)

Jazani, B. *Veghaye Si Saleh-ye Akhir* (*The Events of the Past Thirty Years*) (Fedaiyan Press, Tehran, n.d.)

—— *Tarh-e Jamei-Shenasi va Mabani-ye Jonbesh-e Enghelabi-ye Iran* (*A Sociological Sketch of the Revolutionary Movement*) (no pub., Tehran, 1355)

—— *Tarikh-e Si Saleh* (*A Thirty-Year History*) (Kargar Press, Tehran, 1357)

—— *Tarikh-e Ejtemai-Eghtesadi dar Dowreh-ye Moaser* (*A Socio-economic History of the Present Era*) (Maziar Publications, Tehran, 1358)

Kambakhsh, A. *Jonbesh-e Kargari dar Iran* (*The Working Class Movement in Iran*) (Tudeh Press, Tehran, n.d.)

Kasravi, A. *Bahaigari* (*Bahaism*) (Azadegan Press, Tehran, 1323)
—— *Sufigari* (*Sufism*) (Azadegan Press, Tehran, 1323)
—— *Shiigari* (*Shiism*) (Azadegan Press, Tehran, 1324)
—— *Davari* (*Judgement*) (Azadegan Press, Tehran, 1325)
—— *Tarikh-e Mashruteh-ye Iran* (*A History of the Constitutional Movement in Iran*) (Amir Kabir Press, Tehran, 1340)
Kianuri, N. *Enghelab-e Bozorg va Shokuhmand-e Mihan-e Ma* (*The Great Revolution of Our Country*) (Tudeh Press, Tehran, 1358)
—— *Hezb-e Tudeh-ye Iran Che Miguyad* (*What does the Tudeh Party Say?*) (Tudeh Press, Tehran, 1358)
—— *Ma va Chapgarayan* (*We and the Infantile Left*) (Tudeh Press, Tehran, 1358)
Khomeini, R. *Kashf ol-Asrar* (*Revealing the Secrets*) (Chap Islamiyeh, Tehran, 1324)
—— *Khomeini va Jonbesh, Majmueh-ye Nameh-ha va Sokhanraniha* (*A Collection of Khomeini's Letters and Speeches*) (Ponzdah Khodad Publications, Tehran, 1352)
—— *Velayat-e Faghih* (*The Rule of the Theologian*) (Amir Kabir Press, Tehran, 1358)
—— *et al. Hokumat-e Jomhuri-ye Islami* (*Essays on Islamic Government*) (Fadak Publications, Tehran, 1358)
Khosrovi, K. *Jamei-ye Dehgani dar Iran* (*The Peasant Community in Iran*) (Payan Publications, Tehran, 1357)
Komiteh-ye Nabard (a political group) *Barresi-ye Amari-ye Do Referandum* (*A Statistical Analysis of Two Referenda*) (no pub., n.p., Dey 1358)
Kumala Party *The Proposals of the Kurdish Peace Mission* (no pub., n.p., 1358)
Malek, H. *A Report on the Agricultural Situation* (Centre for Iranian Research, Tehran, 1357)
Masarrat, M. *Az Bohran-e Ejtemai ta Enghelab-e Ejtemai* (*From a Social Crisis to a Social Revolution*) (Nada Publications, Tehran, 1358)
'M.J.' *Veghaye-e Enghelab* (*A Chronology of the Revolution*) (Ettelaat Publications, Tehran, 1357)
Mobarezin-e Azadi-ye Kargar (a political group) *Enghelab-e Naghes* (*The Incomplete Revolution*) (no pub., Tehran, 1358)
Mobarezin-e Rah-e Kargar (a political group) *Tahlili az Sharayet-e Jamei ye Rustaiye Iran* (*An Analysis of the Rural Conditions in Iran*) (no pub., Tehran, 1357)
Mojahedin-e Khalq *Dowreh-ye Zamamdari-ye Karter* (*The Administration of President Carter*) (Mojahedin Press, Tehran, 1357)
—— *Sharhe Tasis va Tarikhche-ye Sazeman-e Mojahedin* (*The Establishment and History of the Mojahedin*) (Mojahedin Press, Tehran, 1357)
—— *Jonbesh-e Khalq-e Tabriz* (*Uprising in Tabriz*) (Mojahedin Press, Tehran, 1358)
—— *Mohemtarin Tahavolat-e Siasi az Khordad 1357 ta Nakhosvaziri-ye Bakhtiar* (*The Most Important Events from 1357 to Bakhtiar's Premiership*) (Mojahedin Press, Tehran, 1358)
—— *A Report on the Aryamehr Steel Industry and Agricultural Company* (Mojahedin Press, Tehran, 1358)
Momeni, B. *Sima-ye Rusta-ye Iran* (*A Picture of the Iranian Village*) (Payvand Publications, Tehran, 1356)
'Moslem Students Following the Line of Imam' *Efshaye Amperializm* (*Imperialism Exposed*) (The Embassy Documents, 2 vols., no pub., Tehran, 1358)
Mosaddeq Press *Mosaddeq va Movazeneh-ye Manfi* (*Mosaddeq and Negative Equilibrium*) (Amir Kabir Publications, Tehran, 1357)
—— *Mosaddeq va Nehzat-e Melli-ye Iran* (*Mosaddeq and the Nationalist Movement*) (Confederation of Iranian Students in Europe, Tehran, 1357)

Mostazafin Foundation *Khalq-e Kurd-e Iran* (*The Kurds of Iran*) (2 vols., Mostazafin Press, Tehran, 1358)
—— *Velayat-e Faghih* (*The Rule of the Theologian*) (Mostazafin Press, Tehran, 1358)
Mottahedin-e Khalq (a political group) *A Report on Strikes in the Oil Fields* (no pub., n.p., Dey 1357)
Naini, M. *Tanbih-ol Mella va Tanzih-ol Omma: Dar Asas va Osul-e Mashrutiyat* (*Concerning the Foundations and Principles of Constitutional Government*) (no. pub., Tehran, 1335)
Nebard-e Rah-e Kargar (a political group) *A Report on Factories Belonging to the National Bourgeoisie* (no pub., Tehran, 1358)
Nazem ol-Mulk Kermani *Tarikh-e Bidari-ye Iranian* (*A History of the Awakening of the Iranians*) (Bonyad-e Farhang Press, Tehran, 1346)
Nuri, A. *Setiz-ha va Sazesh-haye Borzhuizi va Ruhaniyat* (*The Conflicts and Compromises between the Bourgeoisie and the Clergy*) (Dayk Publications, Tehran, 1358)
Pahlavi, M. *Majmueh-ye Sokhanraniha va Payamha* (*A Collection of the Shah's Speeches and Messages*) (2 vols., no pub., Tehran, n.d.)
—— *The White Revolution* (Imperial Library, Tehran, 1967)
—— *Be Suye Tamaddon-e Bozorg* (*Towards the Great Civilisation*) (Farhang Press, Tehran, n.d. [1356])
Paykar Organisation *Masele-ye Melli* (*The National Question*) (Paykar Press, Tehran, 1358)
—— *Qanun-e Sud-e Vizheh* (*Workers' Profit-Sharing Law*) (Paykar Press, Tehran, 1358)
Pigulovskaya, N. *et al. Tarikh-e Iran az Dowreh-ye Bastan ta Payan-e Sedeh-ye Hezhdahom* (*A History of Iran from Ancient Times to the End of the Eighteenth Century*), trans. from Russian by K. Keshavarz (Institute of Social Research, Tehran, 1346)
Pishgam Organisation *Qarna* (Pishgam Press, Tabriz, 1358)
—— *A Report on the Fishermen in the Shilat Area* (Pishgam Press, Tehran, 1358)
Qasseml, A. *Oligarshi ya Khandan-haye Hokumatgar-e Iran* (*Oligarchy or the Ruling Families of Iran*) (4 vols., Roz Publications, Tehran, 1354, 1355, 1356, 1357)
Qum Theological College *Jonbesh-e Islami be Rahbari-ye Imam Khomeini* (*The Islamic Movement Led by Imam Khomeini*) (no pub., Qum, 1350)
—— *Zendeginame-ye Imam Khomeini* (*A Biography of Imam Khomeini*) (Fadak Publications, Tehran, 1357)
Rah-e Kargar (a political group) *Enghelab-e Kurd* (*The Kurdish Revolution*) (Roozbeh Press, Tehran, 1358)
—— *Fashizm: Kabus ya Vaqeiyat* (*Fascism: Nightmare or Reality*), nos. 1-5 (no pub., n.p., 1358)
Razmandegan-e Rah-e Kargar *Shoura-ye Nemayandegan va Majles-e Moassesan* (*The Representative Council and the Constituent Assembly*) (no pub., Tehran, 1358)
Rezai, A. *Nehzat-e Hosseini* (*Hossein's Movement*) (Mojahedin Publications, Tehran, 1354)
'Safari' *Vaze Konuni-ye Eqtesad-e Iran* (*The Present Conditions of the Iranian Economy*) (no pub., Tehran, 1356)
Sami, K. *Estratezhi-ye Enghelab-e Iran* (*The Strategy of the Iranian Revolution*) (no pub., Tehran, 1358)
Sazeman-e Enghelabi *Nehzat-haye Kargari-ye Iran Pas az 1320* (*The Working Class Movements in Iran after 1320*) (Sorkh Publications, Tehran, 1350)
Sazeman-e Vahdat-e Komonisti (a political group) *Naqsh-e Ruhaniyat dar Gozar-e*

Ghodrat (*The Role of the Clergy in the Transition of Power*) (no pub., Tehran, 1358)

Seyed Mehdi *Ruhaniyat* (*The Clergy*) (no pub., Tehran, 1358)

Shajii, Z. *Nemayandegan-e Majles-e Shoura-ye Melli dar Bisto Yek Dowreh ye Qanungozari* (*Members of Parliament in Twenty-One Legislative Sessions*) (Institute for Social Research, Tehran, 1345)

Shariati, A. *Ummat va Imamat* (*Community and Leadership*) (Ershad Press, Tehran, 1349)

—— *Entezar, Mazhab-e Eteraz* (*Expectation, the Religion of Protest*) (Ershad Press, Tehran, 1350)

—— *Fatemeh Fatemeh Ast* (*Fatemeh is Fatemeh*) (Ershad Press, Tehran, 1351)

—— *Masuliyat-e Shia Budan* (*The Responsibility of Being a Shiite*) (Ershad Press, Tehran, 1350)

—— *Tashayo-e Alavi va Tashayo-e Safavi* (*Alavi Shiism and Safavi Shiism*) (Ershad Press, Tehran, 1351)

Shirazi, P. *Enghelab-e Iran va Mabani-ye Rahbari-ye Imam Khomeini* (*The Revolution and the Leadership of Imam Khomeini*) (Ettelaat Publications, Tehran, 1357)

Soltani, F. *Ettehadiyeh-haye Dehqani* (*Peasant Unions*) (Pishgam Press, Tehran, 1358)

Sotanzadeh, A. *Asnad-e Tarikhi-ye Jonbesh-e Kargari-ye va Sosial Demokrasi-ye Iran* (*Documents about the Working Class and Social Democratic Movements in Iran*) (Jomhuri Press, Tehran, 1357)

Soudagar, M. *Roshd-e Ravabet-e Sarmayedari dar Iran: 1304-1340* (*The Growth of Capitalism in Iran*) (Pazand Publications, Tehran, n.d.)

—— *Barresi-ye Eslahat-e Arzi: 1340-50* (*An Analysis of the Land Reforms 1961-71*) (Pazand Research Institute, Tehran, 1351)

Tabari, E. *Iran dar Dowreh-ye Reza Khan* (*Iran in the Reign of Reza Khan*) (Tudeh Press, Tehran, 1356)

—— *Barkhi Masael-e Hadd-e Enghelabe Iran* (*Some Important Issues of the Iranian Revolution*) (Tudeh Press, Tehran, 1358)

Tabatabai, M. *Ravabet-e Iran va Gharb* (*The Relations between Iran and the West*) (no pub., Tehran, 1355)

5. Newspapers and Periodicals

Ayandegan, daily (Tehran, 1975-80)

Bamdad, daily (Tehran, 1979-81)

Besuye Hezb, weekly, the political and theoretical journal of the Tudeh Party

Donya, quarterly, the theoretical journal of the Tudeh Party

The Economist (London, 1973-80)

Enghelab-e Islami, daily (published by A.H. Bani-Sadr, 1979-81)

Ettehad-e Chap, weekly journal of the Organisation for the Unity of the Left (1979-80)

Ettelaat, main daily (Tehran, 1977-81)

Jomhuri-ye Islami, the organ of the Islamic Republican Party (1979-82)

Jonbesh, daily (published by A.A. Haj Seyed Javadi, 1979-81)

Jonbesh-e Kargari, weekly organ of the Organisation for the Creation of a Working Class Movement (1979-80)

Journal of Labour and Social Insurance, weekly (published by the Ministry of Labour, the Social Insurance Organisation, 1965-78)

Kar, weekly, the organ of the Fedaiyan-e Khalq Organisation (1979-82)

Kayhan, a main daily (Tehran, 1973-82)

Khalq, the political and theoretical organ of the Ranjbaran Party (1979)

Lanjan, weekly, journal of the workers of Mobarekeh in Esfahan (1979)

Mardom, daily newspaper of the Tudeh Party (1979-81)

Mobarez, the organ of the Organisation of the Militant Workers of Iran (1979-80)

Mojahed, daily newspaper of the Mojahedin-e Khalq Organisation (1979-80)

New York Times (1977-80)

Omid-e Farda, weekly organ of the Organisation of Democrat Students (1979)

Ommat, weekly organ of the Jama Party (1980)

Paygam-e Emruz, daily (Tehran, 1979-80)

Paykar, weekly organ of the Paykar Organisation (1979-81)

Paykar-e Khalq, biweekly, organ of the Revolutionary Marxist Group (1979-80)

Pishtaz, journal of the Progressive Workers of the Oil Industry (1979)

Rahai, weekly journal of the Organisation of Communist Unity (1979-81)

Rah-e Kargar, weekly, the organ of the Mobarezin-e Rah-e Kargar (1979-81)

Ranjbar, newspaper of the Ranjbaran Party (1979)

Riga-ye Gel, weekly, the organ of the Kurdish Fedaiyan-e Khalq (1979-81)

Setad, journal of the Organisation of the Revolutionary Mass of Students (1979)

Shoura-ye Hambastegi, weekly, the organ of the Solidarity Council of the Ethnic Nationalities (1979-80)

Shuresh, weekly, the organ of the Kurdish Kumala Party (1980)

Tehran Economist, weekly, (1965-78)

Tufan, weekly, the organ of the Communist Party of the Workers and Peasants of Iran (1979-82)

Tufan, biweekly, the organ of the Marxist-Leninist Organisation of Tufan (1979-81)

Turkoman Sahra, news-sheet of the Central Peasant Union of Turkoman Sahra (1980)

Zahmatkeshan, weekly, the journal of the United Workers of the Steel Industry (1979)

INDEX